Forensic Mental Health Nursing

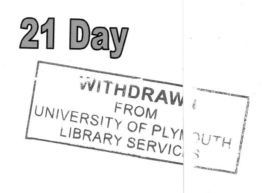

University of Plymouth Library

Subject to status this item may be renewed
via your Voyager account

http://voyager.plymouth.ac.uk

Exeter tel: (01392) 475049
Exmouth tel: (01395) 255331
Plymouth tel: (01752) 232323

Forensic Mental Health Nursing

Interventions with People with 'Personality Disorder'

Edited by the
National Forensic Nurses' Research and
Development Group
Phil Woods (Chair), Alyson Kettles (Deputy Chair) and
Richard Byrt

Chapter reviews by Mary Addo, Anne Aiyegbusi, Michael Coffey,
Mick Collins, Mike Doyle, Gavin Garman and Carol Watson

QUAY
BOOKS

A division of MA Healthcare Ltd

Quay Books Division, MA Healthcare Ltd, St Jude's Church, Dulwich Road, London SE24 0PB

British Library Cataloguing-in-Publication Data
A catalogue record is available for this book

© MA Healthcare Limited 2006

ISBN 1 85642 300 X

Printed by Gutenberg Press Ltd, Gudja Road, Tarxien, Malta

Contents

Contents

Contributors

Mary Addo

Mary Addo, MEd, MA Soc Sci (Aberdeen) DMS, PgCertTLT (Aberdeen), RMN, EN (G) (Aberdeen), is a Lecturer/Practice Education Lecturer in Mental Health Nursing for The Robert Gordon University based at Aberdeen, Scotland. She is completing her PhD research at the Centre for Advanced Studies in Nursing, University of Aberdeen, on the experience of trained nurses working with sex offenders in secure care settings. She has published on forensic nursing and related issues in books and journals, and is a member of the National Forensic Nurses Research and Development Group.

Anne Aiyegbusi

Anne Aiyegbusi, RMN, MSc, PGCE, PGCert Social Science Research Methods, Diploma in Forensic Psychotherapeutic Studies, trained in the use of the Adult Attachment Interview, is Consultant Nurse for Women's Secure Services at West London Mental Health NHS Trust. Anne has a special interest in personality disorder and complex mental health needs and has extensive clinical experience in these areas. She has published articles and presented at conferences for many years, focusing most recently on the emotional impact on nurses of working on the frontline of forensic mental health services with service users who have experienced early psychological trauma. Anne is completing a PhD and the subject is managing the nurse–patient relationship with people who have personality disorders.

Chris Ashwell

Chris Ashwell, RMN, DipNurs, LLB(Hons), is Research and Security Liaison Nurse, Rampton High Security Hospital, Nottinghamshire Healthcare NHS Trust. He provides expert advice to clinicians on aspects of security. His research interests are primarily the measurement and comparison of security provision in different forensic health care providers across the United Kingdom.

Paul Burbery

Paul Burbery, RMN, DipCogTh, coordinates the Sex Offender Treatment Programme for the Adult Forensic Mental Health Services Directorate, part of Bolton, Salford and Trafford Mental Health Trust. He is also a Cognitive Behavioural Therapist with the Directorate's Forensic Psychotherapies Department providing CBT for both in- and outpatients with a range of mental health concerns and personality disorders.

Richard Byrt

Dr Richard Byrt, RMN, RNLD, RGN, PhD, BSc (Hons), is Lecturer-Practitioner, Nursing, at Arnold Lodge medium secure unit, Nottinghamshire Healthcare NHS Trust and the School of Nursing and Midwifery, De Montfort University, Leicester.

Michael Coffey

Michael Coffey, RMN, RGN, BSc, MSc, is Lecturer in Community Mental Health Nursing at the School of Health Science, Swansea University. Michael's PhD research focuses upon attempts by mental health nurses and others to intervene as experienced by people receiving forensic mental health care in the community, with an emphasis on developing professional practice. He is co-editor of *Forensic Mental Health Nursing: Current Approaches* with Chris Chaloner and of *The Handbook of Community Mental Health Nursing* with Ben Hannigan.

Mick Collins

Mick Collins, BA (Hons), Diploma Health Care Research, RMN, is Senior Nurse Research and Development at Rampton Hospital, Nottinghamshire Healthcare NHS Trust. He is also an Honorary Research Fellow at the University of Nottingham. He has spent 13 years in high-security forensic research and has published a wide range of related papers. Mick has a particular interest in the fields of risk assessment and risk management, which have been the focus of his research activity for the past five years.

Steffan Davies

Dr Steffan Davies, MB, ChB, MRCPsych, MBA, is Senior Lecturer in Forensic Rehabilitation Psychiatry at the University of Nottingham and Honorary consultant Forensic Psychiatrist at Rampton High Security Hospital Nottinghamshire Healthcare NHS Trust. His research interests include long-term outcomes from psychiatric services, measurement of security and therapeutic environments.

Jim Dooher

James Dooher, RMN, MA, FHE Cert Ed, Dip HCR, ILTM, CRS, is Principal Lecturer and Academic Lead for Mental Health Nursing at De Montfort University.

Michael Doyle

Michael is a Forensic Nurse Consultant in Manchester, England. He is also undertaking a Post-doctoral Research Fellowship investigating risk assessment in mental health services. A Qualified RMN, he also has a BSc (Hons) in Community Health and an MSc in Individual and Family Cognitive Therapy from the University of Manchester. He complete his PhD in 2003. He has provided extensive training in risk and related subjects since 1996 and has a particular interest in systematic approaches to risk assessment and management.

Karen D'Silva

Dr Karen D'Silva is a Forensic Consultant Psychiatrist working with the Forensic Outreach Personality Disorder Team in Leicester. She has an interest in supporting the involvement of service users in the development and evaluation of services.

David Duffy

Dr David Duffy, BA (Hons), MSc, PhD, RMN, is a Nurse Consultant in Suicide and Self-Harm employed by Bolton Salford and Trafford Mental Health NHS Trust. David coordinated the National Suicide Prevention Strategy for England, published in 2002, has researched, practised and trained in clinical risk for many years, and is the editor, with Dr Tony Ryan, of *New Approaches to Suicide Prevention* (Jessica Kingsley, 2004).

Roberta Graley-Wetherell

Roberta Graley-Wetherell is a founding member and former National Coordinator of the United Kingdom Advocacy Network and Founder Chairperson of the European Network of Users and Ex-Users in Mental Health. Roberta runs a freelance mental health training and development consultancy.

Linnette James

Linnette James, RN, BSc (Hons), is a staff nurse who is working in an acute mental health setting. Linnette is also a poet and songwriter during her spare time.

Alyson M. Kettles

Dr Alyson M. Kettles, PhD, MSc (London), BSc (Dundee), RMN, RGN, RNT, PGCEA (Surrey), AMIBiol, ILTM, is Research and Development Officer (Mental Health) for NHS Grampian and is based at the Royal Cornhill Hospital in Aberdeen, Scotland. She is also Honorary Lecturer for the Centre for Advanced Studies in Nursing at the University of Aberdeen. Her personal portfolio of research has had a forensic focus for the last ten years. She is a well-known author of mental health and forensic nursing articles and books.

Tom Pocock

Tom Pocock, RNMH, BSc (Hons) is a Senior Staff Nurse in an adolescent and family mental health unit in Leicester. He has a keen interest in poetry.

'R'

'R' has been a patient in a secure environment for over ten years. He is a skilled musician and communicator, and continues to cultivate a wide-ranging interest in the arts. He is currently in the pre-discharge phase of his treatment.

Rachel Studley

Rachel Studley is a mental health trainer and student, with interest and experience in education related to individuals said to have 'personality disorder'. She runs a mental health website.

Carol Watson

Carol Watson, RMN, RGN, RNT, MPhil, is the Associate Director of Nursing and Midwifery NHS Education for Scotland. Carol has worked in research, education and practice in high secure settings. Her main focus has been in facilitating the development of post-registration clinical competencies in mental health generally and forensic mental health nursing particularly.

Jean Woodally

Jean Woodally, RMN, is a Senior Staff Nurse for NHS Grampian at The Blair Unit, Royal Cornhill Hospital, Aberdeen. She has over 20 years in psychiatry, 10 of them in the forensic area. This is Jean's first attempt at writing for a book. Jean has participated in research activities within the BEST-Index.

Phil Woods

Dr Phil Woods, RMN, RPN, PhD, is an Associate Professor at the College of Nursing, University of Saskatchewan. He has an extensive personal portfolio of forensic related research. He is a well-known author of mental health and forensic nursing articles and books. His specific research interests are risk assessment and management, and violence prediction.

CHAPTER 1

Introduction

Richard Byrt and Phil Woods

Introduction

Welcome to this book on nursing interventions with individuals with personality disorder diagnoses. We hope that you will find it useful, enjoyable to read, and, above all, relevant to your own work and/or other experience with individuals with personality disorders. This book emerged from one of the National Forensic Nurses' Research and Development Group meetings, through what is often the central focus of these: how can we as a Group contribute to the development of forensic nursing and more widely mental health nursing? A seed was planted and this book was born!

As many of the authors in this book point out, people with personality disorders have had a rough deal from some mental health services, and have often been written off as 'untreatable' and perceived negatively by nurses and other professionals (National Institute for Mental Health in England, 2003). There has been a lack of adequate pre- and post-registration education for working with individuals with personality disorders. In addition, there has been a dearth of support and clinical supervision for staff (Bowers, 2002); and until recently, a limited amount of literature to relate to nursing practice. In particular, there has been a lack of research-based evidence to inform specific interventions (Woods and Richards, 2003).

This book aims to fill a gap in the literature. A pioneering text (Barnes, 1968) considered the nurse's role in working with individuals with personality disorders in therapeutic communities; and several generic and forensic mental health nursing texts include chapters on relevant nursing interventions (for example Houghton and Ousley, 2004; Parsons, 2003; Schafer, 2002; Woods, 2001). However, as far as we know, our book is the first to consider a wide range of nursing interventions with people with personality disorders, and to explore related issues.

This introductory chapter will provide a brief introduction to the concept of 'personality disorder' and to the main themes considered in the book.

The concept of personality

Personality has been defined as: 'The distinctive and characteristic patterns of thought, emotion and behaviour that define an individual's personal style of interacting with the physical and social environment' (Smith *et al.*, 2003, p. 705). Since at least the 5th century BC, the literature of many cultures has indicated a fascination with personality and its effects on individuals' behaviours and relationships (Wells and Cowen Orlin, 2003). Livesley (2001, p. 7) comments on the proliferation of definitions of 'personality' used by psychologists. He concludes:

> ... However, a consensus exists about the essential elements of personality, and an *understanding of these elements clarifies our ideas about personality disorder*. First, the term refers to regularities and consistencies in behaviour and forms of experience .... It does not pertain to occasional behaviours, but, rather, to *behaviours that recur across situations and occasions. Personality also refers to consistencies in thinking, perceiving and feeling...* [Emphasis added]

What is 'personality disorder'?

This question is explored in much of this book. By way of introduction, the following points will be made:

- Personality disorder is used as a *diagnostic category*, for example in the International Classification of Diseases (ICD-10) (World Health Organization, 1992) and the Diagnostic Statistical Manual (DSM-IV) (American Psychiatric Association, 1994). As is indicated in several chapters of this book, and in much of the literature (Byrt *et al.*, 2005), some professionals have used diagnoses of specific personality disorders to inform treatment and nursing and other interventions.
- However, sadly, 'personality disorder' has sometimes been used as a *negative label* and a *pejorative judgement*, applied to someone whose behaviours professionals find hard to understand or to like; and who does not appear to respond to attempts to help or to treat (Dolan and Coid, 1993).
- Several authors have reported that *negative professional attitudes* towards individuals with personality disorder cause them considerable problems. The latter add to the difficulties caused by the personality disorder itself, and often exacerbate the traumatic experiences that may have contributed to its development (Castillo, 2003).
- Several authors refer to *controversies about the nature and meaning* of personality disorder. Some critics have commented on the *lack of scientific validity or reliability* of this diagnostic category (Bowers, 2002; Magnavita, 2004; Pilgrim, 2001). ('Validity ... refers to the degree to which an instrument measures what it is supposed to be measuring, while reliability refers to the degree of consistency or accuracy with which the instrument (used under similar conditions) measures the attribute under investigation'; Carter and Porter, 2000, p. 29). In the case

of personality disorder, the 'instrument' is a list of characteristics or signs and symptoms specific to particular personality disorders, as outlined in the International Classification of Diseases (ICD-10) (World Health Organization, 1992) or the Diagnostic Statistical Manual (DSM-IV) (American Psychiatric Association, 1994).

The following points are based particularly on the writings of psychiatrists and psychologists, and are reflected in work by some mental health nurses (Bennett, 2003; Bowers, 2002; Paris, 2004; Perlin, 2001; Tyrer, 2000).

■ Compared with most people in their cultural and social groups, individuals with personality disorders are described as having particularly *fixed, rigid and habitual* (i.e. frequent and repetitious) *patterns of behaviour, thinking and ways of responding to situations.*
■ Personality disorder usually results in *(often considerable) distress* to individuals with this diagnosis, and sometimes, to other people. The personality disorder *adversely affects aspects of the individual's life*, such as his/her close relationships, ability to trust or relate to people, feelings of satisfaction with life, and desired educational, work and other achievements.
■ Individuals with personality disorders *generally lack coping strategies to respond to stress in creative ways* that do not cause harm to themselves and/or others. However, the extent that different personality traits and ways of coping are 'adaptive or nonadaptive' *depends on the individual's culture* (Paris, 2004, p. 139).
■ In general, people with personality disorders do not have signs and symptoms of mental illness as part of the personality disorder. However, some individuals can have *both* a personality disorder *and* a mental illness and/or problems related to alcohol and/or other drugs. This is referred to as a *dual (or even a triple) diagnosis.* (The care of individuals with personality disorder and alcohol/other drug problems is considered in Chapter 13).

What causes personality disorder?

This is probably the $1,000,000 question, and if health professionals had the answer, perhaps we would not need to publish this book. The actual causes of personality disorder are unclear from the literature, but research is continually progressing in this area and some clear indicators have emerged. A useful summary is given in Gelder *et al.* (2001), and by Bennett (2003). These authors refer to the following factors:

■ **Genetic**: Studies of twins reared apart suggest that antisocial personality disorder (but not other types of personality disorder) has a genetic component (Gelder *et al.*, 2001).
■ **Cerebral functioning**: Electroencephalogram (EEG) abnormalities have been found in some individuals with antisocial personality disorder, but Gelder *et al.* (2003, p. 176) conclude that the evidence for such abnormalities 'causing' antisocial personality disorder is 'weak'.
■ **Low levels of brain 5-hydroxytryptamine (5-HT) neurotransmission** 'have been reported in patients with impulsive and aggressive behaviour. It has been suggested that the same abnormalities may be relevant to antisocial personality disorder' (Gelder *et al.* 2001, p. 176).

However, Gelder *et al.* also suggest that the evidence for this is limited. 5-hydroxytryptamine (5-HT) is a neurotransmitter: a chemical message passing from one neuron (nerve cell) to another (Gray and Bressington, 2004). This neurotransmitter appears to be involved in impulsivity and aggression and their expression (Gelder *et al.*, 2001).

■ **Serious neglect and/or physical, sexual and emotional abuse in childhood** has been found in many individuals with personality disorders, especially those with borderline personality disorder and antisocial personality disorder (Bennett, 2003).

■ **Considerable conflict in relationships with parents and other significant people** has been suggested as important in some people with personality disorders (Bateman and Fonagy, 2004).

■ **'Failure to learn normal social behaviour'** (Gelder *et al.*, 2001, p. 176) or to learn the benefits of antisocial behaviours has been postulated as a causative factor in antisocial personality disorder.

■ **'Attachment theory'** postulates that the features of personality disorder, and the associated distress, are caused, at least in part, by a lack of 'attachments' with parents or other adults in parental roles (Jeffcote and Travers, 2004, p. 24f):

> ...When a child's caregivers do not respond to her [or his] anxiety, or respond with rejection, anger or fear, or abuse her [or him] physically or sexually, she [/he] must find ways of surviving and achieving some sort of safety as best she [/he] can. This may mean shutting overwhelming or unacceptable experiences and feelings out of consciousness, heightening her[/his] own attachment behaviour to obtain some attention, even if it is punitive or aggressive attention... [Because of the individual's early experiences], the idea of any continuity [consistency] in others' behaviour may be lacking altogether, or 'caring' relationships may only be understood as exploitative and abusive...

■ **Response to trauma** has been postulated as contributing to the behaviours and reactions of some individuals with personality disorders, particularly borderline personality disorder. Some authorities have likened borderline personality disorder, in particular, to post-traumatic stress disorder. Trauma is often associated, in individuals with personality disorder, with childhood neglect, abuse and lack of attachment (Castillo, 2003) (see Chapter 6 of this book).

■ **Spiritual factors**, such as a loss of hope, purpose or meaning may both result from, and contribute to the effects of personality disorder. Spiritual factors in relation to individuals with personality disorder do not appear to have been widely considered in the literature (see Chapter 5 of this book).

■ **Sociological explanations: stigmatisation, labelling, negative discrimination and social exclusion**. Finally, some sociologists consider that the problems faced by individuals with personality disorder are related, at least in part, to the attitudes of other people (e.g. those in wider society, or held by some professionals). These attitudes may result in *stigmatisation* and *labelling*, where the individual is seen as different, inferior and perceived to have negative attributes (e.g. everything he or she does may be judged to be 'manipulative'). Some people with personality disorders also face *negative discrimination* and *social exclusion* (lack of access to opportunities that most of us have; Sayce, 2000). These issues are discussed in Chapter 4. Stigmatisation, labelling, negative discrimination and social exclusion may occur particularly in individuals with personality disorder from minority ethnic groups or who are lesbian, gay, bisexual or transsexual (see Chapters 5 and 8).

Topics covered in this book

In **Chapter 2**, Phil Woods considers the *types of personality disorders* outlined in the International Classification of Diseases (ICD-10) (World Health Organization, 1992) and the Diagnostic Statistical Manual (DSM-IV) (American Psychiatric Association, 1994). Phil also considers aspects of *assessment* and the differences and similarities between 'personality disorder' and 'psychopathic disorder'. He concludes with a consideration of the components of 'effective treatment' (p. 16) for individuals with personality disorders.

Chapter 3 includes Richard Byrt's consideration of the *social consequences* of a 'personality disorder' diagnosis and the effects of specific personality disorders on individuals. A brief account of the history of 'personality disorder' is followed by a consideration, with a contribution by Jim Dooher, of *social and political attitudes* towards people with personality disorders, with reference to media presentations (mostly related to images of violence) and the 'dangerous and severe personality disorder' programme.

Chapter 4 considers *service users' views* and *professional attitudes*, both positive and negative. These topics are explored through the perspectives of three people with service user experience (Rachel Studley, 'R' and Roberta Graley-Wetherell); and contributors with professional (Karen D'Silva) or student nurse (Linnette James and Tom Pocock) experience. This chapter includes two poems by Linnette and Tom; and a review, by Richard Byrt, of relevant research and of websites and organisations for individuals with personality disorder and their informal carers. This chapter, and other parts of the book, indicate the importance of positive professional attitudes.

In **Chapter 5**, Mary Addo gives a detailed account of the *spiritual and cultural needs* of people with personality disorders. She points out that individuals with a personality disorder often experience a lack of hope and meaning. Mary considers the nature of spirituality; and the role of the nurse in meeting the individual's spiritual and cultural needs. She refers to the importance of 'cultural competence' and 'cultural awareness, knowledge and sensitivity' (p. 69), and considers related *ethical issues*.

In **Chapter 6**, Anne Aiyegbusi discusses the *'emotional impact* of working with people with personality disorders' (p. 81) in relation to the problems that many of these individuals have experienced in past relationships. Anne explains that early abusive experiences can become replicated in relationships with staff, whom the individual has difficulty in trusting. Despite the individual's need for understanding, professionals may respond with negative attitudes and exclusion from services.

Carol Watson and Alyson McGregor Kettles, in **Chapter 7**, comment on the lack of relevant *staff education, training and support*, a point made by other contributors. Carol and Alyson refer to the need for primary healthcare professionals and 'service planners and managers' (p. 93), as well as mental health nurses, to receive appropriate education and supervision to reduce 'staff burnout and low morale' (p. 93). Education, rather than focusing on narrow competencies, should enable staff to examine attitudes and appreciate service users' perspectives in relation to 'complex legal, ethical and interpersonal... issues' (p. 94).

Gender and sexuality issues are considered in **Chapter 8** by Anne Aiyegbusi and Richard Byrt. This chapter highlights the need for nurses to be sensitive to the specific needs of women with personality disorders, in relation to their frequent experiences of early trauma. Individuals' psychosexual needs and deprivations are considered. The chapter concludes with a review of nursing interventions with people with personality disorder who are gay, lesbian, bisexual or transsexual; and a need for awareness of the discrimination that many of these individuals have experienced.

In **Chapter 9**, Michael Coffey reminds us that many individuals with personality disorders receive care from generic mental health teams. Michael considers how research findings on *community interventions* with individuals with mental illness can be applied to the care of service users with personality disorders. Relevant principles include establishing a therapeutic alliance, trust, respect and engagement. The chapter concludes with a consideration of the need to engender hope through effective social support, enabling 'problem-solving behaviours' (p. 127) and risk assessment and risk management.

Mike Doyle and David Duffy point out that '*risk assessment and risk management* are key components of clinical practice' (**Chapter 10**, p. 135). Mike gives a detailed review of instruments to measure psychopathy and the risk of harm to others. He includes a critical consideration of the reliability and 'predictive validity' (p. 139) of various measures. David considers self harm as an 'expression of personal distress' (p. 143) in relation to assessments which seek to appreciate individuals' perspectives, previous experiences and meanings. The chapter concludes with an account of Mike Doyle's (1998) risk management cycle.

In **Chapter 11**, Mick Collins, Steffan Davies and Chris Ashwell consider *assessment of security need*. They stress the importance of maintaining safe environments to ensure that other nursing interventions and treatment are effective, and the need for levels of security proportionate to the individual's assessed risk. However, there are wide variations in aspects of security across supposedly similar services. Physical, procedural and relational security are outlined. The chapter concludes with a description of Mick Collins' and Steffan Davies' (2001) Security Needs Assessment Profile, which can 'build a comprehensive picture of the security requirements of individual patients' (p. 156).

Alyson McGregor Kettles and Jean Woodally (**Chapter 12**) consider *observation with engagement*. Research has found that observation levels were related to nurses' subjective judgements, rather than more objective assessments (Kettles *et al.*, 2004). Alyson and Jean outline problems from the observation of individuals with personality disorders, including a tendency to 'perpetuate... behaviours' (p. 164). The nature of engagement, in relation to the 'person to person relationship' is explored. The authors conclude that further research is needed to establish the benefits of 'observation and/or engagement' (p. 170).

Chapter 13, by Alyson McGregor Kettles, reports research on the high prevalence of *substance misuse* amongst individuals with personality disorders. This is outlined in relation to particular types of personality disorder. Alyson refers to the lack of agreement on the appropriateness of particular aetiological (causative) models; and the paucity of literature on nursing interventions with people with the *dual diagnosis* of personality disorder and substance misuse. Nursing interventions are described. These include screening for readiness for treatment; assessment; the maintenance of positive attitudes and a therapeutic nurse–patient relationship; and aspects of limit-setting.

In **Chapter 14**, Richard Byrt outlines aspects of the social environment and types of therapeutic groups in *therapeutic communities*. There is a review of the nurse's role, in relation to the nurse–resident relationship and communication; and enabling residents to develop inner controls, strengths, talents and involvement in responsibility. The nurse's role in crises, activities and therapeutic groups is considered. Self-awareness, transference and countertransference are outlined, as is the need for effective staff communication and support. The chapter concludes with a review of relevant research findings and views of former residents.

Mike Doyle, Anne Aiyegbusi and Paul Burbery outline, in **Chapter 15**, *specialist psychological approaches*. They suggest that some of these 'have shown promise' (p. 210), with individuals with personality disorders, despite the lack of conclusive evidence for the effectiveness of nursing interventions (Woods and Richards 2003). 'A *psychodynamic nursing approach*' can explain individuals' behaviours in relation to early 'adverse developmental experiences' (p. 211), reflected in later relationships with professionals. The latter need to recognise this to avoid perpetuating the individual's experience of rejection and abuse. The same chapter outlines *cognitive behavioural therapy* concerned with 'problem orientation' in the 'here and now' (p. 215), particularly related to the beliefs underlying individuals' behaviours and coping strategies. *Schema-focused therapy* can change ineffective strategies in relationships and problem solving; and enable nurses to communicate more effectively with, and understand, service users.

Finally, in **Chapter 16**, Alyson McGregor Kettles, Phil Woods and Richard Byrt *draw together important themes* from the whole book.

References

American Psychiatric Association (1994) *Diagnostic and Statistical Manual of Mental Disorders*, 4th edn (DSM-IV). American Psychiatric Association, Washington.

Barnes, E. (ed.) (1968) *Psychosocial Nursing: Studies from the Cassel Hospital*. Tavistock, London.

Bateman, A. and Fonagy, P. (2004) *Psychotherapy for Borderline Personality Disorder*. Oxford University Press, Oxford.

Bennett, P. (2003) *Abnormal and Clinical Psychology: An Introductory Textbook* (Chapter 11). Open University Press, Maidenhead.

Bowers, L. (2002) *Dangerous and Severe Personality Disorder: Response and Role of the Psychiatric Team* (Chapter 1). Routledge, London.

Byrt, R., Wray, C. and 'Tom'. (2005) Towards hope and inclusion: nursing interventions in a medium secure service for men with 'Personality Disorders'. *Mental Health Practice*, **8**(8), 38–43.

Carter, D. E. and Porter, S. (2000) Validity and reliability. In: Cormack, D. (ed.) *The Research Process in Nursing*, 4th edn (Chapter 3). Blackwell Science, Oxford.

Castillo, H. (2003) *Personality Disorder: Temperament or Trauma?* Jessica Kingsley, London.

Collins, M. and Davies, S. (2005) The Security Needs Assessment Profile: a multidimensional approach to measuring security needs. *International Journal of Forensic Mental Health*, **4**(1), 39–52.

Dolan, B. and Coid, J. (1993) *Psychopathic and Antisocial Personality Disorders: Treatment and Research Issues*. Gaskell, London.

Doyle, M. (1998) Clinical risk assessment for mental health nurses. *Nursing Times*, **94**(17), 47–49.

Gelder, M., Mayou, R. and Cowen, P. (2001). *Shorter Oxford Textbook of Psychiatry*, 4th edn (Chapter 7). Oxford University Press, Oxford.

Gray, R. and Bressington, D. (2004) Pharmacological interventions and electro-convulsive therapy. In: Norman, I. and Ryrie, I. (eds.) *The Art and Science of Mental Health Nursing: A Textbook of Principles and Practice* (Chapter 11). Open University Press, Maidenhead.

Houghton, S. and Ousley, L. (2004) The person with a personality disorder. In: Norman, I. and Ryrie, I. (eds.) *The Art and Science of Mental Health Nursing: A Textbook of Principles and Practice* (Chapter 21). Open University Press, Maidenhead.

Jeffcote, N. and Travers, R. (2004) Thinking about the needs of women in secure settings. In: Jeffcote, N. and Watson, T. (eds.) *Working Therapeutically with Women in Secure Mental Health Settings* (Chapter 1). Jessica Kingsley, London.

Kettles, A. M., Moir, E., Woods, P., Porter, S. and Sutherland, E. (2004) Is there a relationship between risk assessment and observation level? *Journal of Psychiatric and Mental Health Nursing*, **11**(2), 156–164.

Livesley, W. J. (2001) Conceptual and taxonomic issues. In: Livesley, W. J. (ed.) *Handbook of Personality Disorders: Theory, Research and Treatment* (Chapter 1). Guilford Press, New York.

Magnavita, J. J. (2004) Classification, prevalence and etiology of personality disorders: related issues and controversy. In: Magnavita, J. J. (ed.) *Handbook of Personality Disorders: Theory and Practice* (Chapter 1). John Wiley and Sons, Inc., Hoboken, New Jersey.

National Institute for Mental Health in England (2003). *Personality Disorder: No Longer a Diagnosis of Exclusion*. Department of Health, London.

Paris, J. (2004) Sociocultural factors in the treatment of personality disorders. In: Magnavita, J. J. (ed.) *Handbook of Personality Disorders: Theory and Practice* (Chapter 7). John Wiley and Sons, Inc., Hoboken, New Jersey.

Parsons, S. (2003) The person with a diagnosis of borderline personality disorder. In: Barker, P. (ed.) *Psychiatric and Mental Health Nursing: The Craft of Caring* (Chapter 35). Arnold, London.

Perlin, C. K. (2001) Social responses and personality disorders. In: Stuart, G. W. and Laraia, M. T. (eds.) *Principles and Practice of Psychiatric Nursing*, 7th edn (Chapter 23). Mosby, St Louis.

Pilgrim, D. (2001) Disordered personalities and disordered concepts. *Journal of Mental Health*, **10**, 253–265.

Sayce, L. (2000) *From Psychiatric Patient to Citizen: Overcoming Discrimination and Social Exclusion*. Macmillan, Basingstoke.

Schafer, P. (2002) Nursing interventions and future directions with patients who constantly break rules and test boundaries. In: Kettles, A. M., Woods, P. and Collins, M. (eds.) *Therapeutic Interventions for Forensic Mental Health Nurses* (Chapter 4, pp. 56–71). Jessica Kingsley, London.

Smith, E. E., Nolen-Hoeksema, S., Frederickson, B. and Loftus, G. R. (eds.) (2003) *Atkinson and Hilgard's Introduction to Psychology*, 14th edn. Thomson Wadsworth, Belmont, CA.

Tyrer, P. (2000) *Personality Disorders: Diagnosis, Management and Course*, 2nd edn. Butterworth Heinemann, Oxford.

Wells, S. and Cowen Orlin, L. (2003) *Shakespeare: An Oxford Guide*. Oxford University Press, Oxford.

Woods, P. (2001) Personality disorders. In: Dale, C., Thompson, T. and Woods, P. (eds.) *Forensic Mental Health – Issues in Practice*. Ballière Tindall, London.

Woods, P. and Richards, D. (2003) Effectiveness of nursing interventions in people with personality disorders. *Journal of Advanced Nursing*, **44**(2), 154–172.

World Health Organization (1992) *The ICD-10 Classification of Mental and Behavioural Disorders: Clinical Descriptions and Diagnostic Guidelines*. World Health Organization, Geneva.

CHAPTER 2

Types of personality disorder

Phil Woods

Introduction

This chapter will focus on the types of personality disorder, with reference to classifications in International Classification of Diseases (ICD-10) (World Health Organization, 1992) and Diagnostic Statistical Manual (DSM-IV) (American Psychiatric Association, 1994). The main presentation of different types of personality disorder is also summarised according to the classification descriptions. Theories of aetiology, with particular reference to recent research and the implications for nursing interventions, are also given.

It should be pointed out early in this chapter that in England and Wales personality disorder diagnosis is often clouded by the legal category of psychopathic disorder. According to the current Mental Health Act 1983 psychopathic disorder is defined as: 'a persistent disorder or disability of mind (whether or not including significant impairment of intelligence) which results in abnormally aggressive or severely irresponsible conduct'. This is further clouded by the different meanings that psychopathic disorder can have: the legal classification, as noted above; it is a clinical diagnostic construct or category in some classifications; and the vernacular as a term of derogation (Moran, 1999, p. xi). It has also acquired a disparaging implication in clinical work particularly when a patient is identified as 'a psychopath' or as 'psychopathic', with the implication that the patient is untreatable. The term has survived increasingly widespread criticism as recorded in many official reports and professional publications and has attracted cogent arguments for its replacement. The Draft Mental Health Bill (Department of Health, 2004) has removed the term 'psychopathic disorder', suggesting that a diagnosis of mental disorder will be made. Therefore one has to assume this will mean a diagnosis of personality disorder where appropriate. However, the term 'psychopath' is regarded as a separate clinical construct (Hare, 1998) which is perhaps most closely associated with the diagnostic classifications of anti-social personality disorder and dissocial personality disorder (see Dolan and Coid, 1993).

For an effective diagnosis of personality disorder to be made, systematic assessment first has to take place. For those clinicians currently able to make these diagnostic assessments (and currently this does usually include nurses), research has predominately focused on examining the numerous self-report and interview schedules which assist in the classification of personality disorders (e.g. Clark *et al.*, 1997; Maffei *et al.*, 1997; Perry, 1992; Zimmerman, 1994). Comparisons are frequently made with the current diagnostic categories of ICD-10 and DSM-IV or the factor structures of abnormal and normal personality (e.g. Blais and Norman, 1997; Livesley *et al.*, 1994; Parker, 1998; Strack and Lorr, 1997).

Moran (1999, p. 2) comments on how by their very nature the personality disorders present a multitude of measurement problems, as they are diagnosed in an interpersonal context and are nearly totally dependent on the characteristic patterns of social interaction. Grubin and Duggan (1998) indicate that a core assessment battery of instruments should relate to specific treatment targets (pre- and post-test), e.g. diagnosis, impulsivity, hostility, empathy and defence style, and additionally should be more specific to some programmes addressing arson, sex offending and self-harm. Meux and McDonald (1998) state that assessment is the gatekeeper to treatment (and often the progress through it); and it should assist in determining management strategies. There is general agreement that current assessment methods are probably inadequate and that assessment cannot be separated from treatment issues. Meux and McDonald (1998) make some key points:

> ... it is important to use both dimensional and categorical approaches; it should involve multi-disciplinary collaboration; assessment methods should provide vertical descriptions of disorder within the individual (biological; cognitive; behavioural; and social issues) as well as protective factors (intra-personal and environmental factors) and co-morbidity with other mental disorders; as interview, observation and history are the most reliable forms of assessment these should form the bulk of the process.

It is important that hypothesis generation through assessment should include aetiology (pre-disposing factors) – any variable that may have made the individual vulnerable to develop the problem; precipitating events – any specific trigger event which appear to generate the problem; and maintaining factors. Turkat and Maisto (1985) indicate that the modification of social behaviour involves four key areas which are specific to assessment: social attention, information processing, response emission, and feedback.

One of the main problems inherent in the diagnosis of personality disorder is whether or not a dimensional or a categorical approach should be used. However, in the absence of any answer to this vigorous academic theoretical debate, personality disorders are diagnosed either through the Diagnostic and Statistical Manual of Mental Disorders (DSM-IV) (American Psychiatric Association, 1994) or the International Classification of Diseases (ICD-10) (World Health Organization, 1992).

DSM-IV

The American Psychiatric Association (1994) developed a multi-axial system to assist clinicians to plan treatment and predict outcome. There are five axes included in the DSM-IV:

- Axis I: clinical disorders and other conditions that may be a focus of clinical attention
- Axis II: personality disorders and mental retardation

- Axis III: general medical conditions
- Axis IV: psychosocial and environmental problems
- Axis V: global assessment of functioning

The diagnosis of personality disorders according to the Manual (p. 630) requires an evaluation of the individual's long-term patterns of functioning, and the particular personality features must be evident by early adulthood. The personality traits that define these disorders must also be distinguished from characteristics that emerge in response to specific situational stressors or more transient mental states.

The assessment of personality disorders should assess the stability of the personality traits over time and across different situations. Although a single interview with the person is sometimes sufficient for making the diagnosis, it is often necessary to conduct more than one interview and to space these over time. Assessment may also be complicated by the fact that the individual may not consider the characteristics that define a personality disorder problematic. To help overcome this difficulty, supplementary information from other informants may be helpful.

The DSM-IV manual lists general diagnostic criteria for a personality disorder as:

- An enduring pattern of inner experience and behaviour that deviates markedly from the expectations of the individual's culture. This pattern is manifested in two (or more) of the following areas: cognition (i.e. ways of perceiving and interpreting self, other people and events); affectivity (i.e. the range, intensity, liability, and appropriateness of emotional response); inter-personal functioning; and impulse control.
- The enduring pattern is inflexible and pervasive across a broad range of personal and social situations.
- The enduring pattern leads to clinically significant distress or impairment in social, occupational, or other important areas of functioning.
- The pattern is stable and of long duration and its onset can be traced back at least to adolescence or early adulthood.
- The enduring pattern is not better accounted for as a manifestation or consequence of another mental disorder.
- The enduring pattern is not due to the direct physiological effects of a substance (e.g. a drug of abuse, a medication) or a general medical condition (e.g. head trauma).

DSM-IV describes 10 specific personality disorders grouped into three clusters based on descriptive similarities:

- Cluster A: includes paranoid, schizoid and schizotypal personality disorders.
- Cluster B: includes anti-social, borderline, histrionic and narcissistic personality disorders
- Cluster C: includes avoidant, dependent and obsessive-compulsive personality disorder.

Psyweb.com (accessed 16 February 2005) provides an excellent summary of the main presentation features for each of the 10 types and these are reproduced in Box 2.1.

Box 2.1: Main presentation features of DSM-IV personality disorders (source http://www.psyweb.com/Mdisord/jsp/personalityDis.jsp).

- **Antisocial personality disorder**: Lack of regard for the moral or legal standards in the local culture, marked inability to get along with others or abide by societal rules. Sometimes called psychopaths or sociopaths.
- **Avoidant personality disorder**: Marked social inhibition, feelings of inadequacy, and extremely sensitive to criticism.
- **Borderline personality disorder**: Lack of one's own identity, with rapid changes in mood, intense unstable interpersonal relationships, marked impulsivity, instability in affect and in self-image.
- **Dependent personality disorder**: Extreme need of other people, to a point where the person is unable to make any decisions or take an independent stand on his or her own. Fear of separation. Submissive behaviour. Marked lack of decisiveness and self-confidence.
- **Histrionic personality disorder**: Exaggerated and often inappropriate displays of emotional reactions, approaching theatricality, in everyday behaviour. Sudden and rapidly shifting emotion expressions.
- **Narcissistic personality disorder**: Behaviour or a fantasy of grandiosity, a lack of empathy, a need to be admired by others, an inability to see the viewpoints of others, and hypersensitive to the opinions of others.
- **Obsessive-compulsive personality disorder**: Characterized by perfectionism and inflexibility; preoccupation with uncontrollable patterns of thought and action.
- **Paranoid personality disorder**: Marked distrust of others, including the belief, without reason, that others are exploiting, harming, or trying to deceive him or her; lack of trust; belief of others' betrayal; belief in hidden meanings; unforgiving and grudge holding.
- **Schizoid personality disorder**: Primarily characterized by a very limited range of emotion, both in expression of and experiencing; indifferent to social relationships.
- **Schizotypal personality disorder**: Peculiarities of thinking, odd beliefs, and eccentricities of appearance, behaviour, interpersonal style, and thought (e.g. belief in psychic phenomena and having magical powers).

ICD-10

Chapter 5 of ICD-10 contains classification codes for Mental Disorders. These are:

- Organic, including symptomatic, mental disorders (F00–F09).
- Mental and behavioural disorders due to psychoactive substance abuse (F10–F19).
- Schizophrenia, schizotypal and delusional disorders (F20–F29).
- Mood (affective) disorders (F30–F39).
- Neurotic, stress-related and somatoform disorders (F40–F48).

- Behavioural syndromes associated with physiological disturbances and physical factors (F50–F59).
- Disorders of adult personality and behaviour (F60–F69).
- Mental retardation (F70–F79).
- Disorders of psychological development (F80–F89).
- Behavioural emotional disorders with onset usually occurring in childhood or adolescence (F90–F98).

The ICD-10 classifies personality disorders to include a variety of clinically significant conditions and behaviours, each of which are classified according to clusters of traits which correspond to the most frequent or conspicuous behaviour manifestations. General diagnostic guidelines are given as:

> Conditions not directly attributable to gross brain damage or disease or to another psychiatric disorder, meeting the following criteria: markedly disharmonious attitudes and behaviour, involving usually several areas of functioning, e.g. affectivity, arousal, impulse control, ways of perceiving and thinking, and style of relating to others; the abnormal behaviour pattern is enduring, of long standing, and not limited to episodes of mental illness; the abnormal behaviour pattern is pervasive and clearly maladaptive to a broad range of personal and social situations; the above manifestations always appear during childhood or adolescence and continue into adulthood; the disorder leads to considerable personal distress but this may only become apparent late in its course; the disorder is usually, but not invariably, associated with significant problems in occupational and social performance.

ICD-10 classifies personality disorders into 10 specific categories. The classification also gives some characteristics which are also summarized below (source `http://www3.who.int/icd/vol1htm2003/fr-icd.htm`):

- **Paranoid personality disorder (F60.0)**: excessive sensitivity to setbacks, unforgiveness of insults; suspiciousness; tendency to distort experience by misconstruing the neutral or friendly actions of others as hostile or contemptuous; recurrent suspicions, without justification, regarding the sexual fidelity of the spouse or sexual partner; and a combative and tenacious sense of personal rights; excessive self-importance; excessive self-reference.
- **Schizoid personality disorder (F60.1)**: withdrawal from affectional, social and other contacts with preference for fantasy, solitary activities, and introspection; limited capacity to express feelings and to experience pleasure.
- **Dissocial personality disorder (F60.2)**: disregard for social obligations, and callous unconcern for the feelings of others; gross disparity between behaviour and the prevailing social norms; behaviour not readily modifiable by adverse experience, including punishment; low tolerance to frustration; low threshold for discharge of aggression, including violence; tendency to blame others, or to offer plausible rationalizations for the behaviour bringing the patient into conflict with society.
- **Emotionally unstable personality disorder (F60.3) – either impulsive (.30) or borderline type (.31)**: definite tendency to act impulsively and without consideration of the consequences; the mood is unpredictable and capricious; liability to outbursts of emotion and an incapacity to

control the behavioural explosions; tendency to quarrelsome behaviour and to conflicts with others. *The impulsive type*: emotional instability and lack of impulse control. *The borderline type*: disturbances in self-image, aims, and internal preferences; chronic feelings of emptiness; intense and unstable interpersonal relationships; tendency to self-destructive behaviour, including suicide gestures and attempts.

- **Histrionic personality disorder (F60.4)**: shallow and labile affectivity; self-dramatization; theatricality; exaggerated expression of emotions; suggestibility; egocentricity; self-indulgence; lack of consideration for others; easily hurt feelings; continuous seeking for appreciation, excitement and attention.
- **Anankastic personality disorder (F60.5)**: feelings of doubt; perfectionism; excessive conscientiousness; checking and preoccupation with details; stubbornness; caution; rigidity; insistent and unwelcome thoughts or impulses that do not attain the severity of an obsessive-compulsive disorder.
- **Anxious (avoidant) personality disorder (F60.6)**: feelings of tension and apprehension insecurity and inferiority; continuous yearning to be liked and accepted; hypersensitivity to rejection and criticism with restricted personal attachments; tendency to avoid certain activities by habitual exaggeration of the potential dangers or risks in everyday situations.
- **Dependent personality disorder (F60.7)**: pervasive passive reliance on other people to make one's major and minor life decisions; great fear of abandonment; feelings of helplessness and incompetence; passive compliance with the wishes of elders and others; weak response to the demands of daily life; lack of vigour may show itself in the intellectual or emotional spheres; often a tendency to transfer responsibility to others.
- **Other specific personality disorders (F60.8)**
- **Personality disorder, unspecified (F60.9)**

Implications for nursing interventions

Any interventions undertaken in forensic mental health care should have at their root the reduction of risk or dangerousness and any associated offending behaviours. As the main presentation of the personality disorders is behavioural it would appear sensible to focus effort on the behavioural repertoires manifested as a result of the disorder.

It is clear from clinical experience and well supported in the literature that antisocial or challenging behaviours associated with personality disorders are often well established since early childhood. Moran (1999) discusses these in relation to childhood conduct disorder; childhood hyperactivity; delinquency; childhood temperament; childhood victimization; and coercive child rearing. Dolan and Coid (1993) report that research has demonstrated that those who show conduct disorder in childhood, have poor peer relationships, and come from disordered and deprived family backgrounds, with parents displaying mental illness, criminality and abusive behaviour, are more likely to have personality disorder in adulthood. They extensively discuss all these natural history issues and the reader is directed towards this text.

So where should assessment focus to develop potential interventions? Links (1996) indicates that assessment and its related treatment should focus on three areas (1) self-determination (2) role functioning and (3) the clinician maintaining hope. Grubin and Duggan (1998) comment that treatment issues should focus on individual functioning, specific symptoms and behaviours, or more distant outcomes, i.e. offending. In perhaps the most comprehensive review to date of the treatment of antisocial personality disorders, Dolan and Coid (1993) conclude that there was little evidence of sufficient methodological quality to suggest that any particular approach to treatment was effective. Eleven years on, the Government is funding extension research through its personality disorder and Dangerous and Severe Personality Disorder (DSPD) research programmes. The results of these studies will undoubtedly add much to the current evidence base.

Allnutt and Links (1996, p. 23) state that it is clinically useful to consider behavioural deficits of the personality disorders from their optimal DSM-IV criteria:

1. Antisocial: criminal, aggressive, impulsive and irresponsible behaviours.
2. Avoidant: the avoidance of any occupational activity which may mean interpersonal contact for them. This avoids the possibility of their greatest fear of criticism, disapproval or rejection.
3. Borderline: frantic avoidance of either imagined or real abandonment.
4. Dependent: others need to be responsible for their major areas of living.
5. Histrionic: uncomfortable in interpersonal situations when they are not the centre of attention.
6. Narcissistic: a grandiose sense of self-importance.
7. Obsessive-compulsive: perfectionism is seen to interfere with daily living.
8. Paranoid: ideas that others are exploiting, harming or deceiving are apparent.
9. Schizoid: no desire or enjoyment for close relationships.
10. Schizotypal: behaviour, speech, appearance or thinking are eccentric or peculiar.

Often treatment for personality disordered individuals is psychotherapeutic or cognitive behavioural. Underpinning the psychotherapeutic approach is the psychodynamic approach to therapy, where emphasis is given to the individual's personality structure and development; therapy is aimed at developing insight and understanding into feelings and addressing maladaptive defence mechanisms. Dolan and Coid (1993) indicate poor outcome with individual and outpatient psychotherapy, and more success with group and inpatient psychotherapy.

Cognitive and behavioural approaches are perhaps the most widely used at present in forensic services. These programmes usually offer a skills- or social skills-based approach to therapy. Behavioural therapy has been shown to be more successful; however, this only addresses current environmental antecedents and consequences of behaviour. Cognitive–behavioural approaches question individuals' maladaptive irrational thoughts, thus providing new cognitions to replace these. Cognitive therapy works at a dual level of manifested behavioural problems and inferred schema. Moreover, according to Andrews *et al.* (1990), Antonowicz and Ross (1994), Hollin (1993) and Tennant *et al.* (1999), effective treatment must include:

- A sound theoretical base
- Multi-faceted programming
- An individualized assessment of need
- Targeting of crimogenic needs
- Use of active and structured behavioural and social learning techniques

■ Modelling of prosocial attitudes
■ A cognitive–behavioural emphasis inclusive of social cognitive skills training.

Tennant *et al.* (1999) describe a behavioural approach to caring for personality disorders, based around developing trust and a therapeutic relationship, employing a multidisciplinary assessment focusing on symptoms and offending behaviours. More specifically the approach involves: a functional assessment of problem and offence-related behaviours; assessment using the Hare Psychopathy Checklist; standardized psychiatric assessment (e.g. impulsivity, empathy, sexual interest, aggression, blame); pre- and post-test intervention psychological measures (e.g. sexual offending, arson, anger management); and monitoring and recording of behaviours.

It is beyond the scope of this chapter to provide comprehensive accounts of the treatment methods currently being tried with personality disorders. Indeed, many of the later chapters in this text discuss these. However, Stowell-Smith (2000) provides insight into psychodynamic psychotherapy, personality disorder and offending; Jones (2000) into therapeutic community in a forensic setting; McGuire (2000) into problem-solving training with secure hospital patients; and Jackson and Martin (2000) into relating neurological and neuropsychological deficits to antisocial personality and offending behaviour.

Conclusion

It is clear that personality disorders manifest in a variety of behavioural repertoires. They often defy true assessment and measurement. Frameworks that exist to assist with diagnosis have been heavily criticised in the literature. Thus, until such a time as forensic mental health professionals are either able to accurately speculate to effectively determine future behaviours, or effective methods of treatment are found which actually reduce risk or dangerousness in the long term, personality disordered individuals will continue to stretch the imagination and resources of forensic mental health services (Woods, 2001).

References

Allnutt, S. and Links, P. S. (1996) Diagnosing specific personality disorders and the optimal criteria. In: Links, P. (ed.) *Clinical Assessment and Management of Severe Personality Disorders*. American Psychiatric Press, Washington.

American Psychiatric Association (1994) *Diagnostic and Statistical Manual of Mental Disorders*, 4th edn (DSM-IV). American Psychiatric Association, Washington.

Andrews, D. A., Zinger, I., Hodge, R. D. *et al.* (1990) Does correctional treatment work? A clinically relevant and psychologically informed meta-analysis. *Criminology*, **28**, 369–404.

Antonowicz, D. H. and Ross, R. R. (1994) Essential components of successful rehabilitation programmes for offenders. *International Journal of Offender Therapy and Comparative Criminology*, **38**, 97–104.

Blais, M. A. and Norman, D. K. (1997) A psychometric evaluation of the DSM-IV personality disorder criteria. *Journal of Personality Disorders*, **11**(2), 168–176.

Clark, L., Livesley, W. J. and Morey, L. (1997) Personality disorder assessment: the challenge of construct validity. *Journal of Personality Disorders*, **11**(3), 205–231.

Department of Health (2004). *Draft Mental Health Bill*. Department of Health, London.

Dolan, B. and Coid, J. (1993) *Psychopathic and Antisocial Personality Disorders: Treatment and Research Issues*. Gaskell, London.

Grubin, D. and Duggan, C. (1998) *Staff Support and Interventions*. High Security Psychiatric Services Commissioning Board, London.

Hare, R. D. (1998) Psychopaths and their nature: Implications for the mental health and criminal justice systems. In: Millon, T., Simonsen, E., Birket-Smith, M. and Davis, R. D. (eds.) *Psychopathy: Antisocial, Criminal and Violent Behaviour*. Guilford Press, New York.

Hollin, C. (1993) Advances in psychological treatment of delinquent behaviour. *Criminal Behaviour and Mental Health*, **3**, 142–157.

Jackson, H. and Martin, J. (2000) Relating neurological and neuropsychological deficits to antisocial personality and offending behaviour. In: Mercer, D., Mason, T., McKeown, M. and MacCann, G. (eds.) *Forensic Mental Health Care: a Case Study Approach*. Churchill Livingstone, Edinburgh.

Jones, L. (2000) Therapeutic community in a forensic setting. In: Mercer, D., Mason, T., McKeown, M. and MacCann, G. (eds.) *Forensic Mental Health Care: a Case Study Approach*. Churchill Livingstone, Edinburgh.

Links, P. (1996) *Clinical Assessment and Management of Severe Personality Disorders*. American Psychiatric Press, Washington.

Livesley, W. J., Schroeder, M. L., Jackson, D. N. and Jang, K. L. (1994) Categorical distinctions in the study of personality disorder: implications for classification. *Journal of Abnormal Psychology*, **103**(1), 6–17.

Maffei, C., Fossati, A., Agostoni, I., Barraco, A., Bagnato, M., Deborah, D., Namia, C., Novella, L. and Petrachi, M. (1997). Interrater reliability and internal consistency of the structured clinical interview for DSM-IV Axis II personality disorders (SCID-II), version 2.0. *Journal of Personality Disorders*, **11**(3), 279–284.

McGuire, J. (2000) Problem-solving training: pilot work with secure hospital patients. In: Mercer, D., Mason, T., McKeown, M. and MacCann, G. (eds.) *Forensic Mental Health Care: a Case Study Approach*. Churchill Livingstone, Edinburgh.

Meux, C. and McDonald, B. (1998) *Assessment and diagnostic criteria*. High Security Psychiatric Services Commissioning Board, London.

Moran, P. (1999) *Anti-Social Personality Disorder: an Epidemiological Perspective*. Gaskell, London.

Parker, G. (1998) Personality disorders as alien territory: classification, measurement and border issues. *Current Opinion in Psychiatry*, **11**, 125–129.

Perry, J. C. (1992) Problems and considerations in the valid assessment of personality disorders. *American Journal of Psychiatry*, **149**(12), 1645–1653.

Stowell-Smith, M. (2000) Psychodynamic psychotherapy, personality disorder and offending. In: Mercer, D., Mason, T., McKeown, M. and MacCann, G. (eds.) *Forensic Mental Health Care: a Case Study Approach*. Churchill Livingstone, Edinburgh.

Strack, S. and Lorr, M. (1997) The challenge of differentiating normal and disordered personality. *Journal of Personality Disorders*, **11**(2), 105–122.

Tennant, A., Davies, C. and Tennant, I. (1999) Working with the personality disordered offender. In: Chaloner, C. and Coffey, M. (eds). *Forensic Mental Health Nursing: Current Approaches*. Blackwell Science, Oxford.

Turkat, I. D. and Maisto, S. A. (1985) Personality disorders: application of the experimental method to the formulation and modification of personality disorders. In: Barlow, D. H. (ed.) *Clinical Handbook of Psychological Disorders*. Guilford Press, New York.

Woods, P. (2001) Personality disorders. In: Dale, C., Thompson, T. and Woods, P. (eds.) *Forensic Mental Health – Issues in Practice*. Baillière Tindall, London.

World Health Organization (1992) *The ICD-10 Classification of Mental and Behavioural Disorders: Clinical Descriptions and Diagnostic Guidelines*. World Health Organization, Geneva.

Zimmerman, M. (1994). Diagnosing personality disorders: a review of issues and research methods. *Archives of General Psychiatry*, **51**, 225–245.

CHAPTER 3

The social consequences of a 'personality disorder' diagnosis

Richard Byrt with a contribution by Jim Dooher

Introduction

> ... For the service user, finding out that you have a diagnosis of personality disorder can be a traumatic and bewildering experience. All too often, such a diagnosis brings with it a change in attitude from other people.

> ... You only have to read the negative terminology in ... [ICD-10] and [DSM-IV] to realise that there is little hope associated with a diagnosis of personality disorder (PD) ...

(Castillo *et al*. 2001, p. 17: International Classification of Diseases (ICD-10: World Health Organization, 1992) and Diagnostic Statistical Manual (DSM-IV: American Psychiatric Association, 1994) are discussed in Chapter 2 of this text).

> ...When people experience mental or physical health problems, they like to be able to put a name to their difficulty .... This diagnosis, this 'label', allows you to get a handle on your problem, to find information about it, and perhaps even empower you to take steps towards your own recovery (Ashman, 2001, p. 30f).

The above quotes, both by former service users, indicate that 'personality disorder' can be perceived as either a stigmatising label or a helpful diagnosis, with implications for nursing and other interventions. Few diagnoses appear to arouse such strong feelings. This chapter will consider attitudes (defined in Box 3.2; p. 26) in society, with particular reference to the media and political decision making. The rationale for considering these topics is that the literature, including research findings, suggests that self-awareness is a crucial basis for nursing and other interventions with individuals with personality disorder (Aiyegbusi, 2004; Bowers, 2002; Schafer, 2002; see also Chapter 4 of this text). It is suggested that this self-awareness is related to an appreciation of the influence on professionals' attitudes of those expressed in wider society.

Critiques of 'personality disorder'

Chapter 2 considers types of personality disorder delineated in the two major classificatory systems used in psychiatry: the International Classification of Diseases (ICD-10) (World Health Organization, 1992) and the Diagnostic Statistical Manual (DSM-IV) (American Psychiatric Association, 1994). Some psychiatrists and other mental health professionals have found these classifications of 'types' of personality disorder useful in relation to the diagnosis of features or symptoms that cause distress to the individual and, sometimes, to others. Some authors have argued that, despite limitations, the existing classifications have implications for the understanding of individuals and the implementation of treatment and other interventions to relieve and reduce distressing symptoms. This is the general view in one medium-secure service for individuals with personality disorders (Byrt *et al.*, 2005; D'Silva and Duggan, 2002).

However, many critics (including some service users, sociologists and mental health professionals) have questioned the extent that 'personality disorder' is a meaningful, helpful, or scientifically valid or reliable category (Blackburn, 2000; Castillo, 2003; Magnavita, 2004b; Pilgrim, 2001). The need to consider cultural factors in relation to diagnoses of personality disorder has also been emphasised (Paris, 2004). It has been argued that problems in these areas restrict the utility of diagnoses and their relevance for treatment and other interventions.

> ... The [Diagnostic Statistical Manual] approach has limited clinical utility. Diagnostic overlap is a major problem, and there is limited evidence that current categories predict response to treatment ... DSM diagnoses are too broad and heterogeneous to use in investigations of biological and psychological mechanisms, forcing investigators to use alternative constructs and measures ... (Livesley, 2001a, p. 6f).

Diagnosis or label?

Wing (1978) stated that a psychiatric diagnosis is of value only if it informs decisions about appropriate treatment for the patient, rather than stigmatising or labelling him/her. (Labelling is defined in Box 3.2; p. 26) Sanders and Tudor (2001, p. 147) refer to the importance of approaches to diagnoses that are 'person-centred': i.e. based on Carl Rogers' humanistic approach, and valuing, and taking seriously, the individual's experiences. However, both service users and professionals have criticised ways in which service users with personality diagnoses have been labelled and written off as 'untreatable' (Campling and Birtle, 2001; Castillo, 2003; Pilgrim, 2001):

> They are not pitied for their symptoms but condemned for their moral failings (Pilgrim, 2001, p. 258, quoted in Byrt *et al.*, 2005, p. 38).

> ... Personality disorder appears to be an enduring pejorative judgment, rather than a clinical diagnosis ... (Lewis and Appleby, 1988, p. 44, quoted in Castillo, 2003, p. 19).

Campling and Birtle (2001) suggest alternative terms, including 'disorganised attachment' and 'emotionally unstable'. Magnavita (2004b, p. 9) argues for the use of 'personality dysfunction', instead of personality disorder, not only as the former would be less negative, but because it 'is a more fluid construct that allows for changes in the manner in which a person's personality functions'. However, are alternative names for personality disorder necessarily less stigmatising? According to one former service user:

> ... Information on PD [personality disorder] that is useful to a person struggling with one, is hard enough to come by, as it is. A name change will only make this situation worse.

> ... Changing the label will not eradicate the stigma and the prejudice ... currently attached to PD. It will simply attach itself to the new label.

> ... The effort should be on changing how PDs are viewed in the mental health profession, amongst the public and the media .... If we drive the stigma from the label, it merely becomes a name once again ... (Ashman, 2001, p. 30f).

Some authors have commented that psychiatric diagnoses are influenced by the values of professionals and by political and economic motivations in wider society (Busfield, 2001; Pilgrim, 2001; Sanders and Tudor, 2001). Pilgrim (2001, p. 256), citing Levenson (1992), argues that many features of 'personality disorder' involve 'a failure to conform to social norms'; and that 'personality disorder' is, therefore a meaningless category, since it could be used to describe people who break social norms, including opposition to tyrannical political regimes or institutionalised racism.

Whatever we call 'personality disorder', there is evidence that it causes suffering to individuals so diagnosed, and sometimes, to others (Magnavita, 2004a). Box 3.1 gives examples, based on the author's experience, but for reasons of confidentiality, actual people are not described. For the sake of clarity, a single personality disorder has been outlined in relation to each individual. However, the literature suggests that individuals often have features of two or more personality disorders (Livesley, 2001a).

The development of 'personality disorder' and related concepts

The literature of many cultures, from at least the 5th century BC, indicates an interest in possible links between personality and mental health problems (Magnavita, 2004b), with, for example, frequent references in Shakespeare (e.g. to Hamlet's melancholy humour: Skultans, 1979).

Did King Richard III have a personality disorder?

Prins (1995, 2001) has given examples of 'personality disorders' from Shakespeare, including the description (below) of Richard III by his mother, the Duchess of York. Prins suggests that this

Box 3.1: The impact of personality disorder on the lives of 'Mahendra', 'May', 'Ted' and 'Hera'.

'Mr Mahendra Patel'

'Mr Mahendra Patel', aged 29, is very fond of his three-year-old son, and is trying to maintain a relationship with him and with his new girlfriend; and at the same time, tour with his band as their drummer. Mahendra has a *paranoid personality disorder*. Since his early teens, he has been extremely suspicious, misinterpreting what people say as evidence that they are against him. On several occasions he has walked up to another man in a club and asked aggressively 'Why are you staring at me?', when he has not, in fact, been stared at, or treated in a discriminatory or negative way. Such challenges tend to involve Mahendra in fights. He finds it hard to trust anyone, including members of his band, and often broods on past wrongs in lonely silence. Unlike many people with a diagnosis of paranoid schizophrenia, Mahendra does not have persecutory delusions (beliefs which are not shared by others in his cultural, religious, educational or social group) or auditory hallucinations (voices) telling him that others are out to get him.

'Ms May Morris'

'Ms May Morris' is a woman of 38. On the rare occasions when she can relax, she likes to play Scrabble at a local club and spend time at home with her girlfriend. May has an *obsessive–compulsive or anankastic personality disorder*. She is so conscientious and concerned about making mistakes that she spends many hours checking her work as an accountant and her domestic arrangements. May sets herself impossibly high standards and often feels guilty – unnecessarily so, in the view of those who know her. May finds it hard to sleep at night as she ruminates about her work. She finds it difficult to be spontaneous or enjoy herself. She allows herself little time to relax or to develop close, satisfying relationships with her girlfriend or with other people.

'Mr Ted Thompson'

'Mr Ted Thompson' is a keen footballer and weightlifter and enjoys clubbing. In addition, he has an *antisocial personality disorder*. Now in his early thirties, for many years he has frequently behaved impulsively, without thinking of the (sometimes serious) effects on himself and others. Last week, he impulsively stole a leather jacket in a shop and took it without thinking, or checking to notice the store detective standing nearby. Ted finds it difficult to feel concern for other people, although he likes to be with a crowd and enjoys riotous parties. He also finds it difficult to experience empathy for others. Sometimes he acts callously for no apparent reason. Ted has difficulty sustaining friendships or close relationships and has assaulted a succession of girlfriends. He finds it hard to stay long in a job, gets bored easily and resents anyone in authority. At times, Ted experiences considerable distress and wishes he could develop his many abilities. He doesn't let on that, underneath, he feels quite sad. Instead, he tends to express his despair through aggression towards other people.

'Ms Hera Horst'

'Ms Hera Horst', aged 27, is a talented artist, sharing a studio with her new husband, whom, she says, is the only person who really understands her. Hera has *borderline personality dis-*

order, and has experienced considerable distress. Her mother suddenly left the family home when Hera was three years old, and she still feels very abandoned. Hera was neglected and physically abused, and, between the ages of eight and eleven years, sexually abused, by her stepfather. Subsequently, Hera had a succession of foster-parents, all of whom found it difficult to cope with Hera's understandable difficulty in containing her anger and distress. Hera often expresses the latter through cutting her arms. (Not all people with borderline personality disorders have adverse childhood experiences: see Rachel Studley's account in Chapter 4.) As a young woman, Hera has had a succession of intense relationships, in which she has swung rapidly from idealising to denigrating her partner, with impulsive expressions of rage and weeping. Hera finds it difficult to trust others because of her early experiences, and feels persistently empty and worthless. Despite considerable talents, recognised by her husband and friends, Hera feels unable to believe in herself. She adds that some professionals have tended to increase her feelings of worthlessness by judging her as 'attention seeking' without seeking to understand the reasons for her behaviour. (This account is influenced by Bennett, 2003, p. 260).

account indicates that the King had psychopathic disorder or antisocial personality disorder. (A problem with Prins' view is that it is difficult to apply contemporary understandings and meanings to a comprehension of past events in a society, with different beliefs and world views: Carr, 1964; Skultans, 1979).

> Thou cam'st on earth to make the earth my hell.
> A grievous burden was thy birth to me;
> Tetchy and wayward was thy infancy;
> Thy School days frightful, desp'rate, wild and furious;
> Thy prime of manhood daring, bold and venturous;
> Thy age confirmed, proud, subtle, sly and bloody,
> More mild but yet more harmful – kind in hatred,
> What comfortable hour can'st thou name
> That ever graced me with thy company?'
> (*Richard III*, Act IV, Scene iv, quoted in Prins (1995, p. 134f).

Early attempts to describe aspects of what are now known as 'personality disorders' were made by the French psychiatrist, Phillipe Pinel in 1801. In the UK, Prichard (1835) used the term 'moral insanity' to refer to mental health problems which did not include delusions. In relation to contemporary diagnosis, Prichard's account of moral insanity included some features of present-day notions of both personality disorder and bipolar mental illness (Livesley, 2001a). Prichard used the term 'moral' to mean 'emotional and psychological and ... not ... the opposite of "immoral"' (Prins, 1995, p. 121). However, Maudsley's (1874) account of 'moral insanity' resembles some aspects of contemporary notions of antisocial personality disorder and of psychopathic disorder. The following extract from Maudsley (1874) sounds similar to present-day debates about whether antisocial personality disorder should be seen as a mental health problem and responded to with treatment or imprisonment:

[Moral insanity] ... has so much the look of vice or crime that many persons regard it as an unfounded medical invention. Much indignation, therefore, has been stirred up when it has been pleaded to shelter a supposed criminal from the penal consequences of his offences; and judges have repeatedly denounced it from the bench as 'a most dangerous medical doctrine'...which in the interests of society should be reprobated .... Of the actual existence of such a form of disease, no one who has made a practical study of insanity entertains a doubt ... (Maudsley, 1874, p. 170. In Skultans, 1975, p. 193f).

Present-day concepts of personality disorder evolved from the work of Schneider in Germany and Henderson in the UK in the first half of the 20th century (Livesley, 2001a). 'Within British and American psychiatry, the concepts of psychopathy and psychopathic personality ... [were] defined ... to describe what we would now call antisocial personality disorder; although the two are not synonymous ... (Livesley, 2001b, p. 6). From the 1930s, there were many studies of psychopathy and antisocial personality disorder, most notably by Henderson (1939), Cleckley (1976) and Hare (1991, 1998). Various types of personality disorder were delineated in the Diagnostic Statistical Manual (DSM) and International Classification of Diseases (ICD) in the second half of the 20th century. Borderline personality disorder was first described in 1938, and extensively studied from the 1960s (Manning, 2001).

Attitudes in wider society towards people with personality disorders

The next part of this chapter will examine the influence of attitudes in wider society. Research has found that media portrayals of individuals with both personality disorder and mental illness are predominantly negative. It has been argued that this both reflects, and contributes to, the widespread stigmatisation, labelling, negative discrimination and social exclusion (see Boxes 3.2 and 3.3) experienced by people with mental health problems, including personality disorders (Philo, 2001; Sayce, 2000; Wahl, 1995).

'Widespread stigmatising and discriminatory attitudes'

Most studies, from the 1950s onwards, report (often widespread) stigmatising and discriminatory attitudes of members of the public towards people with mental health problems, including personality disorders. Sayce (2000) concludes that, in the UK, the amount of this discrimination is similar to the (considerable) prevalence of racism in the 1950s. However, one study in 1997 reported more favourable attitudes (Market and Opinion Research International, 1997, cited in Warner 2001, p. 452). In addition, between 1998 and 2003, 'small, but sometimes significant, reductions in reported negative opinions' were reported in Royal College of Psychiatrist surveys (Crisp *et al.*, 2004, p. 135). However, other surveys have found little or no change in negative attitudes over time; and little or no effect of public education campaigns. More research is needed to establish

---

Box 3.2: Attitudes, stigmatisation, labelling, discrimination and social exclusion.

Attitude
Attitudes have been defined as:

> Favourable or unfavourable evaluations of, and reactions to, objects, people, situations, or other aspects of the world. (Smith *et al.*, 2003, p. G-2)

Stigmatisation
> A stigma '... implies a moral judgment .... Stigma is a difference that is deeply discrediting ... Goffman (1968) ... [argued] that we do not see people with stigmas as fully human. The view that stigmatised [people] are inferior ... results in all sorts of discrimination ...' (Porter, 1998, p. 145, citing Goffman, 1968)

Labelling
In labelling, other people see an individual as having one or a limited number of negative attributes which mark out him/her as radically different from, and inferior to, others. Labelling involves people assuming, for example, that everything an individual says or does is influenced by her/his personality disorder, and thus not to be taken seriously (Pilgrim and Rogers, 1999; Porter, 1998; Warner, 2001). An example would be: 'Don't ever give her any attention. Everything she does is attention-seeking'.

Discrimination
'Negative discrimination' refers to 'unfair treatment' (Sayce, 2000, p. 17). Positive discrimination includes identifying an individual as having particular needs or problems which entitle her/him to particular services.

Unfair or negative discrimination:

> ... serve[s] to separate and exclude individuals from society and from many of the benefits of society, such as equitable access to services like housing, education, health and social support. Discrimination in this way is a form of social exclusion ... (Mason, 2001, p. 3)

---

effective methods to achieve such change (National Institute for Mental Health in England, 2004). A Department of Health (2000) survey reported an increase in fear and intolerance towards mental health service users, possibly reflecting political, public and media concern about the supposed link between mental health problems, including personality disorder, and violence (Radcliffe, 2003, citing Department of Health, 2000).

Research has found that discrimination is compounded for people with mental health problems who are women, are from ethnic minority groups, or are gay, lesbian or transsexual. Stigma, social exclusion and discrimination (including racism, sexism and homophobia) can contribute to individuals' distress and mental health problems (National Institute for Mental Health in England,

---

Box 3.3: Social exclusion (contributed by Jim Dooher).

When individuals with personality disorders experience social exclusion, this is likely to contribute adversely to their problems and experiences. According to the Social Exclusion Unit:

> Social exclusion happens when people or places suffer from a series of problems such as unemployment, discrimination, poor skills, low incomes, poor housing, high crime, ill health and family breakdown. When such problems combine, they can create a vicious cycle.
>
> Social exclusion can happen as a result of problems that face one person in their life. But it can also start from birth. Being born into poverty or to parents with low skills still has a major influence on future life chances. (Office of the Deputy Prime Minister, Social Exclusion Unit, 2004)

Social exclusion is complex and multi-dimensional, and can pass from generation to generation. Social exclusion includes poverty and low income, but is a broader concept and encompasses some of the wider causes and consequences of deprivation.

2004). Nursing interventions with individuals with personality disorder need to be sensitive to their specific needs related to culture, religion and spirituality, gender, age, sexual orientation and identity and specific problems and disabilities (see Chapters 5 and 8 of this text).

Media association of personality disorder with violence

Studies indicate that mistaken ideas about people with mental health problems, including personality disorders, are relatively common; e.g. in relation to the incidence of violence. Most media images of people with mental health problems are negative, with violence being particularly reported, and out of proportion to its actual incidence (Huang and Priebe, 2003; Philo, 2001; Wahl, 1995). However, the National Confidential Inquiry into Suicide and Homicide, which reported in 2001, did not find an increase in the number of homicides committed by people with mental health problems (Appleby *et al.*, 2001).

The portrayal of personality disorder in the media often focuses on antisocial personality disorder and its association with violence (Tyson and Briscoe, 2002), to the exclusion of other types of personality disorder such as those resulting in internalisation of distress and experiences of excessive sadness or guilt. (The latter include depressive and obsessional or anankastic personality disorder: see Box 3.1 and Chapter 2).

In the media, and in some professional writing, the term 'psychopath' is used to describe (and often label) individuals with antisocial personality disorder (Tyson and Briscoe, 2002). (See p. 10 for a discussion of the overlap and differences between psychopathy and antisocial personality disorder.) Often, accounts indicate confusion between mental illness and personality disorder. For example, in *Red Dragon* by Thomas Harris, the protagonist 'is variously labelled as a "psychopath", a "madman" and "crazy" by authorities in the novel' (Wahl, 1995; p. 19, citing Harris, 1981). The term 'psycho' is often used ambiguously in the media to refer to individuals who are 'psychopathic' or have a mental illness. However, national surveys conducted by the Royal College of Psychiatrists have demonstrated 'the public's ability to recognise the ... differences' (Crisp *et al.*, 2004, p. 135) between different types of mental illness.

There are many newspaper reports (Philo *et al.*, 1996), novels (Wahl, 1995) and films (Wedding and Boyd, 1999) portraying individuals described as 'psychopathic'. Whilst most portrayals are unsympathetic, a few are positive. These include Randle McMurphy in *One Flew Over the Cuckoo's Nest* (Kesey, 1962). To some extent, he is presented, in both the novel and the film of the same title, as a hero who is battling against an inhuman and controlling psychiatric system, and who stands up for the rights of other patients (Wedding and Boyd, 1999). The novel suggests that Mr McMurphy's opponent, Nurse Ratched, is the one who is more negatively 'manipulative'.

However, the majority of portrayals of people described as 'psychopathic' emphasise violence, often in a sensational way, and to the exclusion of any consideration of the individual's positive attributes:

Dando killer is vain psychopath
(Laurance, 2003, p. 41, quoting *The Times*, 4 July 2001)

He is evil incarnate ... a psychopath who ... stalks his victims in the twilight of lonely desert roads. A sadistic murderer with religious visions, he tortures his victims before he kills them, and in the palm of each, he has deeply carved his unmistakable mark (Wahl, 1995, p. 75, quoting cover description of Duncan, 1995)

PSYCHO TOWERS
Three Mad Killers and a Child Molester Mix with Theme Park Kids
(Newspaper headline referring to high security hospital patients' trip to Alton Towers theme park: *Sunday Mirror*, 1995, quoted in Phillips, 2003, p. 221)

'Psychopaths': different or part of us?

The above newspaper quotations suggest that people described as 'psychopathic' are different from the rest of us in relation to the nature and intensity of their violence. This is supported by the research of Hare (1991, 1998), who has developed valid and reliable measures of psychopathy. Black (1999) and Hare (1999) have alerted lay people to problems posed by such individuals to other people and to society as a whole. 'To ignore the reality of [psychopathic personality disorder] is to ignore the real lives of troubled individuals whose actions and attitudes set them apart from the norm' (Black, 1999, p. 201).

There is certainly evidence for such problems and arguments for the need to ensure public safety and to meet the needs and rights of victims and survivors of violent offending (Gray *et al.*, 2002). However, it can be argued that there are problems with defining one group of individuals as 'other', as completely 'different' from most people (Cordess, 2002; Prins, 2001). This may result in political and media focus on a relatively small number of people when there is evidence that violence occurs far more frequently within families than from 'psychopathic' strangers (Kemshall and Pritchard, 1999). Some critics have argued that in many Western societies, including the UK, there has been an excessive swing away from the rights of individuals with mental health problems, including those who offend, to an excessive preoccupation with risk and public safety (Gray *et al.*, 2001). Concerns are sometimes expressed through 'moral panics'. The latter involve intense media, political and public concern over a group of people, such as 'psychopaths', who are thought to constitute a far greater threat than is actually the case. The group concerned becomes stigmatised and labelled, and there is often a political response to incarcerate or otherwise control them (Goode and Ben-Yehuda, 1994):

> ... The 1990s have been characterised by an 'exclusive' view of society, which distinguishes the 'deserving majority' which needs to be protected from the 'undeserving, feckless minority', who must be excluded and in many cases, incarcerated (Faulkner, 1997, quoted in Prins, 2001, p. 90)

> We locate the feared, bizarre or psychotic, the criminal, the anarchic, delinquent and shameful, unwanted aspects of ourselves in the vilified 'other'; we then perceive him as potentially dangerous and violent, then label and stigmatise this 'other' ... under the politically dreamed up catch-all title of 'Dangerous Severe Personality Disorder...
> ... In this way, we justify policies that marginalise, compulsorily detain and punish the other for his/her very difference .... We disown unwanted or shameful aspects of ourselves ... in this case by projection (i.e. that belonging to ourselves is attributed to the other). (Cordess, 2002, p. S15, citing Milner, 1987)

'Dangerous people with severe personality disorder'

One apparent response to media publicity, and associated public concern, is the use of the term 'dangerous people with severe personality disorder' (DSPD) by the UK Government, and their development of services for people so described. Several authors have commented that this appears to have been in response to (sometimes sensational) media accounts of the killing, in 1998, of a mother and her young daughter by Michael Stone, who was said to have a 'personality disorder' (Feeney, 2003; Laurance, 2003; Taylor, 2002). In July 1999, the Home Office and Department of Health produced a consultation paper, 'Managing Dangerous People with Severe Personality Disorder'. This suggested two options: maintaining existing structures for services and legislation, with some changes; or new legislation and services for people with 'DSPD'. The latter were said to number a little more than 2000 individuals, almost all men, who presented 'a very high risk to the public':

> ... The law as it stands fails to protect the public from the danger these people represent because in many cases they have been allowed to return to the community, even though they remain dangerous. (Home Office and Department of Health, 1999, p. 3, quoted in Byrt, 2000)

Following this document, and despite opposition from service users and mental health professionals and groups representing their interests, the Government produced a White Paper, 'Reforming the Mental Health Act', part two of which outlined new proposals, based on 'Managing Dangerous People with Severe Personality Disorder'. The White Paper referred to arrangements for assessment in secure units, including transfer from prison and health services, and subsequent treatment and custody for 'DSPD' individuals (Grounds, 2001; HM Government, 2000). Draft Mental Health bills in 2002 and 2004 (Department of Health, 2002, 2004) do not include reference to 'DSPD', possibly because of quite widespread opposition (Feeney, 2003). However, the Government started to plan 'DSPD' services soon after the publication of 'Managing Dangerous People with Severe Personality Disorder' in July, 2000. By early 2005:

> ... There are 250 places available for use in four DSPD units ... 172 of these are in the Prison Service .... The other 80 are in the Health Service [in high security hospitals] (Home Office *et al.*, 2005).

'Dangerous people with severe personality disorder': ethical and other concerns

Various ethical concerns have been raised in relation to Government proposals, and subsequent services for 'DSPD' individuals. Concerns include the following:

■ Various authors have commented on *infringement of individuals' rights*. Government policy related to DSPD allows for the detention of some individuals, solely for what they *might* do (as evaluated by Risk Assessment), not for offences committed (Padfield, 2000; Prins, 2001). Some authors have stated that this infringes the Human Rights Act (1998), although others, including the Government (HM Government, 2000) have argued that this is not the case (Feeney, 2003). Under the Human Rights Act (1998):

> The rights of the detainee under Article 5 (right to liberty and security) and Article 8 (right to respect of privacy and family life) must be weighed against the rights of the public under Article 2 (the right to life). (Feeney, 2003)

■ Another concern is *harm to individuals, including lack of hope*, if they feel they are being detained indefinitely. This might result in increased likelihood of individuals engaging in institutional disturbances if they feel that they have little chance of moving on from the DSPD service (Feeney, 2003). However, the Government has made it clear that people who make progress 'may ... move to a lower level of security, or ultimately, to a supervised placement upon release' (Home Office *et al.*, 2005). Other harms include increased *stigmatisation* (Feeney, 2003).

■ The *lack of precision of Risk Assessments in predicting future risk* may mean that some individuals are detained indefinitely and unjustifiably (Chiswick, 1999; Padfield, 2000). '... In order to successfully prevent one of those deemed ... DSPD from offending in a one-year period, five others, who would not have offended, would have to be detained' (Feeney, 2003, citing Buchanan and Lesse, 2001).

■ It has been argued that DSPD assessments and services *may increase risk*. Individuals with thoughts of violence may be reluctant to admit these for fear of being sent to a DSPD service. 'The very measures designed to reduce the risks to the public may alienate the target group, making monitoring more difficult, and ultimately leading to increased risk' (Feeney, 2003).

■ There is concern that the Government's DSPD policy is largely a *response to political and media pressure* (Prins, 2001).

■ There is disagreement amongst psychiatrists and psychologists about the nature and diagnosis of personality disorder and *the accuracy of diagnostic testing* (Blackburn, 2000).

■ Concern has been expressed about the *inaccuracy of figures* estimating the number of 'DSPD' individuals, and of data used by the Government (Chiswick 2001).

■ There is concern, also, that, despite the expectation that interventions will be evidence-based (NICE, 2005), the Government has invested considerable money:
  – on services which have *not been shown to be effective* in relation to treatment outcomes or the prevention of violent offending (Byrt, 2000).
  – for a group of people who are loosely defined and *not based on reliable diagnostic criteria*. 'There is no proven link between severity of personality disorder and dangerousness' (Feeney, 2003). However, this author points out that, more recently, the Government has used the term 'DSPD' to describe particular services, rather than a category of people.

■ Some critics have argued that, in the prevention of violent offending, it would be more effective to allocate resources to address social factors involved in its genesis: e.g. working with children who are particularly at risk of developing violent behaviours (Kemshall and Pritchard, 1999). However, the paucity of studies on factors preventing antisocial personality disorder and related violence has been described, with the need for further research identified (Farrington, 2003; Moran and Hagell, 2001).

Some positive aspects of DSPD services

Accounts by service users and mental health or legal professionals are not, in general, supportive of Government policy or proposed legislation related to 'DSPD' individuals. However, it can be argued that the programme has contributed positively to research and educational initiatives; and efforts to share relevant experiences of care and treatment through conferences and other means (Home Office *et al.*, 2005)

Byrt (2000), whilst expressing opposition to the DSPD proposals in general, stated that 'it could be argued that the detention of individuals *solely* because of their risk to others was "made more explicit" in "Managing Dangerous People with Severe Personality Disorder"' (Byrt, 2000, p. 14). Under the Mental Health Act 1983, individuals with 'psychopathic disorder', as defined in the Act, can be detained in hospital only if they are 'treatable'. However, many individuals have been detained for long periods in high-security hospitals for long periods solely because of their risk to others (George, 1998; Gunn and Taylor, 1993). If appeal and other procedures (such as those outlined in the Mental Health Bill: Department of Health 2004) ensure individuals' rights, 'this might be more effective than the present system, in preventing prolonged detention of people described at present as having "untreatable psychopathic disorder"' (Byrt, 2000, p. 14).

Other proposed legal measures affecting individuals with personality disorders

Because of considerable disagreement with its proposals, the 2002 Mental Health Bill was rewritten, with another Bill produced in September 2004 following further consultation (Department of Health, 2004). Critics of the later Bill have expressed concern about proposals to considerably extend 'powers to enforce treatment and ... detain people with mental illness or personality disorder' (Batty, 2004, p. 2). These include arrangements to compulsorily provide assessment and treatment in the community and to formally detain individuals who seem to 'pose a risk to the health and safety of another person without having to show that they refuse care and treatment on a voluntary basis' (Mind, 2005). The Bill proposes, also, that mental health professionals should decide the appropriateness of compulsory treatment for individuals with personality disorders (Department of Health, 2004). Critics of the Bill include the Mental Health Alliance, consisting of over sixty service user and professional organisations. The Alliance and other critics have argued that proposals in the Bill, if they become law, would result in an increased number of people being compulsorily detained, with an infringement of the rights of these individuals, including people with personality disorders (Batty, 2004; Mental Health Alliance, 2005; Mind, 2005).

Conclusion

'Personality disorder' as a diagnostic category has been criticised for being meaningless, stigmatising and lacking scientific validity and reliability. However, some service users and professionals consider that it has positive implications for treatment and nursing and other interventions. A review of the development of 'personality disorder' and related concepts indicates a long history of interest in the links between personality and mental health problems.

Attitudes in wider society are likely to influence both professional attitudes and the services that can be delivered. This is illustrated by a consideration of services for 'dangerous people with severe personality disorder' and related media and political focus on individuals with personality disorders and violent behaviours. In general, research has found widespread negative attitudes, amongst the public and in media reporting, towards individuals with personality disorder.

Acknowledgement

Richard Byrt would like to thank Gavin Garman for his comments on Chapters 3 and 4.

References

Aiyegbusi, A. (2004) Thinking under fire: the challenge for forensic mental health nurses working with women in secure care. In: Jeffcote, N. and Watson, T. (eds.) *Working Therapeutically with Women in Secure Mental Health Settings*, Chapter 8. Jessica Kingsley, London.

American Psychiatric Association (1994) *Diagnostic and Statistical Manual of Mental Disorders*, 4th edn (DSM-IV). American Psychiatric Association, Washington.

Appleby, L., Shaw, J., Sherratt, J., Amos, T., Robinson, J., McDonnell, R. (2001). *Safety First: the National Confidential Inquiry into Suicide and Homicide by People with Mental Illness*. Department of Health, London.

Ashman, D. (2001) Desperately seeking understanding. *Mental Health Today*, October, 30–31.

Batty, D. (2004) Draft mental health bill. *The Guardian*, 9 September 2004. Accessed through: http://www.http://society.guardian.co.uk/mentalhealth/story/0,8510,836476,00.html.

Bennett, P. (2003) *Abnormal and Clinical Psychology: An Introductory Textbook*. Open University Press, Maidenhead.

Black, D. W. (1999) *Bad Boys, Bad Men: Confronting Antisocial Personality Disorder*. Oxford University Press, New York.

Blackburn, R. (2000) Treatment or incapacitation? Implications of research on personality disorders for the management of dangerous offenders. *Legal and Criminological Psychology*, **5**, 1–21.

Bowers, L. (2002) *Dangerous and Severe Personality Disorder: Response and Role of the Psychiatric Team*. Routledge, London.

Buchanan, A. and Lesse, M. (2001) Detention of people with severe personality disorders: a systematic review. *Lancet*, **358**, 1955–1959.

Busfield, J. (ed.) (2001) *Rethinking the Sociology of Mental Health*. Blackwell Publishers, Oxford.

Byrt, R. (2000) Dangerous Proposals? A Response to 'Managing Dangerous People with Severe Personality Disorder'. *Mental Health Practice*, **3**(10), 12–17.

Byrt, R., Wray, C. and 'Tom' (2005) Towards hope and inclusion: nursing interventions in a medium secure service for men with 'personality disorders'. *Mental Health Practice*, **8**(8), 38–43.

Campling, P. and Birtle, J. (2001) The need for an NHS policy on the role of therapeutic communities in the treatment of 'personality disorder'. *Therapeutic Communities*, **22**(2), 131–142.

Carr, E. H. (1964) *What Is History*? Penguin, Harmondsworth.

Castillo, H. (2003) *Personality Disorder: Temperament or Trauma*? Jessica Kingsley, London.

Castillo, H., Allen, L. and Coxhead, N. (2001) The hurtfulness of a diagnosis: user research about personality disorder. *Mental Health Practice*, **4**(9), 16–19.

Chiswick, D. (1999) Preventive detention exhumed and enhanced. *Psychiatric Bulletin*, **23**, 703–704.

Chiswick, D. (2001). Dangerous severe personality disorder: from notion to law. *Psychiatric Bulletin*, **25**(8), 282–283.

Cleckley, H. (1976). *The Mask of Sanity*. Mosby, St Louis.

Cordess, C. (2002) Proposals for managing dangerous people with severe personality disorder: new legislation and new follies in a historical context. *Criminal Behaviour and Mental Health*, **12**(2), S12–S19.

Crisp, A., Cowan, L. and Hart, D. (2004) The college's anti-stigma campaign, 1998–2003. A shortened version of the concluding report. *Psychiatric Bulletin*, **28**, 133–136.

Department of Health (2000) Secondary source, cited in: Radcliffe, M. (2003) Word power. Can people with mental health problems take the sting out of stigma by reclaiming pejoratives? *The Guardian*, 16 July 2003. Accessed 31 October 2003: http://www.society.guardian. co.uk/mentalhealth/story/0,8150,998751,00.html

Department of Health (2002). *Mental Health Bill*. Cm 5538. The Stationery Office, London.

Department of Health (2004) *Mental Health Bill*. Cm 6305. The Stationery Office, London.

Department of Health (2005) Website: http://www.doh.gov.uk/.

D'Silva, K. and Duggan, C. (2002) Service innovations: development of a psychoeducational programme for patients with personality disorder. *Psychiatric Bulletin*, **26**, 268–271.

Farrington, D. P. (2003) Advancing knowledge about the early prevention of adult antisocial behavior. In: Farrington, D. P. and Coid, J. W. (eds.) *Early Prevention of Adult Antisocial Behavior*, Chapter 1. Cambridge University Press, Cambridge.

Feeney, A. (2003) DSPD. *Advances in Psychiatric Treatment*, **9**, 349–359.

George, S. (1998). More than a pound of flesh: a patient's perspective. In: Mason, T. and Mercer, D. (eds.) *Critical Perspectives in Forensic Care: Inside Out*, Chapter 7. Macmillan, Basingstoke.

Goffman, E. (1968) *Asylums. Essays on the Social Situation of Mental Patients and Other Inmates*. Penguin Books, Harmondsworth.

Goode, E. and Ben-Yehuda, N. (1994) *Moral Panics: the Social Construction of Deviance*. Blackwell, Oxford.

Gray, N., Laing, J. M. and Noakes, L. (eds.) (2001) *Criminal Justice, Mental Health and the Politics of Risk*. Cavendish Publishing, London.

Grounds, A. (2001) Reforming the Mental Health Act. Editorial. *British Journal of Psychiatry*, **139**, 387–389.

Gunn, J. and Taylor, P. (1993) *Forensic Psychiatry: Ethical, Clinical and Legal Aspects*. Butterworth Heinemann, Oxford.

Hare, R. (1991) *The Hare Psychopathy Checklist – Revised*. Multi-Health Systems, Toronto.

Hare, R. (1998) The Hare PCL-R: some issues concerning its use and misuse. *Legal and Criminological Psychology*, **3**(1), 99–119.

Hare, R. D. (1999) *Without Conscience: The Disturbing World of the Psychopaths Among Us*. Guilford Press, New York.

Harris, T. (1981) *Red Dragon*. Bodley Head, London.

Henderson, D. (1939) *Psychopathic States*. W. E. Norton, New York.

HM Government (2000) *Reforming the Mental Health Act. Part 2. High Risk Patients*. Cm 5016-II. The Stationery Office, London.

Home Office and Department of Health (1999) *Managing Dangerous People with Severe Personality Disorder: Proposals for Policy Development*. Home Office/Department of Health, London.

Home Office, HM Prison Service and Department of Health (2005) *DSPD Programme*. Website: http://www.dspdprogramme.gov.uk/.

Huang, B. and Priebe, S. (2003) Media coverage of mental health care in the UK, USA and Australia. *Psychiatric Bulletin*, **27**, 331–333.

Kemshall, H. and Pritchard, J. (eds.) (1999) *Good Practice in Working with Violence*. Jessica Kingsley, London.

Kesey, K. (1962) *One Flew Over the Cuckoo's Nest*. Methuen: London.

Laurance, J. (2003) *Pure Madness: How Fear Drives the Mental Health System*. Routledge, London.

Lewis, G. and Appleby, L. (1988) Personality disorder: the patients psychiatrists dislike. *British Journal of Psychiatry* **153**, 44–49.

Liderth, S. (2003) Untitled. In: Bree, A., Campling, P. and Liderth, S. Empowerment in mental health: the therapeutic community model. In: Dooher, J. and Byrt, R. (eds.) *Empowerment and the Health Service User*, Chapter 10, pp. 149–151. Quay Books, Mark Allen Publishing, Dinton, Salisbury.

Livesley, W. J. L. (ed.) (2001a) *Handbook of Personality Disorders: Theory, Research and Treatment*. Guilford Press, New York.

Livesley, W. J. (2001b) Conceptual and taxonomic issues. Chapter 1 in: Livesley, W. J. (ed.) (2001a) *Handbook of Personality Disorders. Theory, Research and Treatment*. The Guilford Press, New York.

Magnavita, J. J. (ed.) (2004a) *Handbook of Personality Disorders: Theory and Practice*. John Wiley & Sons, Hoboken, New Jersey.

Magnavita, J. J. (2004b) Classification, prevalence and etiology of personality disorders: related issues and controversy. In: Magnavita, J. J. (ed.) *Handbook of Personality Disorders: Theory and Practice*, Chapter 1. John Wiley & Sons, Hoboken, New Jersey.

Manning, N. (2001) Psychiatric diagnoses under conditions of uncertainty: personality disorder, science and professional legitimacy'. In: Busfield, J. (ed.) *Rethinking the Sociology of Mental Health*, Chapter 5. Blackwell Publishers, Oxford.

Market and Research Opinion International (1997) Secondary source, cited in: Warner, R. (2001) Community attitudes towards mental disorder. In: Thornicroft, G. and Szmukler, G. (eds.) *Textbook of Community Psychiatry*, Chapter 38. Oxford University Press, Oxford.

Mason, T. (2001) Introduction. In: Mason, T., Carlisle, C., Watkins, C. and Whitehead, E. (eds.) *Stigma and Social Exclusion in Healthcare*, Chapter 1. Routledge, London.

Maudsley, H. (1874). *Responsibility in Mental Disease*. London, Henry S. King and Co. Excerpts in: Skultans, V. (1975) *Madness and Morals: Ideas on Insanity in the Nineteenth Century*. Routledge and Kegan Paul, London.

Mental Health Alliance (2005) Website: http://www.mentalhealthalliance.org.uk/

Mind (2005) Website: http://www.mind.org.uk/

Moran, P. and Hagell, A. (2001) *Intervening to Prevent Antisocial Personality Disorder: A Scoping Review. Home Office Research Study 225*. Home Office Research and Statistics Directorate, London.

National Institute for Clinical Excellence (2005) Website: http://www.nice.org.uk/.

National Institute for Mental Health in England (2004) *From Here to Equality: A Strategic Plan to Tackle Stigma and Discrimination on Mental Health Grounds, 2004–2009*. Department of Health, Leeds.

Office of the Deputy Prime Minister, Social Exclusion Unit (2004) *Taking Stock and Looking to the Future: Emerging Findings*, p. 4. Social Exclusion Unit, Office of the Deputy Prime Minister, London; http://www.socialexclusion.gov.uk/page.asp?id=213.

Padfield, N. (2000) Detaining the dangerous. Editorial. *The Journal of Forensic Psychiatry*, **11**(3), 497–500.

Paris, J. (2004) Sociocultural Factors in the Treatment of Personality Disorders. In: Magnavita, J. J. (ed.) *Handbook of Personality Disorders: Theory and Practice*, Chapter 7. John Wiley & Sons, Hoboken, New Jersey.

Parsons, S. (2003) The person with a diagnosis of borderline personality disorder. In: Barker, P. (ed.) *Psychiatric and Mental Health Nursing: The Craft of Caring*, Chapter 35. Arnold, London.

Phillips, R. (2003) The good, the bad and the ugly: the role of local radio as a medium for overcoming prejudice. In: Dooher, J. and Byrt, R. (eds.) *Empowerment and the Health Service User*, Chapter 18. Quay Books, Mark Allen Publishing, Dinton, Salisbury.

Philo, G. (2001). Media and mental illness. In: Davey, B., Gray, A. and Seale, C. (eds.) *Health and Disease: A Reader*, Chapter 10. Open University Press, Buckingham.

Philo, G., McLaughlin, G. and Henderson, L. (1996) Media content. In: Philo, G. (ed.) *Media and Mental Distress*, Chapter 4. Glasgow Media Group, Longman, London.

Pilgrim, D. (2001) Disordered personalities and disordered concepts. *Journal of Mental Health*, **10**, 253–265.

Pilgrim, D. and Rogers, A. (1999) *A Sociology of Mental Health and Illness*, 2nd edn. Open University Press, Buckingham.

Porter, S. (1998) The social interpretation of deviance. In: Birchenall, M. and Birchenall, P. (eds.) *Sociology as Applied to Nursing*, Chapter 7. Baillière Tindall/Royal College of Nursing, London.

Prichard, J. C. (1835) *A Treatise on Insanity*. London, Marchant. Excerpts in: Skultans, V. (1975) *Madness and Morals: Ideas on Insanity in the Nineteenth Century*. Routledge and Kegan Paul, London.

Prins, H. (1995) *Offenders, Deviants or Patients?*, 2nd edn. Routledge, London.

Prins, H. (2001). W(h)ither psychopathic disorder? A view from the UK. *Psychology, Crime and Law*, **7**, 89–103.

Radcliffe, M. (2003). *The Guardian: Society Supplement*. 16 July, p. 120f.

Sanders, P. and Tudor, K. (2001) This is therapy: a person-centred critique of the contemporary psychiatric system. In: Newnes, C., Holmes, G. and Dunn, C. (eds.) *This is Madness Too: Critical Perspectives on Mental Health Services*, Chapter 14. PCCS Books, Ross on Wye.

Sayce, L. (2000) *From Psychiatric Patient to Citizen: Overcoming Discrimination and Social Exclusion*. Macmillan, Basingstoke.

Schafer, P. E. (2002) Nursing interventions and future directions with patients who constantly break rules and test boundaries. In: Kettles, A. M., Woods, P. and Collins, M. (eds.) *Therapeutic Interventions for Forensic Mental Health Nurses*. Jessica Kingsley, London.

Skultans, V. (1975) *Madness and Morals: Ideas on Insanity in the Nineteenth Century*. Routledge and Kegan Paul, London.

Skultans, V. (1979) *English Madness: Ideas on Insanity, 1580–1890*. Routledge and Kegan Paul, London.

Smith, E. E., Nolen-Hoeksema, S., Frederickson, B. and Loftus, G. R. (eds.) (2003). *Atkinson and Hilgard's Introduction to Psychology*, 14th edn. Thomson Wadsworth, Belmont, CA.

Taylor, P. (2002) The institutionalisation of a concept. *Criminal Behaviour and Mental Health*, **12**, S5–S11.

Tyson, M. and Briscoe, J. (2002) Towards establishing more effective collaboration in the care of people with personality disorders. In: Nolan, P. and Badger, F. (eds.) *Promoting Collaboration in Primary Mental Health Care*, Chapter 7. Nelson Thornes, Cheltenham.

Wahl, O. F. (1995) *Media Madness: Public Images of Mental Illness*. Rutgers University Press, New Brunswick.

Warner, R. (2001) Community attitudes towards mental disorder. In: Thornicroft, G. and Szmukler, G. (eds.) *Textbook of Community Psychiatry*, Chapter 38. Oxford University Press, Oxford.

Wedding, D. and Boyd, M. A. (1999) *Movies and Mental Illness: Using Films to Understand Psychopathology*. McGraw-Hill, Boston.

Wing, J. (1978) *Reasoning about Madness*. Oxford University Press, Oxford.

World Health Organization (1992) *The ICD-10 Classification of Mental and Behavioural Disorders: Clinical Descriptions and Diagnostic Guidelines*. World Health Organization, Geneva.

CHAPTER 4

Service user experiences and professional attitudes

Richard Byrt, Roberta Graley-Wetherell, 'R', Rachel Studley, Karen D'Silva, Linnette James and Tom Pocock

What words come into your head when you hear the term 'personality disorder'?: an exercise

(a) What words come into your head when you hear the term 'personality disorder?'
(b) What do most of these words have in common?
(c) Where have you heard these words?
(d) Can these words be seen as 'symptoms'?
(e) Do patients with: (i) diabetes; (ii) schizophrenia get described in this way?

When Student Nurses consider the questions above, they often say that they have heard professionals use words like 'attention-seeking' and 'manipulative' (Byrt *et al.*, 2005). This chapter includes service user accounts of both positive and negative staff attitudes, as well as their experiences of nursing and other interventions. These thought-provoking accounts are followed by overviews of research on the attitudes of nurses and other professionals towards individuals with 'personality disorders' and of service user experiences. The chapter concludes with a consideration of relevant organisations and websites for service users and informal carers.

My experience of borderline personality disorder

*Rachel Studley – Madnotbad (*http://www.madnotbad.co.uk/*)*
I was diagnosed with borderline personality disorder (BPD) after having extensive contact with the psychiatric system for a couple of years. Initially, I was diagnosed with schizophrenia. I heard voices, had fully fledged delusions, visual hallucinations, little motivation and a very disjointed

thinking head. Before I sought help, I'd used self-harm as a way of coping with my experiences. During my time at university, it became so entrenched that I cut many times a day. It helped with the voices, the intense anxiety and the depersonalisation. It made me feel alive and it mediated some of the self-hate I was feeling. I used it both as a punishment and a reward: ('If I go to the shop, I can cut', 'If I get the milk in, I can cut'). Self-harm enabled me to keep up the pretence that things were OK. Eventually, it stopped working, that's when I broke down fully and got an all-expenses-paid holiday to the psych ward.

Once I began to get help, the self-harm didn't just disappear. This eventually led the psychiatrist and nursing team to diagnose me with BPD. I was also having big mood swings, feeling numb and empty, and they found my behaviour hard to understand. I wasn't able to explain myself as I didn't have much insight into it myself. I was also very paranoid and wasn't able to trust them enough to try. I also had a history of trauma, and so fitted the profile to some extent.

I remember the ward round they changed my diagnosis. Nothing was said explicitly, they just talked about some of my symptoms and said that they thought a therapeutic community was the only real option. They gave me a leaflet to read, which scared the hell out of me, and left me to think about it. Later I discovered that this meant that I now had BPD and not a *bona fide* 'mental illness'.

Strangely enough, with this one relatively seemingly harmless meeting, the whole tone of the care I received changed. Some *staff* were still excellent, but others were colder towards me. I was told that I was wasting their time and that I shouldn't be on a mental health ward. That if I overdosed again, I shouldn't expect to be admitted. It was as if, with one wave of the diagnostic wand, I was 'bad' and no longer 'mad'. Part of my problem was a deep sense of self-hate, and being treated in this way just fed into it. The general line that I was given was 'take responsibility'. This is a fine idea, but it doesn't actually help to continually bash you around the head with it in the hope that it'll actually happen. It had taken a long time for me to become so distressed, I'd lost the skills I needed and felt very out of control. I needed to take back control gradually – handing it back so suddenly when nothing had changed was a recipe for disaster. To be honest, it felt like a punishment.

During my treatment, I felt language in itself had become twisted and judgemental. Words like 'boundaries', 'acting out', 'manipulation', 'attention-seeking' and 'responsibility' were commonplace. The meanings I got from them came from the context in which they were used. When someone wasn't able to talk to me, they'd cite 'boundary issues'. When I did something they judged as wrong, I was 'acting out'. If I was in pain and hurt myself, I was 'attention-seeking' and 'manipulative'. In truth, I was bouncing off the walls and very little was making sense. Suddenly, the world around me had become as chaotic and dysfunctional as I was. Unsurprisingly, it made my internal chaos that much worse.

The way that my symptoms, feelings and actions were interpreted changed dramatically with the new diagnosis. Very little was seen in simple terms and people kept trying to make links – it was like a game of join the dots, except the dots were important events in my life. I'm all for finding reason in any kind of mental distress, but the problem I faced was that the reasons they found weren't fitting. They were stereotypes. My parents came under a lot of fire. I couldn't ask for better, more supportive and nurturing family; however, many professionals couldn't tally this with my mental state. They tried to get me to see that I had a 'deep-seated anger' at them, or that we were 'too close'. They were made to feel at fault, and for a while they probably felt they were. My whole family was traumatised by the 'care' I was receiving.

I think there's something about personality disorder labels that helps everyone in the situation to lose perspective. As a chaotic person, I was reacting on impulse a lot of the time, and so were the people involved in my care. Some of their impulses were caring and supportive, others were less so. In all this time I hadn't actually changed at all. I was still the same person, regardless of my diagnosis. That attitudes shifted so drastically is telling of a deeper problem, I think.

After a particularly bad period of treatment I looked further into BPD and I decided to seek a second opinion. Eventually, with a fresh pair of eyes, I was pronounced 'mad' and not 'bad' once more. The psychiatrist was able to be more objective as they weren't embroiled in the chaos of the previous few years and I was rediagnosed with schizoaffective disorder. This, again, resulted in a huge shift in my care. This also proved to be one of the catalysts for my recovery – it removed the brick wall that had been keeping me and my care team in a stalemate.

I do believe that at one stage I fitted the criteria of BPD. I also feel that my problems could have been explained in a number of ways. I think it would have been more helpful if people dealt with the symptoms I presented, instead of a label. The BPD label encouraged people to make leaps of judgement, to adopt certain stances and to see things in a certain light. Whenever the label is more visible than the individual, it's a dangerous thing. Being a borderline prevented people from accepting me as me.

Now, a number of years later, I am doing all the things that I've been told I would never be able to do. I am in a long-term stable relationship, I live independently, I am back at college, I run a mental health website, I am a mental health trainer, I have bucketloads of responsibility and I can (generally) cope. I still have mental health problems, and sometimes these are quite severe. But I have a balance and stability that was previously lacking.

How did I get to this point? It's not rocket science. There was no magic therapy or intervention that changed my life. By pure luck, I found a voluntary organisation which offered outreach support. They gave me stable, practical and positive support. I was able to come to trust my keyworkers and feel safe enough to try new things. Most importantly, I felt that they believed and accepted my experiences without second guessing them. Their recovery-based approach gave me the opportunity to become an expert in my own mental health, and learn to manage it. I no longer looked to others to fix me and became confident that I didn't need them to. This, and the support given to me by family, friends and other survivors, was worth more to me than any kind of formal therapy.

My advice to you – a diagnosis can be a useful rough guide, but it doesn't mean that everyone with that diagnosis acts, feels or needs the same things. This is especially true with personality disorders, as the criteria are so diverse, as are the reasons a person is given the label. It can be used as a diagnostic dumping ground when the patient is seen as difficult, frustrating or resistant. Be aware that it's easy to become blinkered and never forget that behind every label, there is a person who needs your help. You can make such a difference just by being respectful, caring and not letting the stereotypes blind you to their uniqueness.

My experience of personality disorder treatment in high secure and medium secure environments

'R'

I was first admitted to a psychiatric hospital when I was 19, and had a number of different episodes of depression and stress/anxiety-related illnesses until I was 30. I was in various psychiatric units where the doctors didn't know what they were treating me for – whether to diagnose me as having depression or not. I was making suicide attempts and there was no real diagnosis. Personally, I didn't have much faith in them, but then I didn't want to admit the depth of the problem. I was consistently running away from treatment.

When I was 31, in a crisis, I experienced anxiety, stress, and depression, suicidal and murderous thoughts. I went on to commit an extremely serious offence. I then saw various doctors in prison who collectively agreed: 'This man has a personality disorder, sufficient to deem him as psychopathic'. The court then sent me to a high secure hospital on their recommendation.

It was the first time I had ever heard the term 'personality disorder'. I thought, 'Oh great, so now I'm a psychopath, and what's this personality disorder bullshit all about?'. They said they had to say various things to get me treated. I thought at first that hospital would be an easy ride. I was wrong.

What was interesting was the perception of personality disorder at the high secure hospital, especially amongst patients: 'All personality disorders (PDs) are psychopaths' – and I really don't think half the staff thought differently. There was a personality disorder unit at the hospital which I did not want to go to because I did not want to be labelled a psychopath, and I was afraid to live among 'psychopaths' on the unit. I was also concerned I would be branded 'sex offender' in the hospital, as there were patients there who were in for those kinds of offences. One doctor did call me a psychopath, and I knew this wasn't right.

So a lot of my treatment took place in a ward in the main part of the hospital. I had two years' psychotherapy, and then I was referred to a specialist for borderline personality disorder. Here, in my present medium secure personality disorder unit, I have been found to have borderline traits, but have been given a different diagnosis.

When, in the high secure hospital, they diagnosed me as having borderline personality disorder, and I read about its characteristics, I thought 'This is me!'. This was helpful because I realised I was in the hospital for the right reasons. It took a load off my mind.

I did dialectical behaviour therapy, which was exceptionally useful, particularly emotional regulation, and mindfulness [important aspects of dialectical behaviour therapy, or DBT]. My experience was that you got what you put into it – if you failed to engage with it, you would not get anything. I was in such a tortured state of mind; I'd have done anything to help myself.

After this, I was moved on to a rehabilitation ward which was mixed, with mentally ill and personality disordered patients. Again, different staff had different understandings, and I heard the term 'psychopath' many times. This annoyed me a great deal. Ultimately, mentally ill and personality disordered offenders were separated onto different wards.

From the rehabilitation ward, I was recommended to go to a medium secure personality disorder unit. Up until the time I left, the environment of the rehabilitation ward wasn't nearly structured enough. There were people with entrenched problems who had been there years. But the high secure hospital was basically a holding place, though some patients were beginning to be moved on. My present consultant psychiatrist from the medium secure personality disorder unit came to see me, and eventually I got here.

The personality disorder unit here was a whole new chapter. When I came, it was completely different from the high secure hospital, more structured, and far stricter. I had not been challenged in the morning meetings, as happens here. One of the first things was that I was re-diagnosed. I feel there could be more information about your diagnosis – if you have a dependent personality disorder, what does this mean? What are the antecedents? What are the things in the person's history that caused this? At the high secure hospital, there was a four-leaf booklet on borderline personality disorder. This was useful, but you don't get it here. There is a psycho-education leaflet, but it's not enough. I thrive on written information, although not all patients do. The more information I get, the better.

In this unit, individual sessions with my consultant psychiatrist happen once a week, and are very helpful. We just sit and talk. I opened up about things, and he's fed things back to me. We established a dialogue. At the high secure hospital, the consultants only spoke to you every few weeks, and seemed to sit on a 'high chair', surrounded by staff. You very rarely got to speak alone, face to face. But every place has its own culture. The two consultants here speak to patients and staff on a more equal basis. I felt at the high secure hospital, they kept at a distance. If a doctor is prepared to sit down with you individually, then you know he's got your interests at heart, that you're not just a number. You then get the full benefit of their expertise. I had seven consultant psychiatrists at different times when I was at the high secure hospital. I'm very thankful that's not the case here.

There's a problem-solving methodology here at the personality disorder unit. I didn't key into at all, at first. I got tremendous benefit when I did understand what it's all about. However, I had to do two problem-solving presentations before I understood, and I'm not sure all the staff have got a grasp of it. You have to work through a structured methodology every time. It's helpful in defining problems, and you come up with a plan of action as a result.

Nursing staff are mostly very good. My (multidisciplinary) clinical team are very helpful in identifying issues. However, I have felt that sometimes, nursing staff are so involved in paperwork that they don't have time to work with patients. I'm impressed with the nurse in charge here: she challenges patients on a regular basis. She's on top of the environment, if things go awry, she brings it to our attention. She doesn't let things just slip. She gives an impression of caring for the environment. I've known this not happen enough. I don't want to knock the high secure hospital, but there was more of a prison culture there. It wasn't as consistent.

As a consequence of what I did and my diagnosis, I've have to make a massive readjustment. I'm empowered to work towards a more fulfilling life, but am not free to do what I want. I understand that everything I do and say is written down, including things I haven't thought important. There's a whole new language: 'boundaries', 'appropriateness', 'aggressive', 'passive aggressive'. My relationships are very carefully scrutinised. Even if I make someone a compliment, it can be taken the wrong way. It feels a bit pathological here. If you see a female nurse as attractive, this can be deemed as questionable or inappropriate because staff and patients have these boundaries. I wonder if things are sometimes fed back punitively. They seem to define something as a problem by their own set of rules. Nurses here are trained to observe everything, write it down, and feed back. You say 'it's not a problem', but they say 'we feel it is'. As a patient, you can wonder if it is significant, and whether you're problem-solving things for their benefit. You feel you've lost your sense of ownership, your sense of identity. You want to feel empowered. Some staff are better at it than others – but it can be draconian.

But overall, I think the unit is pretty good.

A multidisciplinary team approach is absolutely invaluable on a small unit such as this. It's not just therapists, it's nurses themselves who know what's going on. But, also, the occupational therapists are superb. They run groups side by side with the nurses and a community outreach team. It's all very consistent. All patients choose to be here, and for those who are here for a good length of time, it's beneficial. The staff do a very good job coordinating, and all have a clear idea of what they're doing. The strong part of this ward is its sustained ethos. Approaches to people with personality disorders are maintained by all the staff. At the high secure hospital, I was fighting to get the right treatment. Here, it's the complete opposite. I feel more respected, and the environment is positive and progressive. But although I've said critical things about the high secure hospital, there were a lot of very good things there. It was not a great time at all, but I did establish good relationships and support.

For anyone working with individuals with personality disorders, I'd say there's no substitute for experience. If you're going to get trained, find a well-run place such as this unit.

A service user view of therapeutic interventions for personality disorder

Roberta Graley-Wetherell

Since my teenage years, I have carried the label of Borderline Personality Disorder. It took me many years to come to terms with this, partly because of the stigma surrounding the label, but also because I never really understood what this meant. I did not understand that there were many types of personality disorder, and I thought that I was a borderline psychopath, which really frightened me and reinforced my negative beliefs about myself. I was exceptionally lucky to meet a psychiatrist who encouraged me to become involved in the fledgling service user movement of the early 1980s, giving me the confidence to find out much more about my diagnosis and Personality Disorders generally. Perhaps one of the most empowering statements came from a psychiatrist who said that *'behind each personality disorder there is a personality and behind each personality there is a person'*. This statement underlines my belief that everyone is an individual who needs to have a treatment plan individually tailored to his or her needs. Services need to move away from the process of placing patients into groups determined by their symptoms and behaviour patterns. I now understand that each label is just shorthand for a group of symptoms or behaviour patterns, but that does not mean that we are all the same. We each have a different path which led us to behave in the way we do.

My experience has been that individuals respond in different ways because they are unique: what works for one person will not always work for another. Even if they are displaying the same symptoms and patterns of behaviour, their past experiences and emotional upsets will have been different and this will play a big part in how they respond. The care programme approach has encouraged staff to treat patients as individuals with their own care plan based on individual need, rather than a 'one size fits all' approach.

Talking Treatments are usually seen as the best way forward by mental health service users, and for patients with a diagnosis of Personality Disorder, this is really the only option, unless they have other mental health issues co-existing with the diagnosis: e.g. depression. Medication can be very useful for patients with such problems, but the underlying personality issues need to be addressed with 'Talking Treatments'. I believe that nurses should be given opportunities and encouraged to do additional training in these skills, but they do need to remember that it does not work for everyone.

Sometimes, group dynamics and environment will have an effect on the outcome. Group therapy can be very difficult to facilitate and I have met patients who felt very damaged after group therapy, so it is important that the facilitator is well trained and fully understands the consequences of steering the group in certain ways. I was talking to some patients from a high secure hospital who had been attending group therapy for sex offenders. Their reaction was varied. Most of them said they had got some benefit from the sessions until the boundaries were pushed too far. They felt that sometimes, they were made to share information which they felt should only be dealt with on a one-to-one basis. The patients were all males living on various wards throughout the hospital and at various stages in their journeys through the system. One patient was pushed and pushed by the facilitator to reveal in depth the details of his offence until he finally gave in and 'confessed' all to the group. The other members of the group were horrified by the details and the patient then suffered many different responses from his peers. Some threatened physical violence, some merely withdrew and refused to participate in the group again, and others blackmailed him for cigarettes, other goods and sexual favours, threatening to tell the rest of the hospital population the details, unless he complied with their demands.

When thinking about individual therapy, on a personal level I benefited greatly from cognitive behavioural therapy (CBT), although this was hard to access for me personally and I welcome the new initiatives of having nurses trained in CBT. The waiting lists for psychologists remain very long and if nurses can start the process, this is a great help, even if the patient needs more intense work with a specialist later on.

The most helpful interventions I have used are self-help therapies. Although I have been asked to write about helpful nursing interventions, I do feel that nurses can help by supporting patients to attend self-help groups. However, nurses should also understand how these groups work, as patients will need to be encouraged to attend.

Self-help can be far less stigmatising and certainly feel less threatening than traditional therapeutic interventions. There is no power structure as everyone attending the group has equal input and ownership. Self-help groups that I have attended have been to address depression, self-harm and addictions. Each group was run in a different way but all of them helped me to cope with self-destructive behaviour, poor self-worth and an inability to cope with my emotions (Wetherell and Graley-Wetherell, 2003).

I attend a support group for people with addiction problems, which is a 12-step programme. The meetings which I attend are available all over the UK, and have many members who have been diagnosed with a personality disorder (alcohol and substance abuse are diagnostic symptoms in DSM-IV: see Chapter 2). Almost all of these people are now living productive lives with no offending behaviour and often in stable relationships. The 12-step programme is cognitive in its approach; it encourages members to be totally honest, not only with others but also to themselves. Members are encouraged to reflect daily on the way they respond to others and to admit when they have been wrong in any way. In meetings, members are encouraged to share their feelings and their experiences. This helps individuals cope with their emotions without having to use drugs or alcohol; in turn, members find that all other aspects of their lives get better. It becomes easier to cope with relationships, self-worth can be built up and ego increased. Without drugs and alcohol, members are less likely to be violent and are more likely to respond positively to professional help with anger management, etc. There are 12-step groups for all types of problems, including eating disorders, which again is common amongst women with a borderline personality disorder diagnosis. The groups do have a policy of autonomy and anonymity but will work with the professional services in both hospital and prison settings, if requested. Some of the groups you might seek help from are Alcoholics Anonymous, Narcotics Anonymous and Overeaters Anonymous. There are also similar groups for the relatives and friends of the addict or alcoholic (Al-anon). These groups are available for free and have no waiting list. There are groups all over the world and millions of men and women have been released from their addictions by using them.

Also, for patients who use self-harm as a coping strategy, self-help can assist in finding new, less damaging, ways of coping with intense emotions. These can be brand new ways such as using ice or elastic bands rather than cutting and burning, or helping patients to reduce possible physical damage by giving information on where to cut, and how to dress wounds and keep cutting implements and lacerations sterile. The National Self Harm Network (1999) has produced a manual called *The Hurt Yourself Less Workbook* and this has proved to really help reduce the physical damage.

I have really struggled in the past with the help I have been given. Sometimes, it was totally ineffective, other times I was dismissed as being non-treatable. I believe that most patients with a Personality Disorder can be helped by good quality interventions, but they have to be tailored to individual need. Nurses need access to quality training programmes and most of all, services should not give up on people because of the diagnostic label attached to them. I no longer take drugs, I do not drink alcohol and I have very rarely cut myself in the past ten years. I hold down a full-time job and have a very stable relationship. That is all I ever wanted. Sometimes I was very angry and frustrated with services because the help they offered did not meet my need. However, in the end, I found a good balance between self-help and professional help which allowed me to reach the stage in my life I now find myself. Most of the time I am happy being me: something I thought for years I would never feel.

Professional attitudes: the move from 'therapeutic nihilism'

The above accounts describe both professionals who were prepared to be non-judgemental and appreciate individuals' perspectives, and evidence of 'therapeutic nihilism'. The latter term has been used to describe refusals to provide treatment or other interventions, and/or to assume that individuals will not respond to these (Dolan and Coid, 1993). It is suggested, also, that therapeutic nihilism includes professionals' judgements that people with personality disorder diagnoses are 'bad not mad' (in the words of Rachel Studley), and staff refusal to engage therapeutically with individuals or to take their experiences seriously.

Several authors point out that many services have refused treatment for individuals with personality disorder (Dolan and Coid, 1993; National Institute for Mental Health in England, 2003a; Perkins and Repper, 1996). The latter authors refer to 'blanket' refusals to treat people with personality disorder or to provide treatment unless individuals conform to expectations which they cannot meet, or which do not meet their needs. However, several studies have found that some mental health professionals are willing, and, in some cases, keen, to work with these individuals (Bowers, 2002; Cope, 1993; Sallah, 1999). In 2003, The Department of Health made it clear that all NHS Trust providers of mental health services must make specialist provision, with appropriate staff education, for people with personality disorder (National Institute for Mental Health in England, 2003a, 2003b). Department of Health funding has been made available for these services (Department of Health, 2005).

Richard Byrt, Roberts Graley-Wetherell, 'R', Rachel Studley, Karen D'Silva, Linnette James and Tom Pocock

Professionals' moral judgements and negative attitudes

Research indicates that nurses' and other professionals' attitudes are influenced, to some extent, by those in wider society. '... Mental health professionals ... sometimes hold [mainly negative] attitudes ... which are similar to those of the general public ...' (Warner, 2001; p. 453).

Much of the literature, including research studies, by both service users and professionals, includes comments about the moral judgements that professionals tend to make of individuals with personality disorders (Bowers, 2002; Castillo, 2003; Crichton, 1997; Mercer *et al.*, 1999; Pilgrim, 2001). Words normally used to morally evaluate behaviour are applied to people with this diagnostic category. Pilgrim (2001, p. 256) concluded: 'the diagnosis of [personality disorder] does not constitute a version of medical science, it is simply the medical codification of ordinary moral judgements'. Peck (1988), cited in Prins (1994), commented that psychological testing, as well as subjective judgements, could lead to professionals making moral evaluations. Professionals' judgemental attitudes are indicated in the accounts of many service users:

> ... Three days after my admission, I noticed the nursing staff treating me differently. No conversation was entered into and I barely received any eye contact ... I was told they thought I had borderline personality disorder.
> ... I have to prove that I'm trustworthy, that I don't manipulate, that I won't take and take. I know that if I am greeted without preconceived ideas, then I am treated with respect. Too often, I am greeted warily, if at all, simply because of those three words that make up a misleading diagnosis that is not representative of my difficulties or of me ... (Elsie, quoted in Ashman, 2001, p. 30)

Research has found evidence of negative attitudes of nurses and psychiatrists towards individuals with personality disorders, including perceptions that the latter are 'hostile, manipulative, complaining and suffering from a stigmatised illness' (Carr-Walker *et al.*, 2004, p. 266, citing Ganong *et al.*, 1987). More positive attitudes have been found amongst nurses working in specialist units for individuals with personality disorders (Bowers, 2002; Perseius *et al.*, 2003). Markham (2003, p. 595) found that mental health nurses:

> ... expressed less social rejection towards patients with a diagnosis of schizophrenia, and perceived them to be less dangerous than patients with a borderline personality disorder .... Staff were least optimistic about patients with a borderline personality label, and were more negative about their experience of working with this group.

Similarly, Crichton (1997) found that nurses working in secure settings were more likely to censure individuals for violent behaviours, and recommend sanctions if they had a personality disorder, rather than a mental illness diagnosis. This was particularly the case with women with personality disorders.

Carr-Walker *et al.* (2004, p. 265) found that, in a prison-based pilot assessment unit for people with 'dangerous and severe personality disorder':

> ... Prison officers' attitudes were more positive than those of psychiatric nurses in all aspects of the [Attitude to Personality Disorder Questionnaire] .... Prison officers indicated

that they felt more liking for and interest in contact with personality disordered prisoners, less fear and helplessness, less anger, were more optimistic regarding treatment and less frustrated. The [Staff Attitude to Personality Disorder Interview] revealed that nurses expressed more concern about caring for and managing personality disordered patients, and felt more vulnerable and less accepting towards them. Prison officers conveyed more confidence in their own abilities and felt less vulnerable.

Most studies of staff attitudes are concerned with one or a few units, often in secure settings. It is therefore difficult to be sure of the generalisabilty of findings to staff working elsewhere.

Notions of 'evil'

Rachel Studley, in her account on p. 39, indicates some staff members' changes of attitudes when it was concluded that she was 'bad not mad'. Several authors have considered notions of 'evil' in relation to individuals with personality disorders, especially antisocial personality disorder. Crichton (1997) argues that dichotomous judgements, whereby some individuals are seen as 'mad' and others (mostly those with personality disorders) are seen as 'bad', should be avoided. He proposed that many mental health inpatients, including those with personality disorders, are able to exercise judgement and responsibility; and that they should be held to account for 'misdemcanours' and 'rule-breaking', where this is the case. Crichton (1997, p. 36) considered that 'clinical policies and guidelines must recognise the influence of moral judgement, and introduce systems that recognise the reasonableness of these judgements through education, staff support and systems of appeal'.

The literature suggests that some nurses working in high secure hospitals have unreflectively seen people with antisocial personality disorder solely as 'evil'; and have been unable to critically consider their (the nurses') perceptions. In Mercer *et al.*'s (1999) study, nurses were less likely to view individuals with mental illness in this way. Staff perceptions of evil were influenced by wider public and media perceptions and related to the moral dilemma of caring for individuals with personality disorder who had committed serious crimes that evoked, understandably, strong reactions in professionals. However, if nurses were unable to progress beyond these perceptions, this raised questions about the effectiveness of nursing interventions.

Mercer *et al.* (1999) point out that the nurses in their study combined both public and professional understandings of patients with personality disorders and offending histories. This may reflect recent developments in UK law 'to seek an uneasy and not very workable compromise between punitive and rehabilitative values, with an emphasis on the former' (Prins, 2001, p. 90).

Bowers (2002) commented that nurses with negative attitudes to individuals with personality disorders were unable to learn therapeutic, non-hostile responses to patients' negative behaviours. These nurses' reactions appeared to result in 'self-fulfilling prophecies' (p. 119), where certain behaviours of patients became reinforced. In addition, the 'negative attitude nurses were very much more likely to report negative impacts of work on their lives outside hospital' (p. 121), with increased experiences of stress and adverse effects on close relationships.

> ## Box 4.1
>
> Bowers (2002) found, from his research in high secure hospitals, that aspects of nurses' positive attitudes, which enabled them to work with patients with personality disorders, included:
>
> 1. **'Professionalism**: a commitment to provid[ing] a high standard of service, regardless of who the client is, or what has been done ...'
> 2. **'Individualised care**: everyone is unique and has to be understood as a product of his or her own ... history ... with a rejection of ... labelling ... and stereotyping ...'
> 3. **'Prevention** ... of further crime and harm to others ...'
> 4. **'Illness**: seeing patients' behaviour as symptomatic of an illness, thereby absolving them from blame.'
> 5. **'Abuse reminder**: ... remembering ... the patient's history of abuse and suffering ...'
> 6. **'Universal humanity**: recalling that we, including PD patients, are members of the human race, and are deserving of equality, human rights, compassion ...
> 7. **'Behaviour/person split**: drawing a distinction between PD patients' behaviour, which could be seen as bad, and the patients themselves, who are not.'
> 8. **'Person-first**: meeting the patients first, getting to know them as persons, before finding out about their index offences or reading the case notes ...'
> 9. **'Non-judgementalism** ...'
> 10. **'Reasoning** ... explaining the reasons behind restrictions ... in a *respectful* way ... thus avoiding confrontation ...'
> 11. **'Expressing [feelings] to colleagues**, rather than to patients' and using support from colleagues to work effectively with patients.
> 12. **'Understand**: striving for psychological understanding ... of ... patients' behaviour ... '
> 13. **'Perseverance**: willingness to try again after failure ... determination, patience.'
> 14. **'Facilitating complaints** ...'
>
> (Bowers, 2002, p. 89f)

One criticism of labelling theory is that it does not explain the existence of features of mental health problems that occur in the absence of labelling by others (Pilgrim and Rogers, 1999). Bowers (2002) found that, no matter how positive nurses were towards patients with personality disorders, they (the nurses) were still sometimes the recipients of behaviours, such as intimidation, which caused them considerable stress. Nevertheless, Bowers found that nurses with positive attitudes were able to maintain therapeutic relationships with patients, despite such behaviours, and avoided labelling them.

Bowers (2002, p. 124) reported wide repertoires of creative coping strategies used by these 'positive attitude' nurses (see Box 4.1).

> ... The love and care ... towards PD patients was probably enhanced and supported by their moral commitments (for example, to 'universal humanity') and ... 'individualised care').

How this translated into actual action towards patients is not clear ... but it seems likely that these nurses would spend more time in direct interaction ... be more tolerant of poor behaviour and struggle harder to reach an understanding of it...'

Education and staff attitudes

The National Institute for Mental Health in England (NIMHE) has highlighted the needs for 'staff selection, supervision, education and training' (NIMHE, 2003a, p. 43), related to a 'personality disorder capabilities framework'. Among other goals, this enables nurses and other professionals to appreciate service users' and carers' perspectives and avoid rejection of individuals (NIMHE, 2003b; Box 4.2).

Since the publication of 'The Personality Disorder Capabilities Framework', relevant education for a variety of staff has been provided. A study of one 'multi-agency course' found considerable attitude change, improved confidence and enhanced communication between staff in different services (Rigby and Longford, 2004, p. 337).

The attitudes of some staff are reflected in the poems in Box 4.3.

The next part of this chapter includes a review of research and other writing on service users' views.

Box 4.2: 'Underlying principles' of 'the personality disorder capabilities framework'.

Training/training programmes should:

- '... Be based on respect for the human rights of service users and their carers.'
- '... Consider how best to reflect the views and experiences of service users and carers.'
- '... Be aimed at breaking the cycle of rejection at all levels, including self-rejection, the social support system, practitioners and the wider health and social care systems.'
- '... Encourage patient/client autonomy and the development of individual responsibility.'
- '... Be multi-agency and multi-sectoral.'
- '... Support team and organisational capacity, as well as that of individual practitioners.'
- '... Be connected to meaningful lifelong learning and skill escalator programmes.'
- '... Be based on promoting learning in approaches to treatment and care that are supported by research evidence, where it exists.'

(NIMHE, 2003b, p. 22)

Box 4.3: From poems based on the authors' experience as student nurses.

From 'The Stigma that Precedes Me as a "PD"' by Linnette James
There're several scars that are prominent on both my arms
        They see this as attention seeking
I'm unable to tolerate people who are critical of me, especially when they're giving opposing views
        They say I'm being manipulative
I scream, I break things and even occasionally attack the nurse in charge
        This, they call challenging behaviour
They see the surface of me as a man, they judge me based on what's obvious to the eye.

If only they could see the turmoil in me

If only they could see the trauma from my past

If only these nurses would take the time ...

If only they weren't so fearful of what they lack the knowledge to understand

If only support and coping strategies were readily available as criticism were

Then and only then, would they begin to understand ...

If only they weren't so fearful of what they lack the knowledge to understand

If only support and coping strategies were readily available as criticism were

Then and only then, would they begin to understand.

From 'Personality Disorder Made Flesh', by Tom Pocock
'i'm a PD'
      said the young man.
          'isn't that just a label?'
             i said.
               'no, a fact'
                  he said.

i wanted to ask him more.
      who decided?
          why was he all too willing
            to accept this 'fact'?

there's a manual called the DSM,
      a book,
          hardback and hard-nosed.
            some experts' views.
               it tells people they are not the same as you and i.

> or maybe they are.
> only more so.
>
> personality disorder they call it.
> natural reaction i call it.
> natural reaction to fear.
> natural reaction to abuse.
> natural reaction to no love.
> no stability,
> no support.
> all the innate good made lifeless.
>
> instead, why not
> a celebration of the good
> in each?
> ascribing labels like
> friend, father, fellow human,
> if indeed labels there must be.
>
> for there is not one that I have met
> where a fundamental goodness
> did not burn
> behind their eyes,
> half-closed through shielding life's unpleasantness,
> but opened through the acceptance of others.
>
> and one day,
> they might move in next door to you
> and borrow sugar
> and come round for drinks.
> and if you never knew,
> you might never know.

Service users' views

Walker (1999, p. 2) refers to the importance of enabling the voices of individuals with personality disorders to be heard. Their accounts can be a useful corrective to writing that is solely from a professional perspective and sensationalist, negative media reports:

> As for many other survivors, there can be a very positive side to speaking and being heard: both ... in therapy, or more publicly ... in a book .... There can be a powerful sense of something positive having come from a dreadful experience: there is a hope and an expectation that others will learn from it ...'

Research on service user views includes the following findings.

Positive and negative staff attitudes

Positive and helpful staff attitudes have been found. Also reported (in Castillo's 2003 research, more frequently) are experiences of rejection, lack of validation of the individual's experience, and negative labelling: e.g. as 'attention-seeking' or 'manipulative' (Castillo, 2003; Castillo *et al.*, 2001; Fallon, 2003). In some instances, rejection has meant a refusal by services to provide treatment or other interventions, despite the individual's distress. This was described by several respondents in Castillo (2003, p. 81):

> A lot of people see you as untreatable – you're not offered the help and support. You're not seen as a human being but as a diagnosis – everything you do is seen in that light (Service user, quoted in Castillo, 2003, p. 81).

Hearing (or not hearing) the diagnosis

Some service users have not been told that they have a personality disorder, and have been given no information about the meaning of this diagnostic category or its implications for care and treatment (Castillo, 2003). Informal carers have also not been given information to help them understand their partner or relative, and their own needs have often been unacknowledged (Deborah, 2003). Some service users have described being told about the diagnosis insensitively, or in ways that made them feel labelled (Castillo, 2003) or alarmed (as indicated in the accounts by 'R' and Roberta Graley-Wetherell earlier in this chapter).

> At the review, nobody took time to explain the diagnosis to me, and all the discussions took place about me, but not involving me. I remember feeling numb and bewildered, as if everyone knew except me. I felt as if there was little or no hope for me (Castillo, 2003, p. 72).

In contrast, Tyrer (1998) has argued the importance of giving feedback on personality disorder diagnoses, with an emphasis on the possibility of change, response to treatment, and the individual's personal responsibility. D'Silva and Duggan (2002) outline a 'psychoeducational programme for [men] with personality disorder' (p. 268) at Arnold Lodge medium secure unit. This gives oral and written information about the personality disorders experienced by the individual, causative factors, and the consequences for himself, his relationships and specific treatment programmes to address problems.

Some individuals have noticed changes in attitudes once their diagnosis was established, often accompanied by an exclusion from services, despite their despair and depression (Castillo, 2003; Fallon, 2003). Also reported are professional expectations (sometimes formally stated in a contract) which the service user sees as unrealistic or with which he or she disagrees (Castillo, 2003; Perkins and Repper, 1996). Several authorities see consistent preparedness to work with individuals, despite the difficulties, as essential to successful outcomes (Bowers, 2002; Prins, 1995).

Respondents in the study by Perseius *et al*. (2003) described their 'experience of discontinuity and feelings of betrayal' (p. 223) when staff decided to stop working with them.

Staff qualities, particularly 'the capacity for being caring and understanding' (Ryan *et al*., 2002, p. 259) were considered by patients to be the second most important aspect of a high-security personality disorder service. In Castillo's (2003) research, of 50 individuals, 44% said that there had been adverse consequences from their diagnosis in relation to how they had 'been supported/treated' (Castillo, 2003; p. 81). However, 20% reported some positive or improved attitudes amongst staff. A few individuals stated that their diagnosis had made 'no difference' or reported 'good support' in general. In the study by Perseius *et al*. (2003), respondents reported lack of staff understanding and respect in services that they had used in the past. In contrast:

> The patients narrated the great respect, understanding and confirmation they have encountered in [their current] dialectical behaviour therapists. Some of the patients said that it was the first time, in a long history of psychiatric contact, they felt respected, understood and confirmed ...' (Perseius *et al*., 2003, p. 222).

Respondents in other studies have reported satisfaction with specialist interventions, both in relation to the interventions used, and staff attitudes, compared with more generic mental health services (Castillo, 2003; Liderth, 2003).

Nehls (1999) outlines the importance of 'safeguarding opportunities for dialogue' (Perlin, 2001, p. 443). Relationships with staff and people significant in the individual's life were seen by respondents to be important in studies by Castillo (2003) and Fallon (2003). Developing therapeutic relationships with staff was thought to be particularly crucial, in view of individuals' previous adverse experiences with relationships, both with parents and with professionals. Such experiences made it difficult for many people to trust others (Castillo, 2003; Fallon, 2003; Perseius *et al*., 2003):

> The qualities that facilitated sustained relationships were demonstrated by people who were calm, patient, knowledgeable, flexible, empathic and interested in them as people. Having all experienced negative attitudes, [the respondents] were sensitive to negative attitudes. People who were 'straight' with them and set clear boundaries without being punitive or judgemental, were identified as people they could dare to trust ...
> ... The participants identified relationships with other people as the single most important thing they had received from the service (Fallon, 2003; pp. 398 and 399).

The importance to individuals of opportunities to negotiate with staff, and have a say in decisions about nursing and other interventions is evident in several studies (Breeze, 2002; Breeze and Repper, 1998; Fallon, 2003). 'Where negotiation was lacking, the participants felt that the service did not trust them, and they had to constantly "prove" themselves' (Fallon, 2003, p. 398).

Respondents in several studies have emphasised the importance of *validation*: acknowledgement, acceptance and understanding of the individual and his or her problems (Linehan, 1993; Perseius *et al*., 2003). This includes staff's efforts to listen, and attempt to understand the individual's experience of distress, with many service users describing both positive and negative examples (Castillo, 2003; Fallon, 2003; Liza, 1999; Perseius *et al*. 2003). Important areas of understanding include 'awareness of the relationship between a person's current behaviour and past life events' (Fallon, 2003, p. 399); 'understanding self-harm' (Perlin, 2001, p. 443, citing Nehls, 1999); and appreciating the individual's need for safe containment of his or her feelings (Fallon, 2003), whilst avoiding unnecessary and custodial practices (Norton and Dolan, 1995; Perseius *et al.*, 2003). Bowers (2003) indicates the importance of understanding 'manipulation', rather than dismissing it, and outlines various interpretations of manipulative behaviour.

Providing effective treatment

Many service users have indicated the importance of treatment and services which are effective, flexible, and take their views and concerns seriously, and have staff experienced in working with individuals with personality disorder (Fallon, 2003; Perkins and Repper, 1996; Ryan *et al.*, 2002). In the latter study, 'physical facilities of the unit' and 'treatment' were seen as important priorities. Many respondents commented on the lack of treatment when they were in prison, prior to their admission to a high secure hospital (Ryan *et al.*, 2002, pp. 262 and 263). The importance of skilled nursing interventions and treatment is indicated in the accounts by 'R' and Roberta Graley-Wetherell earlier in this chapter.

Service users' views in a community outreach service

In a survey of service users' views, prior to setting up an outreach service for individuals with personality disorders discharged from a medium secure service, D'Silva (2004) found that the following 'issues [were] identified by ... current in-patients as important to them in the pre and post discharge phase before returning to the community' (Box 4.4).

This chapter will conclude with a consideration of organisations and websites for service users and informal carers.

Support groups and other organisations set up by service users and their carers

In the last decade, besides a growing interest in service user research related to personality disorder (Castillo, 2003), there has been an expanding movement of service users diagnosed with personality disorder and their carers, and an increasing number of relevant self-help groups and other organisations. In the UK, many members of groups for individuals who self-harm or have experienced abuse have had a diagnosis of personality disorder (Antony-Black, 1999; National Self Harm Network, 2005). Borderline UK, founded by Dale Ashman, is a nationwide network, with the Internet as the main communication channel. The network is involved in campaigns and

Box 4.4: By Karen D'Silva.

Issues identified by the current in-patients as important to them in the pre and post discharge phase if returning to the community.

- Obtaining appropriate housing
- Ensuring they have the correct benefits
- Linking into employment opportunities
- Accessing training in relation to preparing for job interviews, preparing CVs
- Linking into voluntary work
- Linking into educational courses
- Ensuring they are equipped to manage in the community, e.g. budgeting, being able to pay bills
- Advice on structuring time
- Being able to maintain skills and use relapse prevention strategies
- Having a support network
- Being able to develop and maintain relationships

provides leaflets and Internet information for individuals with borderline personality disorder. Professionals are occasionally consulted, but:

> We strongly feel that those of us diagnosed borderline personality disorder are the experts on the subject, and we are more than capable of voicing our opinions and making our case known – we do not need someone to speak for us, or to tell us how to run our lives (Borderline UK, 2005).

There are several other relevant UK websites, specifically for service users and their carers, including sites on borderline and other personality disorders, self-harm and generic mental health charities. Several of the latter, including Mind (2005), have website and printed information on personality disorder. Information on a wide range of relevant organisations and websites is available on the Borderline UK (2005) and Madnotbad (2005) websites. The Association of Personality Disorders (2005) is a service-user-run website which offers a critical perspective, particularly on the 'Dangerous People with Severe Personality Disorder' programme and policy (see Chapter 3).

Relevant service user and carer organisations have been established for several years in North America. These include the New England Personality Disorder Association (2005) and the New York Society for the Study of Multiple Personality and Dissociation (2005). Both these organisations have service user, carer and professional membership. There are also several support groups and websites for people who have been negatively affected by individuals with antisocial personality disorder (e.g. The Emptied Soul Psychopathy Group, 2005) and for individuals with, or caring for people with borderline, passive-aggressive, narcissistic and avoidant personality disorders. Examples include: N-Partners (2005), Online BDP Family Groups and Stigma (2005), Passive-Aggressive Helping Hands (2005), The Avoidant's Homepage (2005) and Wise Mind (2005).

Conclusion

This chapter includes accounts by service users and overviews of research on professionals' attitudes and service user experiences. Whilst positive experiences of professionals and of their interventions have been reported by service users, many individuals experience problems, not only from the distress caused by personality disorders, but from negative staff attitudes. Many service users have reported denial of appropriate services. However, despite past 'therapeutic nihilism', more professionals appear to be keen to work with people with personality disorders. The Department of Health has stated that all Trust mental health service providers must make specialist provision in this area, with appropriate staff education.

Service user accounts in this chapter, as well as research findings, indicate instances of staff rejection and judgementalism, but also examples of consultation and the provision of relevant information. Also stressed is the importance of being listened to and validated by staff, receiving effective treatment, and having professionals experienced in caring for people with personality disorders.

The above findings have obvious implications for the provision of care, interventions, treatment and services by nurses and other professionals.

Finally, there has recently been an increase in the number of organisations and websites for service users with personality disorders and their informal carers.

References

Antony-Black, J. (1999) Multiple personality: a personal perspective. In: Walker, M. and Antony-Black, J. (eds.) *Hidden Selves: An Exploration of Multiple Personality*, Chapter 7. Open University Press, Buckingham.

Ashman, D. (2001) Desperately seeking understanding. *Mental Health Today*, October, 30–31.

Association of Personality Disorders (Asperdis) (2004) Website: http://www.asperdis.org/.

Borderline UK (2005) Website: http://www.wardrobehudson.co.uk/.

Bowers, L. (2002) *Dangerous and Severe Personality Disorder: Response and Role of the Psychiatric Team*. Routledge, London.

Bowers, L. (2003) Manipulation: searching for an understanding. *Journal of Psychiatric and Mental Health Nursing*, **10**, 329–334.

Breeze, J. (2002) User participation and empowerment in community mental health nursing practice in: Dooher, J. and Byrt, R. (eds.) *Empowerment and Participation: Power, Influence and Control in Contemporary Health Care*, Chapter 6. Quay Books, Dinton, Salisbury.

Breeze, J. and Repper, J. (1998) Struggling for control: the care experiences of 'difficult' patients in mental health services. *Journal of Advanced Nursing*, **28**(6), 1301–1311.

Byrt, R., Wray, C. and 'Tom' (2005) Towards hope and inclusion: nursing interventions in a medium secure service for men with 'personality disorders'. *Mental Health Practice*, **8**(8), 38–43.

Carr-Walker, P., Bowers, L., Callaghan, P., Nijman, H. and Paton, J. (2004) Attitudes towards personality disorders: comparison between prison officers and psychiatric nurses. *Legal and Criminological Psychology*, **9**, 265–277.

Castillo, H. (2003) *Personality Disorder: Temperament or Trauma?* Jessica Kingsley, London.

Castillo, H., Allen, L. and Coxhead, N. (2001) The hurtfulness of a diagnosis: user research about personality disorder. *Mental Health Practice*, **4**(9), 16–19.

Cope, R. (1993) A survey of forensic psychiatrists' views on psychopathic disorder. *The Journal of Forensic Psychiatry*, **4**, 214–235.

Crichton, J. (1997) The response of nursing staff to psychiatric inpatient misdeameanour. *The Journal of Forensic Psychiatry*, **8**(1), 36–41.

Deborah (1999). Informing relatives and partners about personality disorder? *Dialogue*, Issue 3, Winter 1999/2000.

Department of Health (2005) Website: `http://www.doh.gov.uk/`.

Dolan, B. and Coid, J. (1993) *Psychopathic and Antisocial Personality Disorders: Treatment and Research Issues*. Gaskell, London.

D'Silva, K. (2004) *F.O.R.T.E. The Forensic Personality Disorder Outreach Team, East Midlands and South Yorkshire: Involving Service Users and Service Providers in the Development of the New Service. Internal report*. Arnold Lodge Medium Secure Unit, Leicester.

D'Silva, K. and Duggan, C. (2002) Service innovations: development of a psychoeducational programme for patients with personality disorder. *Psychiatric Bulletin*, **26**, 268–271.

The Emptied Soul Psychopathy Group (2005) Website: `http://communities.msn.com/TheEmptiedSoulPsychopathychatsite/homepage/`.

Fallon, P. (2003) Travelling through the system: the lived experience of people with borderline personality disorder in contact with the system. *Journal of Psychiatric and Mental Health Nursing*, **10**, 393–400.

Liderth, S. (2003) Untitled. In: Bree, A., Campling, P. and Liderth, S. Empowerment in mental health: the therapeutic community model. In: Dooher, J. and Byrt, R. (eds.) *Empowerment and the Health Service User*, Chapter 10, pp. 149–151. Quay Books, Mark Allen Publishing, Dinton, Salisbury.

Linehan, M. M. (1993) *Skills Training Manual for Treating Borderline Personality Disorder*. Guilford Press, New York.

Liza (1999) 'Liza's story'. In: Walker, M. and Antony-Black, J. (eds.) *Hidden Selves: An Exploration of Multiple Personality*, Chapter 2. Open University Press, Buckingham.

Mad Not Bad (2005) Website: `http://www.madnotbad.co.uk/`.

Markham, D. (2003) Attitudes towards patients with a diagnosis of 'borderline personality disorder': social rejection and dangerousness. *Journal of Mental Health*, **12**(6), 595–612.

Mental Health Alliance (2005) Website: `http://www.mentalhealthalliance.org.uk/`.

Mercer, D., Mason, T. and Richman, J. (1999) Good and evil in the crusade of care. *Journal of Psychosocial Nursing and Mental Health Services*, **37**(9), 13–17.

Mind (2005) Website: `http://www.mind.org.uk/`.

National Institute for Mental Health in England (2003a) *Personality Disorder: No Longer a Diagnosis of Exclusion*. Department of Health, London.

National Institute for Mental Health in England (2003b) *Breaking the cycle of rejection. The personality disorder capabilities framework*. NIMHE, Leeds.

National Self Harm Network (1999) *The Hurt Yourself Less Handbook*. Self Harm Network, Nottingham.

National Self Harm Network (2005) Website: http://www.nshn.co.uk/.

New England Personality Disorder Association (NEPDA) (2005) Website: http://www.nepda.org/.

New York Society for the Study of Multiple Personality and Dissociation (2005) Website: http://www.nyssmpd.org/.

Norton, K. and Dolan, B. (1995) Acting out and the institutional response. *The Journal of Forensic Psychiatry*, **6**, 317–332.

N-Partners (2005) Website: http://communities.msn.com/Npartners/.

Online BDP Family Groups and Stigma (2005) Website: http://www.borderlinepersonalitytoday.com/.

Passive-Aggressive Helping Hands (2005) Website: http://www.passiveaggressive.homestead.com/.

Pembroke, L. R. (ed.) (1996) *Self-Harm: Perspectives from Personal Experience*. Survivors Speak Out, London.

Perkins, R. E. and Repper, J. M. (1996) *Working Alongside People with Long Term Mental Health Problems*, Chapter 14. Chapman & Hall, London.

Perlin, C. K. (2001) Social responses and personality disorders. In: Stuart, G. W. and Laraia, M. T. (eds.) *Principles and Practice of Psychiatric Nursing*, 7th edn, Chapter 23. Mosby, St Louis.

Perseius, K.-I., Ojehagen, A., Ekdahl, S., Asberg, M. and Samuelsson, M. (2003) Treatment of suicidal and deliberate self-harming patients with borderline personality disorder using dialectical behavior therapy: the patients' and the therapists' perceptions. *Archives of Psychiatric Nursing*, **17**(5), 218–227.

Pilgrim, D. (2001) Disordered personalities and disordered concepts. *Journal of Mental Health*, **10**, 253–265.

Pilgrim, D. and Rogers, A. (1999) *A Sociology of Mental Health and Illness*, 2nd edn. Open University Press, Buckingham.

Prins, H. (1994) Psychiatry and the concept of evil. *British Journal of Psychiatry*, **165**, 297–300.

Prins, H. (1995) *Offenders, Deviants or Patients?*, 2nd edn. Routledge, London.

Rigby, M. and Longford, J. (2004) Development of a multi-agency experiential training course on personality disorder. *Psychiatric Bulletin*, **28**, 337–341.

Ryan, S., Moore, E., Taylor, P., Wilkinson, E., Lingiah, T. and Christmas, M. (2002) The voice of detainees in a high security setting on services for people with personality disorder. *Criminal Behaviour and Mental Health*, **12**, 254–268.

Sallah, D. (1999) The treatment, care and management of the psychopathic disorder patient: the nursing contribution. In: Tarbuck, P., Topping-Morris, B. and Burnard, P. (eds.) *Forensic Mental Health Nursing. Strategy and Implementation*, Chapter 3. Whurr Publishers, London.

Szasz, T. (1972) *The Myth of Mental Illness*, Paladin edition. Granada Publishing, London.

The Avoidant's Homepage. Website: http://fiona128.tripod.com/theavoidantshomepage/.

Tyrer, P. (1998) Feedback for the personality disordered. *The Journal of Forensic Psychiatry*, **9**(1), 1–4.

Walker, M. (1999) A century of controversy: multiplicity or madness; memory or make-believe? In: Walker, M. and Antony-Black, J. (eds.) *Hidden Selves: An Exploration of Multiple Personality*, Chapter 1. Open University Press, Buckingham.

Walker, M. and Antony-Black, J. (eds.) (1999) *Hidden Selves: An Exploration of Multiple Personality*. Open University Press, Buckingham.

Warner, R. (2001) Community attitudes towards mental disorder. In: Thornicroft, G. and Szmukler, G. (eds.) *Textbook of Community Psychiatry*, Chapter 38. Oxford University Press, Oxford.

Wetherell, A. and Graley-Wetherell, R. (2003) Self-help: personal perspectives and experiences. In: Dooher, J. and Byrt, R. (eds.) *Empowerment and the Health Service User*, Chapter 17. Quay Books, Dinton, Salisbury.

Wise Mind Recovery Connection for Borderline Personality Disorder. (2005). Website: http://www.wisemindinc.com/.

Culture, spirituality and ethical issues in caring for clients with personality disorder

Mary A. Addo

Introduction

This chapter examines cultural, spiritual and ethical issues involved when working with people from diverse cultural backgrounds diagnosed with a personality disorder. The aim is to contribute to the recognition of culture and spirituality as being of relevance to providing services for people defined as having a personality disorder. For ease of discussion the terms *client* or *person* are used within this chapter to refer to people diagnosed with personality disorder and whose cultural world views are different from the providers of care (nurses) they access.

The UK now features greater cultural diversity due to the presence of various ethnic groups (Cortis, 2004; Narayanasamy, 2001; Social Trends, 2002). Policy directives from the (Department of Health, 1991) place the client at the core of service provision in the UK. The Race Relations Act (1976, 2000) also sets out legal imperatives on how service providers have to address the cultural needs of diverse ethnic communities such that the service provided is reflective of the needs of the particular ethnic group in question.

In addition, policy documents like *Modernising Mental Health Services* (Department of Health, 1998a) and *Modernising Social Care Services* (Department of Health, 1998b) highlighted the need to ensure ethnic inequalities in health care is improved through the education and training of staff. Furthermore, Watson (1990) maintains that cultural needs of ethnic minority patients are not addressed during the educational preparation of health care professionals. The UKCC (1999) study on secure environments also highlighted that the specific needs of patients from diverse cultures are frequently overlooked in the allocation of resources.

If we are to have equity and excellence in health care provision and delivery that meets the diverse needs of everyone in an ethnically diverse country like the UK, having knowledge and an understanding of those cultures is essential. To achieve this, staff are required to be aware of the demographic changes in the population they serve, and of the cultural and health issues of that population (Cortis, 2004).

The person with a personality disorder

Our personality is that unique and distinctive human quality that defines and determines the essence of what we are as human beings (Houghton and Ousley, 2004). Personality, then, is what makes us who we are and how well we know ourselves. However, in developing a personality disorder, there are individuals whose early childhood experiences, following trauma such as serious neglect and physical, emotional and sexual abuse, have led to damaged self-image, relationship problems, fear of abandonment, and self-injurious and impulsive behaviours (Bennett, 2003). These individuals experience distress of all kinds and thereby develop coping strategies which are not always help-ful to them (Bowers, 2002; Tennant and Hughes, 1997; Tennant *et al.*, 2000), leading to maladap-tive behaviours. For more information on types of personality disorder see Chapter 2.

Being labelled as having a personality disorder gives a sense of loss of one's self, where one's identity is lost and replaced with stigma, shame, grief and a feeling of difference. It is during these turbulent times, in which the person diagnosed with a personality disorder's sense of self is chal-lenged by life's afflictions, that his or her definition of who he or she is and the person's successes and accomplishments lose their significance. Instead, it is at this point that the person's existence and those spiritual questions and challenges must be faced (Puchalski and Larson, 1998).

Why cultural and spiritual care in personality disorder

Race, ethnicity and culture in a broad sense are acknowledged as having an influence on one's experience of health care delivery (Narayanasamy, 1999). The need to offer appropriate care that meets the spiritual and cultural expectations of people from diverse cultures is recognised by the NHS through the Patient's Charter and accompanying guidance (Department of Health, 1991). Standard one of the Charter makes reference to all health services to ensure that proper personal consideration is shown to clients. For example, issues of the individual's right to privacy, dignity and religious and cultural beliefs are respected.

This means that no matter how incongruous the cultural beliefs of nurses to that of their cli-ents, they are expected to ensure that the clients' cultural and spiritual needs are identified and met, in an appropriate and sensitive manner regardless of any differences (Department of Health, 1991; NMC, 2002). Nonetheless, where those who provide the care lack the necessary cultural and spiritual knowledge to guide their practice to show respect to the client's cultural values and beliefs, this can often lead to care given based on ignorance, ethnocentrism or discrimination (Aiyegbusi, 2000; Fernando, 1995; Gerrish *et al.*, 1996; Luckmann, 1999).

Burnard (1990) asserts that the spiritual needs of clients are not very well catered for in the nursing profession. Similarly, Gerrish *et al.* (1996) maintain that the cultural care needs for people from diverse ethnic groupings are far from adequate, a view supported by Cortis (2004) and Watkins (2001). We cannot shy away from the cultural and spiritual care needs of personality disorder clients. If we do, then the care offered will be perceived as less than adequate as both culture and spirituality are essential human needs in the context of nursing work that need to be acknowledged.

To reverse this trend requires the cultivation of mutual understanding between nurses as care providers and the wide diversity of cultural groupings from which persons diagnosed as having a personality disorder may come. Becoming knowledgeable and informed about the clients' cultural worldviews, and their impact on providing appropriate care, which empowers them to be in control of their identity, is necessary.

Spirituality and the person with a personality disorder

Spiritual and cultural specific care are expected by clients when they engage with health care services and frontline staff. There are various arguments in the literature supporting the therapeutic gains derived from providing spiritually appropriate care (Narayanasamy, 2002; Puchalski and Larson, 1998; Swinton and Kettles, 1997; Swinton, 2002), of which culture is a component (Leininger, 1995; Narayanasamy, 2001). The lack of any agreed definition and consensus on spirituality (Swinton, 2001) does little to enhance nurses' understanding of this important human need for fulfilment. This view is supported by Highfield (1992) and Ross (1997), asserting that nurses have difficulty in recognising clients' spiritual needs and knowing how to assess these.

Part of the confusion relates to the view that spirituality is religion. However, Swinton (2002) points out that religion is only one aspect of spirituality, a view shared by Harrison (1993) who argues that the word 'spirituality' is often used interchangeably with religion, yet its scope and meaning are more complex. Langford (1989) also contends that spirituality covers more than religion, although a religious framework can be used to make sense of the experience. This implies that religion is only one route through which some people achieve their spiritual quest. Emblen (1992) distinguished religion from spirituality.

Box 5.1: Attributes of religion.

- Systems
- Beliefs
- Organisation
- Mediators, e.g. priest, imam
- Worship
- Practices

Emblen (1992)

Box 5.2: Attributes of spirituality.

- Personal life
- Principle
- Animator
- Being
- God-quality
- Relationship
- Transcendence

Emblen (1992)

Boxes 5.1 and 5.2 shows that religion may shape and inform spiritual matters, but spirituality and spiritual care are not exclusive to religion (Olumide, 1998; Swinton, 2002). Spirituality may embrace religious understandings of illness and death and the acceptance that these are partly culturally determined. According to Olumide (1998), to offer spiritual care implies having a broad understanding of the fundamental differences in outlook between people, coupled with a belief in the underlying sameness of human need.

Definition of spirituality

Swinton (2002, p. 207) offers this definition of spirituality as the

> aspect of human existence that gives it its 'humanness'. It concerns the structures of significance which give meaning and direction to a person's life and helps them deal with the vicissitudes of existence. As such it includes such vital dimensions as the quest for meaning, purpose, self-transcending knowledge, meaningful relationships, love and commitment, as well as the sense of the Holy amongst us. A person's spirituality is that part of them which drives them on towards their particular goals, be they temporal or transcendent.

This definition of spirituality, although it includes religion, is not solely defined by religion. It includes basic human needs such as love, the search for meaning, hope, values, relationships and commitment (Goldberg 1998). These basic human needs also fit with Maslow's (1954) hierarchy of human needs such as safety, self-esteem, sense of belonging and self-actualization. If spirituality is a human need then there is no doubt that regardless of one's race, creed, culture, ethnicity, health status or disability, spirituality is something that we can all experience, and does not belong to and is not owned by church-goers or believers. In this sense spiritually could be viewed as bound to one's cultural worldview. Further definitions of spirituality can be found in Bradshaw (1994), Cobb (2001), Hall (1997) and Swinton (2001).

The implication for nurses working with personality disorder clients from diverse cultural backgrounds is to seek clarification and meaning of what spirituality is from the client's perspective, regardless of their diagnosis or differentness, as this is a personal issue. In fact, Cassidy (1988) asserts that everyone has a spiritual nature that can be touched through the ministration of another 'inclusive of nurses'. In that sense if nursing is perceived as ministration to the health and well-being of personality disordered clients in society, with diverse cultural needs, it demands that care providers must have the appropriate knowledge and skills to do so (Puchalski and Larson, 1998). This will promote the delivery of care that enables personality disorder clients to find meaning and purpose in living (Burnard, 1988a).

Spirituality, healing and the person with a personality disorder

Ross (1994, p. 441) states that:

> An individual entering a hospital will do so with particular spiritual needs. Whether or not these needs are met may determine the speed and extent of their recovery and the level of spiritual well-being and quality of life they experience. It is important, therefore, that they receive the necessary help to meet their spiritual needs.

Within the nursing literature *presencing* is referred to as the act of being with a client in a compassionate manner (Rogers, 1957). It is a way of engaging with the client, as it has the therapeutic effect of empowering and enabling the client to change, to accept, to grow, or to die peacefully (Roach, 1991, p. 15). When a personality disorder client, regardless of cultural background, sexual orientation, gender or disability, feels recognised as a whole person rather than being defined by the label, it is this recognition of the real person behind that label that brings relief and healing to the client by being accepted for what one is with all one's imperfections. When personality disorder clients feel understood and when they feel connected to the other person (nurses) and when they know they have been recognised for who they are, this equates with the ethical principle of respect.

Watkins (2001) argues that for social inclusiveness to become a reality for people with reference to cultural diversity it is important to take clients' world views into consideration. The implication for the helping relationship between the nurse and his or her clients is the acknowledgement of the impact on clients' psychosocial well-being of factors such as stigma, discrimination, social impoverishment and disadvantage, to which cultural care needs can be added.

Davidson (1998) contends that the nurse's role is not only helping the personality disorder client to demystify his or her problems but that the role also involves the nurse to be comforting and nurturing and to provide an encouraging presence. In addition he argues that:

> ... if we can just be with someone no matter what state they are in, without needing to act on them or change them, yet be vibrantly alive to their humanity, then clients do eventually feel sufficiently safe and courageous to tackle aspects of their life which are amenable to development (p. 63)

Compassionate care is central to working with personality disorder clients, as the caring relationship with the client is of paramount importance for spiritual insight to happen (Egan, 1994; Friedemann *et al.*, 2002; Rogers, 1957; Watkins, 2001). Personality disorder clients come to us when they are at their most vulnerable, at times of loss and suffering. In these stages of their life we as nurses providing professional care must help them find meaning, purpose and a sense of harmony in the midst of their suffering, alongside any other treatment interventions that they are offered.

Furthermore, Barker (2003) asserts that in our engagement with the client we must seek to understand the meaning of the client's narratives in the context of the client's beliefs, family and culture. For it is through these narratives that the client's world unfolds and we as care providers gain insight into what it is like for them living with a personality disorder label. It is this insight that enables the nurse to understand better the client's predicament and to offer the appropriate help. For when we as nurses attend to the total needs of the client, including their cultural and spiritual concerns, we are dealing with the total human dimensions of nursing practice (Swinton, 2001).

McCavery (1985) considers the delivery of spiritual care in acute illness by nurses and relates this to ethical principles, such as respect for the person and truth telling. For nurses to provide this aspect of nursing care to clients with a personality disorder requires the skills of active listening and responding in order to allow the patient to express their feelings of anger, frustration, pain, distress or anxiety, and to begin to experience a renewed sense of security and peace. It is upon this interpersonal relationship that the ultimate health outcome for the personality disorder client depends to help make sense of his or her present circumstances.

If the nurse–client relationship is the hallmark of nursing practice and the NMC (2002) requires nurses to treat the client as a unique individual, providing spiritual and cultural care to personality disorder clients requires nurses whose behaviour in their engagement with clients demonstrates love, hope and meaning to the client (Bontell and Bozett, 1990; Bowers, 2002; Health Service Commissioner, 1995).

Assessing spiritual needs of personality disorder clients

Watkins (2001) asserts that the assessment of need should be from the perspective of clients, in that they should be able to negotiate a plan of care that best meets their needs. However, it has been acknowledged in the literature that nurses face challenges in this negotiation process with personality disorder clients regarding assessment and intervention (Coffey, 2000; Houghton and Ousley, 2004; Tennant *et al.*, 2000). Hence there is a need for nurses working with personality disorder clients who are culturally diverse to be able to understand and assess the spiritual needs of clients. This will form the basis upon which appropriate interventions are selected and implemented to provide care that meets the clients' needs for safety, comfort, hope, meaning, growth and development. The ability to engage in a meaningful manner in taking personality disorder clients' history forms the foundation for aiding the decision as to which interventions would be the most appropriate in the given context (Cortis, 2004; Hunt *et al.*, 2003, Puchalski and Larson, 1998; Swinton, 2001, 2002).

Box 5.3: Faith or beliefs, importance or influence, community, address.

Some specific questions to guide spiritual assessment dialogue:

Faith
- What is your faith or belief?
- Do you consider yourself a spiritual or a religious person?
- Does religious faith or spirituality play an important part in your life?
- What things do you believe in that give meaning to your life?

Influence
- Is it important in your life?
- What influence does it have on how you take care of your self?
- How have your beliefs influenced your behaviour during this illness (or health circumstance)?
- What role do your beliefs play in regaining your health?

Community
- Are you part of a spiritual or religious community (or congregation)?
- Is this of support to you and how?
- Is there a person or group of people you really love or who are really important to you?

Address
- How would you like me, your health care provider, to address these issues in your health care?
- Do you have any religious or spiritual issues or concerns that you'd like me to address with you?

Puchalski (1999)

Particular rituals, whether cultural or spiritual, are generally performed at a time of significant transition in one's life, such as being diagnosed and labelled with a personality disorder, leading to a change in one's perception of self and others to the person, and how the person handles this change process. How the individual handles this process is partly influenced by the person's cultural worldview, of which spiritual beliefs are a component. To assess a client's spiritual beliefs requires nurses who are aware of their own spirituality and are competent in cultural knowledge and interpersonal skills. The examples in Boxes 5.3 and 5.4 are spiritual assessment tools that can be used in this context (Puchalski, 1999; Swinton 2002).

Research evidence demonstrates that some nurses feel uncomfortable in assessing the personality disorder client's spiritual needs and providing spiritual care (Carroll, 2001; McSherry, 1998). Part of this problem relates to the lack of preparation for practice in the spiritual aspect of caring for people during their training (McSherry, 1998). The simple questions illustrated about

Box 5.4: The nursing process as a framework for providing individualised spiritual care (Swinton, 2002).

Stages of nursing process	Knowledge required
Assessment	What are spiritual needs, and how can they be assessed?
Planning and intervention	What types of intervention could be applied to meet these needs?
Evaluation	What criteria might we use to determine whether or not a patient's spiritual needs have been met?

beliefs and faith (see Boxes 5.3 and 5.4), when respectfully put to the client, can lead to eliciting a meaningful exploration of the client's spiritual and cultural worldview.

Such opening statements can promote a dialogue enabling both the nurse and the client to share and explore within the therapeutic relationship elements of life that give spiritual sustenance to both the nurse and the client within professional boundaries (Puchalski and Larson 1998). Even if the nurse does not share the client's cultural and spiritual worldview, the nurse has a duty to ensure that this aspect of the client's need is identified and that provision is made to meet that need (Department of Health, 1991; NMC, 2002; Swinton, 2002). Box 5.5 shows some of the benefits of spirituality.

As nurses helping personality disorder clients to take charge of their situation, if we are able to help them fulfil their spiritual needs we have realised what nursing is about: it is about caring for the whole person. To achieve this requires the language of spirituality to be part of our practice, as spirituality is a component of one's culture and there is no human being without a culture of some sort.

Box 5.5: Benefits of spirituality.

■ Religious beliefs and practices, especially in seeking God's help, extend the individual's coping resources and are associated with improvements in health outcome (Pargament *et al.*, 1990)

■ Provides help and comfort in times of great need (Oxam *et al.*, 1995)

■ Rituals like prayer and meditation have been found to make us feel safe and are helpful alongside conventional medical treatments (Hall, 1997)

■ Help people cope with serious illness such as depression, cancer and addictions (Puchalski and Larson, 1998)

■ Positive relationships between measures of religious commitment and health (Levin *et al.*, 1997)

■ Offers hope and comfort in coping with depression (Swinton, 2001)

Culture, health and personality disorder clients

Culture is defined as a system or systems of socially acquired values, beliefs and rules of conduct which delineate the range of accepted behaviours in any given society (Helman, 2000). Cultural background has an important influence on many aspects of our lives, including our beliefs, behaviours, perceptions, emotions, language, religion, rituals, family structure, diet, dress, body image, concepts of space and time, and attitudes to illness, pain and other forms of misfortune; all of which may have important implications for health and health care (Helman, 2000, p. 3). It is recognised in the literature that cultural and social background, gender and sexual orientation make a difference to the sense of connection and the ability of the helper to work in culturally sensitive ways (Helman, 2000; Watkins, 2001).

The issue of culture and its relevance to health care delivery has been demonstrated in the literature (Gerrish *et al.*, 1996; Leininger, 1995; Narayanasamy, 1999). Various cultures have different perceptions and beliefs about the causes of illness, disease, diagnosis and treatment (Helman, 2000). Kleinman (1980) and Burr (1998) assert that a person's culturally embedded ideas about why he or she becomes ill may differ widely from biomedical aetiologies and that clients may maintain these culturally determined explanations even after a medical diagnosis.

For example, in some cultures health-related or life circumstances presented to health care providers may be attributed to some other source, such as a curse from the gods or the result of witchcraft. Such persons may not feel comfortable in sharing or disclosing this with others if they do not feel culturally safe to do so (Papps and Ramsden, 1996). Furthermore, when health care is based on race alone this can lead to misdiagnosis, as illustrated by Marsella (1980) of the differences in depressive experience and disorder from diverse cultures presented in Box 5.6.

Box 5.6: Differing cultural responses to depression.

Country	Depressive pattern
Afghanistan	While suicidal thoughts are absent from this group, numerous similarities exist with Western depressed people such as low mood.
Iraq	This group does not tend to express ideas of unworthiness, self-deprecation or suicidal ideation. Depression is manifested by physical symptoms and paranoid ideation.
India	Suicidal tendencies, sleep difficulties, depressive affect ... feelings of guilt and motor retardation are minimal. The body is used for expressing tension, with the experience of agitation and anxiety being more common.
Indonesia	Loss of vitality and sleep disturbances are common, with the absence of sadness.
Philippines	Depression is infrequent.

Adapted from Marsella (1980)

Kleinman (1980) argues that the Western explanatory models of health and illness are predominantly biological and pathological, whereas the explanatory models of other cultures may be more supernaturalistic. Therefore applying a 'one size fits all approach' in this sense of a model (western worldview) to a client where a different model (non-western) applies may result in misdiagnosis through lack of understanding of the client's cultural meanings. Therefore it can be argued that being labelled as having a personality disorder only has meaning within the cultural context of the particular client.

As such, coping mechanisms for life challenges adopted by personality disorder clients from non-Western cultures may be perceived as symptoms through ignorance of the clients' particular cultural context by care providers in that the symptoms are an outcome of illness rather than a misfortune suffered (Aiyegbusi, 2000). This means double discrimination for ethnic minority people when faced with mental health problems (Fernando, 1995). Ethnocentrism, the belief in the superiority of one's own ethnic group, can be a deeply ingrained tendency and thus understandable, but it is a limiting view if nurses are to deliver humane care that meets the needs of all individuals, regardless of any differentness that exists including personality disorder clients.

Although no one should be denied having ethnocentric views, nurses working with personality disorder clients from diverse cultures should not see the world from their cultural standpoint alone without due regard to the personality disorder clients' cultural views, otherwise issues of accusations of prejudice and discriminatory practices may be levied against nurses (Mazanec, 2003).

Providing culturally appropriate care for personality disorder clients

Stokes (1991) asserts that nursing is not culturally free but culturally determined, and if this is not recognised or understood then nurses become guilty of gross ethnocentrism. Issues in providing culturally appropriate care to clients can be looked at from two perspectives: those originating from providers of the service and those from systems in operation (Mazanec, 2003). Culturally inappropriate care is experienced by clients whose cultural needs have not been met due to poor service design and delivery based on service providers' ignorance and lack of knowledge of the cultural practices and beliefs of the clients they provide the service for. Therefore the service does not meet the needs of those it purports to serve. This occurs when differences exist in clients' worldviews yet providers of the service fail to make any attempts to address this imbalance (Gerrish *et al.*, 1996; Luckmann, 1999).

Racial and cultural disparities in health and health care delivery still persist and evidence within the literature confirms the negative experience of people from diverse racial, ethnic and cultural backgrounds in health care provision often marred by discriminatory practices (Aiyegbusi, 2000; Gerrish *et al.*, 1996; Mind, 1993, 1999; Royal College of Nursing, 1996). Examples of the impact of lack of cultural awareness on race and mental health care are shown in Box 5.7.

This situation illustrates how lack of cultural knowledge of other cultures can contribute to ineffective stances where health and illness are concerned. Learning about other cultures provides the nurse with information on the most common cultural practices of a particular group, which enables the nurse to offer care which is defined as culturally competent. Leininger (1978) describes trans-cultural nursing as a formal area of study and practice in the cultural beliefs,

> ### Box 5.7: Racism in mental health services.
>
> Black people are more likely than white:
>
> - To be diagnosed as suffering from schizophrenia or another form of psychosis
> - To be detained in a locked ward or secure psychiatric unit
> - To be detained under a detention order
> - To be removed to a place of safety by the police
> - To be given higher doses of medication
> - To experience unmet needs
>
> They are less likely:
>
> - To be referred for psychotherapy or counselling
> - To receive an appropriate assessment and intervention at an early stage
>
> Department of Health and Home Office (1992), cited in Watkins (2001)

values and life ways of diverse cultures and in the use of knowledge to provide culture-specific or culture-universal care to individuals, families and groups of particular cultures. This requires the nurse to be culturally competent.

According to Papadopoulos *et al.* (2001) cultural competence is the capacity to provide effective health care taking into consideration people's cultural beliefs, behaviours and needs, asserting further that this includes not just anti-discriminatory policies, but cultural awareness, knowledge and sensitivity (see Box 5.8). It demands that nurses looking after clients with a personality disorder must take into account both their own and the client's cultural worldview and that of the client's family members. To do so without due regard to diversity in this context may contribute towards abuse (Gallop, 1998; NMC, 2002), which may bring harm to personality disorder clients.

It is not good practice to provide care for individuals from diverse cultural backgrounds based on the norms drawn out of the majority culture (Fernando, 1995; Kleinman, 1980; Watkins, 2001). Each person must be considered individually; failure to do so means the Patient's Charter (Department of Health, 1991) is worth nothing. In addition nursing is governed by the ethical principles of doing good to clients and preventing harm regardless of the context of engagement (NMC, 2002).

To help nurses achieve this competence in order to provide person-centred care irrespective of differences will require each nurse to define and understand his or her own culture. The adoption and utilisation of cultural self-assessment tools can be valuable in enabling nurses to formatively check their own professional development in the area of providing culturally appropriate care. For example, clinicians should consider the ways in which clients and families express themselves verbally when discussing the concepts of personality disorder, specific needs and treatment options to evaluate their beliefs and attitudes (Mazanec, 2003). Some of the key points in relation to trans-cultural care are presented in Box 5.9.

Box 5.8: What is cultural competence?

Cultural awareness

Self-awareness

Culture identity

Heritage adherence

Ethno-centric

Cultural competence

Assessment skills

Diagnostic skills

Clinical skills

Challenging prejudice

Discrimination and inequalities

Cultural knowledge

Health beliefs and behaviours

Barriers to cultural sensitivity

Ethno-history

Stereotyping

Sociological understanding

Similarities and variations

Cultural sensitivity

Empathy

Interpersonal communication skills

Trust

Acceptance

Appropriateness

Respect

Papadopoulos *et al.* (2001)

Box 5.9: Trans-cultural care – key points.

■ The cultural needs of personality disorder clients can be met by transcultural nursing

■ Nursing is not culturally free, but embedded in a specific culture which pervades all aspects of care and practices

■ Trans-cultural nursing is about considering culture, specific values, beliefs and practices

■ An understanding of terms such as race, culture and ethnicity is an important feature in working with personality disorder clients

Adapted from Narayanasamy (1999)

This cultural awareness can be achieved through effective communication and use of appropriate language. This enables the personality disorder client to express his or her thoughts and feelings so that these can be understood. The meaning of what is required of the nurse–client relationship is established through negotiation and mutual understanding. Box 5.10 highlights some of

> ## Box 5.10: Barriers to providing culturally appropriate care to personality disorder clients from diverse cultural backgrounds.
>
> - Ignorance of other cultures
> - Language ambiguities and styles of communication
> - Gestures, symbols and the meaning of words used
> - Past experiences
> - Bias and ethnocentric views
> - Expectations of care provider and that of the client
> - Racism
> - Stereotyping and prejudice
>
> Luckmann (1999)

the barriers that contribute to providing culturally appropriate care to personality disorder clients from diverse cultural backgrounds.

The manner in which culturally specific care can be managed is through paying attention to the delivery of care to persons with a personality disorder that is free from intimidation, oppressive attitudes and discrimination. Care needs to be provided in a safe context of sharing, recognising and acknowledging the client's beliefs and values in these situations and working with them. To help nurses achieve this requires established standards and training which serve as exemplary benchmarks for service providers and those at the front-line in delivering such services.

Ethical issues

The NMC (2002) Code of Professional Conduct requires nurses to show respect for the interests and dignity of clients regardless of gender, age, race, ability, sexuality, economic status, lifestyle, culture and religious or political beliefs. The implication of this is that nurses in their engagement with clients should do everything possible within their authority to overcome barriers that hinder appropriate care being offered. Campbell (1984) coined the phrase 'skilled companionship' to describe the relationship between the nurse and the client. This relationship is perceived as both committed but carefully delineated, which implies that nurses working with clients with a personality disorder are in companionship with them through sharing experiences.

However, there are boundaries of space and time which protect both the nurse and the client in this relationship from over-involvement, which can be to the detriment of the well-being of both the nurse and the client (Arnold and Boggs, 2003). In addition, aspects of particular problems with personality disorder clients mean nurses need knowledge of ethical principles to help inform their decision-making process when faced with dilemmas of care. It is recognised that individuals diagnosed as having a personality disorder are perceived as difficult to work with and present major challenges for those working with them. However, these clients have the same need for

---

Box 5.11: Behaviours in specific personality disorders that may inhibit the establishment of therapeutic relationship.

Personality disorder	Associated behaviours
Paranoid	Suspiciousness
Schizoid	Indifference
Schizotypal	Poor social skills
Anti-social	Disregard for others
Borderline	Unstable relationship building
Histrionic	Attention seeking
Narcissistic	Lack of empathy
Avoidant	Socially inhibited
Dependent	Reassurance seeking
Obsessive compulsive	Indecisive

Houghton and Ousley (2004)

See also Bowers (2002) for other ethical issues in working with personality disorder clients.

---

compassionate care, just like any other client. Yet their behaviour makes it difficult to engage with them, and many nurses seem unprepared in their professional role to work effectively with this client group (Murphy and McVey, 2003). Some of the difficulties that nurses face in developing a therapeutic relationship with personality disorder clients are presented in Box 5.11.

The NMC (2002) Code of Professional Conduct identifies standards and expectations required of nurses which influence how they should be operationalised in their professional role, setting out the parameters of professional practice through a series of clauses. Ethical decision making is not a straightforward easy exercise. However, having knowledge of ethical principles can enable the nurse to have a framework for reasoned thought, although this cannot provide universal answers (Royal College of Nursing, 1997).

Rowson (1990) asserts that all clients, regardless of their cultural or spiritual beliefs or diagnosis or differentness, have a right to expect the following:

- Individuality of the client will be respected
- Privacy will be safeguarded
- No unreasonable harm should come to them
- Nothing should be done to them without their consent
- Those looking after the clients should exert their skills on the patients' behalf

Ethical conflicts are bound to emerge when the beliefs and value systems of the nurse contradict those of the client; for example on matters related to health and illness interpretation, choice,

> **Box 5.12: Challenges in working with personality disorder clients.**
>
> ■ Recognising and acknowledging that people with a personality need respect too and compassionate care (Ashman, 2001)
> ■ Maintaining a therapeutic relationship (Bowers, 2002)
> ■ The manipulative and intimidating behaviours of personality disorder clients brings strong feelings from nurses (Bowers, 2002)
> ■ Being non-judgemental towards personality disorder client (Bowers, 2002)
>
> See also Tennant and Hughes (1997) and Tennant *et al.* (2000)

informed consent, advocacy, confidentiality and client autonomy. The fact is that while Western culture places a high value on individual rights and autonomy, these worldviews are not shared by all cultures (Mazanec, 2003). However, the fact that in some non-Western cultures decisions about the welfare of an individual are a collective decision-making process through a consensus effort raises further ethical dilemmas for the nurse who is lacking in cultural awareness of the client's needs.

In these situations ethical dilemmas emerge due to the differing personal beliefs, feelings and principles about what is good or right in the particular situation. This is further compounded by the associated behaviours of personality disordered clients and the difficulty that nurses engaging with them face if they are lacking in the appropriate knowledge base, good interpersonal skills and a willingness to learn from the clients. Murphy and McVey (2003) provide evidence of some of the ethical challenges that nurses engaging with personality disorder clients are confronted with. Issues with the manipulative behaviour of clients and the conflicts that it generates within the nurse–client relationship have been highlighted (Bowers, 2002; Tennant *et al.*, 2000). Box 5.12 highlights some of the challenges in working with personality disorder clients.

It is a daunting task for nurses to handle and to meet all these expectations. Without a sound underpinning of educational preparation and the proper support thereafter, trying to meet these

> **Box 5.13: Guide to ethical problem solving for the nurse.**
>
> The following questions provide a useful starting point when trying to resolve a dilemma:
>
> ■ What is the goal of health care in this situation?
> ■ What are my/the health care team's responsibilities?
> ■ What are the moral/legal rights of everyone concerned?
> ■ What are the interests and expectations of the individuals involved?
> ■ What are the likely outcomes – in terms of benefits and harm – of available options?
> ■ What other moral considerations may be seen as relevant to the situation?
>
> Royal College of Nursing (1997)

expectations can lead to stress. The Royal College of Nursing (1997) clarifies this point when it states that at times there are situations where the nurse in conforming to the law may cause ethical problems, and ethical conviction could contravene the law. This reality justifies the preparation of staff who engage with personality disorder clients to be culturally competent in order not to violate the person's right to cultural safety. Box 5.13 offers a guide to ethical problem-solving for nurses.

For example, if a client with a personality disorder comes from a cultural background that places value on non-medical approaches to dealing with his or her health concerns, this may be a source of conflict for the nurse if he or she espouses Western cultural values and beliefs. Not allowing the client this cultural value in respect to their beliefs and values constitutes providing culturally insensitive and inappropriate care (Gerrish *et al.*, 1996; Kleinman, 1980), which equals abuse (Gallop 1998). However, what the nurse can do is to be open and willing to learn from the client. In this context offering emotional support would be a more respectful choice, ensuring that the client is aware of the available intervention options and of his or her right to choose. Sometimes there is no right way, but as an example the nurse can approach the client in this manner.

The problem is that failure to understand the complex needs of the person with a personality disorder as a whole person places enormous legal, ethical and professional accountabilities on nurses. The knowledge and expertise required for nurses in order to feel confident in their role to engage on a humane professional level with personality disorder clients need to be addressed. It is also important that these nurses are offered support forums that enable the challenge of mind sets to be explored and new learning to emerge (Addo, 2000; Hawkins and Shohet, 1989; Murphy and McVey, 2003).

In fact, Hawkins and Shohet (1989, p. 5) assert that:

> Our experience of supervision is that supervision can be an important part of taking care of oneself, staying open to new learning and an indispensable part of the helper's on-going professional development, self-awareness and commitment to learning, as nursing is a profession which requires a great deal of emotional commitment from its members.

In preparing to work with personality disorder clients there are many personal issues which nurses need to address first, such as personal feelings, values and perceptions (Coffey, 2000; Tennant and Hughes, 1997; Tennant *et al.*, 2000). Bowers (2002) found that despite positive attitudes shown by some nurses to people with a personality disorder, the nurses experienced levels of stress brought on by the behaviours of the clients towards the nurses. However, Bowers maintains that those nurses with positive attitudes fared better in maintaining a therapeutic relationship with the clients, despite the challenging nature of clients' behaviours.

Conclusion

This chapter focused on the relevance of culture, spirituality and ethical issues in the provision of care for people from diverse cultures with a personality disorder and how service providers and nurses can provide culturally appropriate care that takes into account the holistic being of the person. One may ask what culture and spirituality have to do with forensic mental health nurses. The fact is that we need to be able to gain mutuality in understanding in order to appreciate and care appropriately for people diagnosed with a personality disorder whose way of viewing the world is different from those who provide the care. Helping personality disorder clients requires nurses who understand, accept and manage any differences that exist in a sensitive respectful professional manner; are open-minded, knowledgeable, optimistic, well-adjusted and motivated with a strong value base in awareness of diversity issues; and committed to working with clients whose personality has been damaged in some way. It is essential that all stakeholders with an interest in the welfare of personality disorder clients work together collaboratively to break down barriers that impede and stifle the quality of health care to which personality disorder clients from diverse cultural backgrounds are subjected.

Tackling this problem through education for practice is one approach. However, until individual professionals are prepared to remain open to self-confrontation and challenge ingrained personal prejudices because of differences in worldviews, the social inclusion of each member of the community and equity in health care cannot become a reality for all. Promoting a work culture that respects human diversity and values differences that exist between groups of people, it can be argued, is what gives richness to our humanity and existence.

Therefore as nurses we need to be careful not to put people into pre-set boxes, but must be open and prepared to find out who our clients really are, and how they have fused different aspects of their identity together. Until we learn to read the cultural intricacies that we face in the world of nursing work we cannot bridge the cultural gap that separates us and the diversity of clients who seek our help.

References

Addo, M. (2000) The role of the forensic nurse in clinical supervision. In: Robinson, D. and Kettles, A. (eds.) *Forensic Nursing and Multidisciplinary Care of the Mentally Disordered Offender*. Jessica Kingsley, London.

Aiyegbusi, A. (2000) The experience of black mentally disordered offenders. In: Chaloner, C. and Coffey, M. (eds.) *Forensic Mental Health Nursing: Current Approaches*. Blackwell Science, London.

Arnold, E. and Boggs, K. U. (2003) *Interpersonal Relationships: Professional Communication Skills for Nurses*. W. B. Saunders, Philadelphia.

Ashman, D. (2001) Desperately seeking understanding. *Mental Health Today*, October, 30–31.

Barker, P. (2003) Person-centred care: the need for diversity. In: Barker, P. (ed.) *Psychiatric and Mental Health Nursing: The Craft of Caring*. Arnold, London.

Bennett, P. (2003) *Abnormal and Clinical Psychology: An Introductory Textbook*. Open University Press, Maidenhead.

Bontell, K. A. and Bozett, F. W. (1990). Nurses' assessment of patients' spirituality: continuing education implications. *Journal of Continuing Education Nurse*, **21**(94), 17217.

Bowers, L. (2002) *Dangerous and Severe Personality Disorder: Response and Role of the Psychiatric Team*. Routledge, London.

Bradshaw, A. (1994) *Lighting the Lamp: The Spiritual Dimension of Nursing Care*. Scutari Press, Harrow.

Burnard, P. (1988a) Searching for Meaning. *Nursing Times* 84(37), 34-36.

Burnard, P. (1988b) The spiritual needs of atheists and agnostics. *Professional Nurse*, **4**, 130–132.

Burnard, P. (1990) *Learning Human Skills: An Experiential Guide for Nurses*. Butterworth-Heinemann, Oxford.

Burr, J. A. (1998) Some reflections on cultural and social considerations in mental health nursing. *Journal of Psychiatric and Mental Health Nursing*, **5**, 431–437.

Campbell, A. (1984) *Moderated Love: A Theology of Professional Care*. SPCK, London.

Carroll, B. (2001) A phenomenological exploration of the nature of spirituality and spiritual care. *Mortality*, **6**(1), 81–98.

Cassidy, S. (1988) *Sharing the Darkness: The Spirituality of Caring*. Darton, Longman & Todd, London.

Cobb, M. (2001) *The Dying Soul*. Open University Press, Buckingham.

Coffey, M. (2000) Working with sex offenders. In: Chaloner, C. and Coffey, M. (eds.) *Forensic Mental Health Nursing: Current Approaches*. Blackwell Science, London.

Cortis, J. (2004) Meeting the needs of minority ethnic patients. *Journal of Advanced Nursing*, **48**(1), 51–58.

Davidson, B. (1998) The role of the psychiatric nurse. In: Barker, P. and Davidson, B. (eds.) *Psychiatric Nursing: Ethical Strife*. Arnold, London.

Department of Health (1991) *The Patient's Charter*. HMSO, London.

Department of Health (1998a) *Modernising Mental Health Services*. Department of Health, London.

Department of Health (1998b) *Modernising Social Care Services*. The Stationery Office, London.

Egan, G. (1994) *The Skilled Helper. A Problem Management Approach to Helping*. Brooks Cole, California.

Emblen, J. D. (1992) Religion and spirituality defined according to current use in nursing. *Journal of Professional Nursing*, **8**(1), 33–40.

Fernando, S. (1995) Social realities and mental health. In: Fernando, S. (ed.) *Mental Health in a Multi-Ethnic Society*. Routledge, London.

Friedemann, M.L., Mouch, J. and Racey, T. (2002) Nursing the spirit: the framework of systemic organisation. *Journal of Advanced Nursing*, **39**(4), 325–332.

Gallop, R. (1998) Abuse of power in the nurse client relationship. *Nursing Standard*, **12**(37), 43–47.

Gerrish, K., Husband, C. and MacKenzie, J. (1996) *Nursing for a Multi-Ethnic Society*. Open University Press, Buckingham.

Goldberg, B. (1998) Connection: an exploration of spirituality in nursing care. *Journal of Advanced Nursing*, **27**, 836–842.

Hall. J. (1997) The search inside. *Nursing Times*, **93**(40), 367.

Harrison, J. (1993) Spirituality in nursing practice. *Journal of Clinical Nursing*, **2**, 211–217.

Hawkins, P. and Shohet, R. (1989) *Supervision in the Helping Relationship*. Open University Press, London.

Health Service Commissioner for England for Scotland and for Wales (1995) *Annual Report*. HMSO, Scotland.

Helman, C. (2000) *Culture, Health and Illness*, 4th edn. Butterworth-Heinemann, Oxford.

Highfield, M. F. (1992) Spiritual health in oncology patients. *Cancer Nurse*, **15**, 18.

Houghton, S. and Ousley, L. (2004) The person with a personality disorder. In: Norman, I. and Ryrie, I. (eds.) *The Art and Science of Mental Health Nursing: A Textbook of Principles and Practice*. Open University Press, Berkshire.

Hunt, J., Cobb, M., Keeley, V. L. and Ahmedzai, S. H. (2003) The quality of spiritual care: developing a standard. *International Journal of Palliative Nursing*, **9**(5), 208–214.

Kleinman, A. (1980) *Patients and Healers in the Context of Culture: an Exploration of the Borderland between Anthropology, Medicine and Psychiatry*. University of California, London.

Langford, D. (1989) *Where is God in All This?* Countess Montbatten House, Southampton.

Leininger, M. (1978) *Transcultural Nursing: Concepts, Theories and Practice*. John Wiley, New York.

Leininger, M. (1995) *Transcultural Nursing Concepts, Themes, Research and Psychiatry*, 2nd edn. McGraw-Hill: New York.

Levin, J. S., Larson, D. B. and Puchalski, C. M. (1997) Religion and spirituality in medicine: research and education. *Journal of American Medical Association*, **278**, 792–793.

Luckmann, J. (1999) *Transcultural Communication in Nursing*. Delmar, USA.

Marsella, A. (1980) Depressive experience and disorder across cultures. In: Triandis, H. and Draons, J. (eds.) *A Handbook of Cross-Cultural Psychology*, Vol. 6. Allyn & Bacon, Boston.

Maslow, A. H. (1954) *Motivation and Personality*. Harper & Row, New York.

Mazanec, P. (2003) Cultural considerations in end-of-life care: how ethnicity, age, and spirituality affect decisions when death is imminent. *American Journal of Nursing*, **103**(3), 50–58.

McCavery, R. (1985) Spiritual care in acute illness. In: McGilloway, O. and Myco, F. (eds.) *Nursing and Spiritual Care*. Harper & Row, London.

McSherry, W. (1998) Nurses' perceptions of spirituality and spiritual care. *Nursing Standard*, **13**(4), 36–40.

Mind (1993) *Policy on Black and Minority Ethnic People and Mental Health*. Mind Publications, London.

Mind (1999) *Creating Acceptable Communities, Report of the Mind Inquiry into Social Exclusion and Mental Health*. Mind Publications, London.

Murphy, N. and McVey, D. (2003) The challenge of nursing personality disordered patients. *The British Journal of Forensic Practice*, **5**(1), 3–19.

Narayanasamy, A. (1999) Transcultural mental health nursing 1: benefits and limitations. *British Journal of Nursing*, **8**(11), 664–668.

Narayanasamy, A. (2001) *Spiritual Care: A Practical Guide for Nurses and Health care Practitioners*, 2nd edn. Quay Books, Wiltshire.

Narayanasamy, A. (2002) Spiritual coping in chronically ill patients. *British Journal of Nursing*, **11**(22), 1461–1470.

NMC (2002) *The Code of Professional Conduct*. Nursing and Midwifery Council, London.

Olumide, S. (1998) Spiritual Care. *Nursing Management*, **5**(1), 8–9.

Oxam, T. E., Freeman, D. H. and Manheimer, E. D. (1995) Lack of social participation of religious strength and comfort as risk factors for death after cardiac surgery in the elderly. *Psychosomatic Medicine*, **57**(1), 5–15.

Papadopoulos, I. *et al.* (2001) Culturally appropriate care should be at the heart of mental health services. *Openmind*, **110** July/August feature.

Papps, E. and Ramsden, T. (1996) Cultural safety in nursing: the New Zealand experience. *Journal of Qualitative Health Care*, **8**(5), 4917.

Pargament, K. I., Ensing, D. S., Falgout, K., Olsen, B., Van Haitsma, K. and Warren, R. (1990) God help me (1): religious coping efforts as predictors of outcomes of significant life events. *American Journal of Community Psychology*, **18**, 793–824.

Puchalski, C. (1999) A spiritual history. *Supportive Voice*, **5**, 12–13.

Puchalski, C. M. and Larson, D. B. (1998) Developing curricula in spirituality and medicine. *Academic Medicine*, **73**, 970–974.

Roach, M. (1991) The call to consciousness: compassion in today's health world. In: Gaut, D. and Leininger, M. (eds.) *Caring: The Compassionate Healer*, pp. 7–18. National League for Nursing, New York.

Rogers, C. R. (1957) The necessary and sufficient conditions of therapeutic personality change. *Journal of Consulting Psychology*, **21**, 95–103.

Ross, L. (1994) Spiritual aspects of nursing. *Journal of Advanced Nursing*, **19**(3), 439–447.

Ross, L. (1997) The nurses' role in assessing and responding to a patient's spiritual needs. *International Journal of Palliative Nursing*, **3**(1), 37–42.

Rowson, R. (1990) *Introduction to Ethics for Nurses*. Scutari Press, London.

Royal College of Nursing (1997) *Ethical Dilemmas. Issues in Nursing and Health*. Royal College of Nursing, London.

Social Trends (2002) *Social Trends Number 32*. HMSO, London.

Stokes, G. (1991) A transcultural nurse is about. *Senior Nurse*, **11**(11), 402.

Swinton, J. (2001) *Spirituality and Mental Health Care: Rediscovering a Forgotten Dimension*. Jessica Kingsley: London.

Swinton, J. (2002) Spiritual care in forensic nursing: spiritual interventions and future directions for care. In: Kettles, M. A., Woods, P. and Collins, M. (eds.) *Therapeutic Interventions for Forensic Mental Health Nurses*. Jessica Kingsley, London.

Swinton, J. and Kettles, A. M. (1997) Resurrecting the person: redefining mental illness – spiritual perspective. *Psychiatric Care*, **4**(3), 1–4.

Tennant, A. and Hughes, G. (1997) Issues in nursing care for patients with severe personality disorder. *Mental Health Practice*, **1**(1), 10–17.

Tennant, A., Daines, C. and Tennant, I. (2000) Working with the personality disordered offender. In: Chaloner, C. and Coffey, M. (eds.) *Forensic Mental Health Nursing: Current Approaches*. Blackwell Science, London.

UKCC (1999) *Nursing in Secure Environments*. United Kingdom Central Council, London.

Watkins, P. (2001) *Mental Health Nursing: The Art of Compassionate Care*. Butterworth-Heinemann, Oxford.

Watson, H. (1990) Mental Health: Caught between two cultures ... psychiatric care for people from ethnic minorities. *Nursing Times*, **85**(39), 66–68.

CHAPTER 6

The emotional impact of working with people who have personality disorders

Anne Aiyegbusi

Introduction

For the first time in the United Kingdom, there is a clearly identified direction within mental health policy for the development of services for people diagnosed with personality disorders (National Institute for Mental Health in England, 2003a). These particular mental disorders can be conceptualised as disturbances of interpersonal functioning. Because personality disorders are primarily manifest in the interpersonal domain and may not be particularly responsive to some of the widely applied mental health interventions, such as psychopharmacology, it has been stated that service developments have been slow to emerge.

Two main causes have been hypothesised as underpinning the widespread exclusion of personality-disordered people from mental health care and treatment in the UK. The first is that the patients are disliked because of the negative emotional impact they have on professionals and the second is that because services have not developed, there remains little in the way of evidence to inform effective treatment (National Institute for Mental Health in England, 2003a). These two reasons are interlinked, resulting in the exclusion of patients. With the exception of specialist treatment services, experience of working with this patient group has been lacking, militating against the possibility of developing clinical expertise and evidence within most mainstream mental health facilities. As a result, there is a relative dearth of research evidence with regard to what mental health interventions are effective with this population (Warren *et al.*, 2003). However, within the small body of available literature, the interpersonal challenges presented to professionals and the skills and personal qualities required to manage them are described. For example, with regard to the interpersonal challenges, Bowers (2002) found through a survey that one in ten forensic mental health nurses working in high-security hospitals found interpersonal contact with offenders diagnosed with personality disorders aversive, because such people provoke emotionally painful feelings. Similarly, National Institute for Mental Health in England (2003a) suggests that practitioners tend to avoid interacting with patients primarily diagnosed with personality disorders because of the emotional discomfort incurred in doing so. This 'cycle of rejection' is central to understanding the alienation of this population from mental health services (National Institute for Mental Health in England, 2003b).

There is agreement within the literature that professionals working with people diagnosed with personality disorders require specific, appropriate clinical skills (Bateman and Tyrer, 2003; Bateman and Fonagy, 2004; Bowers, 2002; Hinshelwood, 2002; National Institute for Mental Health in England, 2003a,b). These skills include those enabling the effective management of any negative emotional impact created within therapeutic relationships with personality-disordered individuals. However, the results of a recent UK scoping exercise indicate that much work remains to be done with regard to adequately preparing clinicians to work effectively with personality-disordered patients (Duggan, 2002). While there does appear to be some professional consensus about what skills are required and how they may be developed, much of this opinion has not been tested through research findings.

Nurses, with their professional base within the social environments of services, have a particularly challenging role. Furthermore, the main therapeutic tool for mental health nursing is the nurse–patient relationship. Despite this, little formal guidance or training exists to inform nursing practice, leaving nurses, especially those working in the forensic field, vulnerable to high levels of stress (Bowers, 2002).

Personality disorder

There are many models of personality disorder. Perhaps the most widely applied model is that which is contained in the Diagnostic and Statistical Manual. According to the current Diagnostic and Statistical Manual (DSM-IV) (American Psychiatric Association, 1994), personality disorders can be understood as persistent disorders of interpersonal functioning, usually present since early adult life, which lead to emotional distress and social problems for the individual and/or those with whom they are required to have relationships. Ten distinct types of personality disorder are described in DSM-IV (American Psychiatric Association, 1994) and these types are grouped into three clusters. The types and clusters of personality disorder described in DSM-IV are briefly described below in order to provide an overview of what is meant clinically by the term personality disorder.

Types of personality disorder

Cluster A: Odd/eccentric

Paranoid

People with paranoid personality disorder are distrustful of other people and therefore liable to interpret the motives of others as hostile, even when this is not the case. Anger is frequently sustained for long periods of time and violence may occur because of perceived insults or mistreatment. Sustained relationships are difficult to achieve because of lack of trust. The latter characteristic extends to therapeutic relationships.

Schizotypal

People who have schizotypal personality disorder present as loners, with little interest in relationships with other people. Pursuits tend to be of a mechanical nature and are likely to be undertaken solitarily. Uninterested in other people's opinion of them, these people may be perceived as self-absorbed or egocentric.

Schizoid

People with schizoid personality disorder may experience distorted perceptions, speak in a vague or disjointed manner and engage in magical thinking. While not experiencing frank psychosis, their thought processes are unusual and social situations are anxiety-provoking. These features may lead others to perceive them as odd. Social isolation is typically a feature of this type of personality disorder.

Cluster B: Dramatic/emotional

Antisocial

Antisocial personality disorder is characterised by coercive, exploitative behaviour within relationships with other people. Antisocial characteristics include violence to others, deception and persistent failure to honour obligations or responsibilities. Reckless behaviour with no regard for the risk to self or others is another feature of antisocial personality disorder, which, research shows, is present to a high degree in offender populations.

Borderline

This personality disorder is characterised by emotional instability, particularly within the context of relationships with other people. Frantic efforts to avoid abandonment, self-injurious behaviour and impulsivity are amongst the range of volatile features associated with borderline personality disorder. People with borderline personality disorder have been found to use mental health services to a high degree, but effective, research-based psychotherapeutic treatments that have been tested through randomised controlled trials have only become available relatively recently (Linehan, 1993; Bateman and Fonagy, 1999).

Histrionic

People with histrionic personality disorder behave in a dramatic, flamboyant way. Their strong need to be the centre of attention drives their exaggerated conduct. Relationships tend to be shallow and changeable.

Narcissistic

This type of personality disorder describes a grandiose, self-important pattern of relating to other people, whereby a sense of entitled admiration for exaggerated or even fantasised accomplishments leads others to feel belittled, used and diminished. However, this self-important vain demeanour belies a fragile sense of self. People with narcissistic personality disorder are easily wounded emotionally. They are, however, typically insensitive to the feelings of others.

Cluster C: Anxious/fearful

Avoidant

Social situations and relationships are avoided. Fear of negative reactions by other people drive the social avoidance that is central to this personality disorder. Such negative reactions may include being bullied, criticised or humiliated. Therefore a restricted lifestyle is engaged in. People who have this type of disorder are unlikely to seek care or treatment.

Dependent

The passive, clinging and emotionally needy characteristics of this type of personality disorder aim to ensure support from other people, who are inevitably perceived as stronger and more capable. People with dependent personality disorder are vulnerable to exploitation by others.

Obsessive-compulsive

This type of personality disorder is characterised by rigidity and the need to control. Perfectionism and intense attention to detail accompanies a harsh evaluation of self and other people.

Personality disorder and mental health services

The personality-disordered patients who are regarded as particularly challenging to mental health services are largely those who are diagnosed with Cluster B disorders (i.e. antisocial, borderline, histrionic and narcissistic), and also paranoid personality disorder, which is categorised under Cluster A. People who have these disorders are challenging to mental health services and professionals because of their impulsive, high-risk behaviours, the way they treat other people and the accompanying emotional impact they have as a result of the way they externalise their distress and disturbance (Bateman and Tyrer, 2004; Moran, 2002). The risk is that the patients repeatedly create disturbed, damaging relationships with other people, including those tasked with providing care and treatment. The other personality disorders tend to be characterised by self-directed distress.

It has been noted that, from the perspective of research, the categorical model of personality disorder described in DSM-IV (American Psychiatric Association, 1994) is problematic. The norm is for people so diagnosed to fall into more than one diagnostic type. Also, there is a high level of co-morbidity with other types of mental disorder (Moran, 2002; National Institute for Mental Health in England, 2003a,b; Roth and Fonagy, 1996).

Nursing process and practice with regard to personality disorder

The conclusions contained in the national guidance (National Institute for Mental Health in England, 2003a) state that most mental health practitioners regard themselves as insufficiently skilled or informed to work therapeutically with personality-disordered patients. These conclusions are drawn from available research, user views, a number of expert papers and also from the experience of members of the steering group who put the document together. However, the skills needed by practitioners have not been clarified as there is so little research regarding what interventions are effective in the treatment of personality disorders. Of the research that does exist, little could be regarded, in methodological terms, as providing a high level of clinical evidence. That which does refers to psychological and psychotherapeutic interventions, not nursing.

Bowers (2002) noted the absence of literature referring to nursing interventions with people in secure settings diagnosed with personality disorder. Bowers (2002) specifically points to 'the vacuum of practical guidance and research results' and by conducting a survey and qualitative interviews, found that nurses in the three English high-security psychiatric hospitals considered themselves to be poorly trained and to experience high levels of stress in their work with personality-disordered offender patients.

As both Hinshelwood (2002) and Bateman and Tyrer (2004) state, the effective treatment of personality disorder requires an interpersonal process. This interpersonal process is underpinned by a robust clinical framework and is delivered through the effective relational skills of practitioners. In turn, these relational skills may be augmented by particular personal characteristics. By that same principle, Bateman and Fonagy (2004), amongst others, suggest that some personal characteristics may undermine clinical effectiveness with personality-disordered people.

From the available literature, there does appear to be some consensus about the interpersonal skills and personality characteristics necessary for clinicians to work effectively with personality-disordered people. Some criteria have been identified by clinician-researchers who are experienced in the field of personality disorder care and treatment. The criteria appear to be derived directly from that experience rather than as a result of empirical research findings. Exceptions are those characteristics identified by Duggan (2002) in a scoping exercise commissioned to inform national policy guidance (National Institute for Mental Health in England, 2003a) and Bowers (2002) who conducted research into factors underlying and supporting nurses' positive therapeutic attitudes to personality disordered patients. Duggan (2002) employed a structured qualitative approach to identify key skills for multidisciplinary practitioners working with personality disorder. This included conducting semi-structured interviews with stakeholders involved with services recognised as providing high-quality mental health services for people with personality disorder and matching these findings against an existing mental health capability framework (*The Capable Practitioner*: Sainsbury Centre For Mental Health, 2001).

Duggan's (2002) findings claim to identify 'capabilities' required by three levels of practitioner, that is at the point of recruitment, the key worker and the clinical leader. Surprisingly perhaps, few of the identified criteria refer specifically to the interpersonal domain. Those that do are: 'emotional robustness, ability to work in groups and understand group dynamics, knowledge and skill in applying psychotherapeutic and psychodynamic interventions, ability to establish personal boundaries'. Bowers (2002) surveyed nurses in the three English high-security psychiatric hospitals in order to establish what factors underpinned positive therapeutic attitudes to patients with personality disorder. Bowers' (2002) intention was to utilise research findings to inform a support and training strategy to nurture nurses' positive attitudes towards patients with personality disorders. Bowers sent a questionnaire to all nurses employed in the three English high-security psychiatric hospitals and then interviewed a random sample. Nurses identified as having positive attitudes towards personality-disordered patients were able to utilise an inner dialogue to manage their emotional reaction to the patients, were able to concentrate on the patient in the here and now rather than what they had done in the past, and were able to persevere with their relationship with the patient through conflict, which was seen as an opportunity to be therapeutic.

Bowers' (2002) findings appear to concur with the descriptions provided by clinical experts in the field of personality disorder care and treatment (Bateman and Tyrer, 2004; Bateman and Fonagy, 2004; Hinshelwood, 2002). Hinshelwood (2002), the former clinical director of a renowned therapeutic community specialising in the treatment of personality disorders, has, based on clinical experience, described a psychodynamic paradigm for understanding the negative emotional impact that personality-disordered patients have on their professional caregivers. Central to Hinshelwood's (2002) thesis is the concept of abusive care. That is, the personality-disordered patient received abusive early care, which they have identified with. Therefore, when in receipt of mental health care, the personality-disordered patient experiences professionals as abusive and then proceeds to abuse the help offered. On the face of it, this formulation appears to offer some utility to nurses. Clinical experience would also support this formulation.

Case example

Tommy is a 26-year-old man with an early history of emotional deprivation and abuse. He is the fifth of nine children who had all experienced periods of their childhood in care. Tommy's parents had a violent marriage, with Tommy's father serving numerous prison sentences for serious incidents of domestic violence and for assaults that took place outside the home. Throughout Tommy's various periods in care, professionals had noted his apparent identification with this violent father. He was regularly reprimanded for what appeared to be gratuitous violence towards other children, especially girls. Tommy's school teachers also observed this pattern.

By the time Tommy was in his early teens, he was engaging in criminal activities on a regular basis. In particular, he stole cars and committed many acts of burglary. He was known to be a bully and often associated with people regarded as more submissive and easily malleable, therefore enabling Tommy to be in control of the relationships. He developed a reputation amongst his peers for being cold and ruthless, somebody not to be crossed. Vengeful and quick to humiliation, Tommy was often preoccupied by perceived humiliations, plotting ways of seeking adequate revenge on the people he felt slighted by. Although he had no convictions for violence, he regularly got into fights and often used weapons. His victims were people he felt had humiliated him in some way.

As Tommy got a little older, he tended towards exploiting vulnerable young men and coerced them to commit crimes on his behalf. He began to experience periods of low mood, which he masked with large amounts of alcohol and drugs. Tommy had many casual sexual relationships, failing to settle down with any one partner.

Tommy's work history was sketchy, with short periods of employment terminated when he inevitably came into conflict with superiors. At the age of 24 he had secured a job selling insurance. When his sales figures were not as high as he had expected, he began to suspect that his manager was sabotaging his progress. Tommy became obsessed with his manager, who was a woman, fearing that she was poisoning his colleagues' minds against him. This, according to Tommy, explained why his co-workers seemed to be avoiding him and even sniggering at him behind his back. One day, when Tommy felt he could take no more, he decided to show his manager who was really 'the boss'.

Tommy's index offence involved the torture and subsequent violent murder of his manager. When assessed by a psychiatrist in prison, it was felt that he suffered from antisocial, narcissistic and paranoid personality disorders with a co-morbid depression and he was admitted to a high-security psychiatric hospital for treatment under the Mental Health Act (1983) classification of Psychopathic Disorder.

When detained in hospital, Tommy was a particularly difficult patient, refusing help and bullying other patients, and he was suspected of initiating many episodes of organised fraud and deception. Typically, he would apparently coerce less able patients to take out large orders from catalogues and give the items to him; they would then be left with debts they could not pay. Tommy would sell on the goods, earning himself a healthy profit at the expense of other patients who found themselves in financial trouble. Tommy was also suspected of bullying less able patients into making complaints about members of staff he did not like in order to inflict emotional distress on the members of staff in question.

Nursing approach

It could be argued that Tommy's early abusive experience left him with severe personality disorders characterised by a style of relating to the world and the people in it, by coercion and abuse. When in a hospital setting, this persistent style of relating continues, meaning that he is not immediately amenable to care and treatment, responding by continuing to abuse and exploit. For nurses, contact with Tommy is emotionally uncomfortable and they are kept at bay by his misuse of the hospital complaints procedure, albeit through coercing other patients to act out this abuse on his behalf. What then are nurses to do if they are to play an active part in his therapeutic regime? Bowers (2002), based on his research into nurses working with personality disorder in high-security psychiatric hospitals, suggests that a developmental perspective on understanding why Tommy behaves the way he does would be helpful. Indeed, a dynamic therapeutic formulation of Tommy's personality disturbance that takes account of his own early experiences of witnessing extreme violence between his parents could provide an explanation for why he has identified with the aggressor and why he perceives vulnerability as a dangerous state, tantamount to inviting the humiliation involved in being a victim of abuse. Also, this formulation could explain why he cannot emotionally manage the task of being at the receiving end of care, much as Hinshelwood (2002) describes in his thesis about the core difficulty of being a caregiver to people with severe personality disorders.

Holding on to a clinical formulation for a patient such as Tommy requires the nurses involved in his care to be in receipt of high-quality clinical supervision. This supports the nurses in their task, which involves both maintaining a formulation in the face of the patient's disturbing and painful behaviour and managing therapeutic work in the context of the nurse–patient relationship. This work would involve maintaining interpersonal boundaries, therefore neither avoiding difficult contacts with the patient, such as challenging him about his misuse of hospital policies and bullying of other patients, nor reacting in a negative, punitive manner, which Tommy's behaviour is at risk of eliciting due to his emotional provocation of nurses. On the surface, Tommy is attempting to control nursing staff by making it very difficult to engage with him unless it is on his terms, which would involve collusion with his inflated sense of entitlement and narcissistic world view.

Supervision enables a third party to support nurses with regard to thinking about their relationship with Tommy and in planning interventions that aim to discontinue his disturbed way of relating. Managing interpersonal boundaries and remaining in role as a professional caregiver are important tasks for nurses involved in the care of patients like Tommy. These tasks are easier said than done because of the emotional impact Tommy has on nurses who, as previously mentioned, are at risk of either avoiding him, colluding with him or retaliating. What Tommy needs in the first instance is for his carers to manage their tasks. It is the emotional impact of working with him that threatens to derail nurses from their task. For example, anxiety about being persecuted by Tommy through his misuse of hospital complaints procedures may encourage nurses to avoid interacting with him. Alternatively, nurses may find themselves colluding with his antisocial behaviour by facilitating his access to more vulnerable patients for the purposes of fraud and deception, which would also enable them to avoid confrontations or anxiety provoking interactions with him. Tommy's bullying behaviour may also potentially lead to nurses feeling that they need to control him in a punitive way, rather than be controlled in an equally bullying way by him. Such a strategy would also fail to contain his behaviour, as it would merely replicate the abusive style that is central to his personality disorders. The thoughtful, containing but challenging approach to his management that Tommy requires in order to begin to function in a more interpersonally healthy way, is an emotionally demanding task that must be underpinned by proper training and supervision.

Discussion

The picture for mental health nurses appears to be that they are tasked with an emotionally challenging, interpersonal task in contributing to the treatment of personality-disordered patients within health care settings. It is possible that what is so challenging about this task is the patients' perception of nurses as threatening and their subsequent abusive responses. However, from the perspective of formal clinical paradigms, no clear picture is available within the research. From what research is available, it would appear that a minority of nurses are able to apply their own personality characteristics in a positive way, which enables them to at least feel that they are working positively with personality-disordered patients. The majority, however, experience difficulty and may feel emotionally compromised by the process. No research has triangulated surveys and interviews with observations of nurses interacting with personality-disordered patients in the social environments of services. Therefore it is not possible to confirm their subjective experiences.

Out with established, specialist services, little in the way of emotional support, supervision or training is in evidence to enable the development of specific clinical skills or to assist nurses to withstand the negative emotional impact of managing the nurse–patient relationship with people diagnosed with personality disorders. For patients who rely on nurses to contribute to their treatment through the core nursing task of achieving change through a professional, skilled interpersonal process, the experience of mental health services is disappointing. Qualitative research undertaken by service users (Ramon *et al.*, 2001) found, through interviews that people diagnosed with personality disorder described their contact with mental health services and practitioners as unsatisfactory and even upsetting due to professionals' attitudes towards them. This picture is coherent with the descriptions given by service users to the national policy guidance team (National Institute for Mental Health in England, 2003a). Therefore, it would appear to be very clear that if effective services for personality disordered patients are to be developed in this country, the focus for nursing needs to be on the management of the emotional impact that working with this group has on nursing. Training that elucidates the early developmental nature of severe personality disorders may be helpful, and skills to work confidently with the dynamics of relationships seem to be essential, along with ongoing clinical supervision to support the primary clinical task.

References

American Psychiatric Association (1994) *Diagnostic and Statistical Manual of Mental Disorders*, 4th edn (DSM-IV). American Psychiatric Association, Washington.

Bateman, A. W. and Fonagy, P. (1999) The effectiveness of partial hospitalization in the treatment of borderline personality disorder: a randomised controlled trial. *American Journal of Psychiatry*, **156**, 1563–1569.

Bateman, A. W. and Fonagy, P. (2004) *Psychotherapy for Borderline Personality Disorder: Mentalization-Based Treatment*. Oxford University Press, Oxford.

Bateman, A. W. and Tyrer, P. (2004) Services for personality disorder: organisation for inclusion. *Advances in Psychiatric Treatment*, **10**, 425–433.

Bowers, L. (2002) *Dangerous and Severe Personality Disorder: Response and Role of the Psychiatric Team*. Routledge, London.

Department of Health (1983) *The Mental Health Act for England and Wales*. HMSO, London.

Duggan, M. (2002) *Developing Services for People with Personality Disorder: The Training Needs of Staff and Services*. Website: http://www.nimhe.org.uk/.

Hinshelwood, R. D. (2002) Abusive help – helping abuse: the psychodynamic impact of severe personality disorder on caring institutions. *Criminal Behaviour and Mental Health*, **12**, 20–30.

Linehan, M. M. (1993) *Cognitive Behavioural Treatment for Borderline Personality Disorder*. Guilford Press, New York.

Moran, P. (2002) *The Epidemiology of Personality Disorders*. Website: http://www.nimhe.org.uk/.

National Institute for Mental Health in England (2003a) *Personality Disorder: No Longer a Diagnosis of Exclusion: Policy Implementation Guidance for the Development of Services for People with Personality Disorder*. Department of Health, London.

National Institute for Mental Health in England (2003b) *Breaking the Cycle of Rejection: The Personality Disorder Capabilities Framework*. Department of Health, London.

Ramon, S., Castillo, H. and Morant, N. (2001) Experiencing personality disorder: a participative research. *International Journal of Social Psychology*, **47**(4), 1–15.

Roth, A. and Fonagy, P. (1996) Personality disorders. In: Roth, A. and Fonagy, P. (eds.) *What Works for Whom? A Critical Review of Psychotherapy Research*, Chapter 11, pp. 197–215. Guilford Press, New York.

Sainsbury Centre for Mental Health (2001) *The Capable Practitioner: A Framework and List of Practitioner Capabilities Required to Implement the National Service Framework For Mental Health*. Sainsbury Centre for Mental Health, London.

Warren, F., McGauley, G., Norton, K., Dolan, B., Preedy-Fayers, K., Pickering, A. and Geddes, J. R. (2003) *Review of Treatments for Severe Personality Disorder*. Home Office, London.

CHAPTER 7

Education, training and support for staff working with clients with a diagnosis of personality disorder: some thoughts

Carol Watson and Alyson McGregor Kettles

Introduction

People with a diagnosis of personality disorders present particular challenges for staff. Staff should understand the difficulties faced by people with this diagnosis, as well as the behavioural traits that they present. This chapter will discuss the importance of ensuring that practitioners have sufficient knowledge and understanding of personality disorders as well as the skills and attitudes to enable them to engage effectively with both their clients and in clinical supervision, in order that they can manage their own emotions, stress levels, transference and counter-transference in working with these groups of patients. Whilst the focus is primarily on the education required by staff working within forensic services, the needs of all staff, both from the wider mental health arena and also from primary care services will be discussed, along with the implications for public mental health education.

The nature and purpose of professional education

The purpose of professional education is increasingly about role and task. The recent trend in developing competencies reflects this focus, and good competency models ensure that the underpinning knowledge as well as values and attitudes are described and detailed within the competency as well as the skill required (Bedford *et al.*, 1993; Carlisle *et al.*, 1999; Peach, 1999). However, the broader view of education is of an ongoing process which enables the practitioner to develop knowledge and understanding fundamental to their growth and development, and which will impact on both the personal and professional life of the individual (Peach, 1999). This is particularly relevant to the discussion of the education/training needs of practitioners when working with individuals who may have a range of 'disordered' personality traits or be given a diagnosis of personality disorder (McMurran, 2001).

Evidence (see for example Bowers, 2002; Shimmin and Storey, 2000) suggests that clinicians require considerable self-awareness, particularly in relation to counter-transference, and be well rounded, confident and knowledgeable practitioners in relation to this client group. Furthermore, much has been written in the professional press about the effects of working, usually in high secure settings, with these groups of patients, citing increased staff turnover and sickness/absence rates, and the resultant distancing or avoidance of therapeutic engagement by staff that see little or no potential for positive therapeutic progress (Schafer, 2002) (see also Chapter 12 of this text). It would seem essential, therefore, to ensure that foundation-level professional education challenges the stereotype of the untreatable personality disorder with a broader introduction to this umbrella term for what are a range of complex disorders (DSM-IV; American Psychiatric Association, 1994) not all of which will be present in a forensic arena. The World Health Organization Guide to Mental and Neurological Health in Primary Care (WHO, 2002) included personality disorders in their updated guide in the light of morbidity figures from the Office of National Statistics, which indicated that 44 per 1000 adults in Britain may have a diagnosis of a personality disorder (Singleton *et al.*, 2000). This has clear implications for the preparation and support of primary care staff, as well as those in general mental health services.

Professional education must also be seen within a broader context of public education. Recent campaigns on raising public awareness about mental health, and specifically anti-stigma campaigns being promoted by the UK Department of Health (2001), The Scottish Executive Health Department (2002) and the Royal College of Psychiatrists (Crisp, 2003) demonstrate how public perceptions of mental health and mental ill health can be changed over time. However, even within these high profile and highly political campaigns, personality disorder remains somewhat invisible, reinforcing public and professional perceptions that it is different, and that extreme stereotypes are the norm.

Educational approaches, content and methodologies

When considering educational approaches to enable a range of practitioners to engage effectively with individuals who present with complex and challenging problems and behaviours, a reductionist curricular model might not be the most appropriate. This model looks at specific behaviours, for example aggressive behaviour, self-harming behaviour or manipulative behaviour, and describes specific competencies, i.e. knowledge, skills and attitudes which the practitioner needs to develop in order to provide an appropriate therapeutic response. Support and supervision are then given from colleagues/supervisors whilst the practitioner develops first competence and then, with additional practice, guidance and reflection, expertise.

This model is of course appropriate within certain parameters, and essential when following protocol-based interventions. It is based on the assumption of adequate and expert supervision, for example when developing specific psychological interventions, such as Cognitive Behaviour Therapy, or Dialectical Behaviour Therapy, where it is essential for all members of the team to support the approach taken in a consistent way. It is also based on an assumption of a foundation level of underpinning knowledge about the nature of the conditions being treated. It is a little like learning another language. If your first language is English and you decide to learn French or Spanish, there are some principles in common, e.g. use of the same alphabet and many words derived from Latin or Greek. However, if you choose Japanese or Russian the alphabets and derivations are substantially different, and how you go about learning these languages will be different. You will have to go back to very first principles as you are not building on much common knowledge. For mental health practitioners (and service commissioners and managers) working with a range of people with personality disorders it is like learning a very different language and going back to look at some core principles is essential if we are to understand the experience of having this diagnosis and its impact on the lives of our patients and clients. Only when there is a foundation of knowledge and some positive attitudes and beliefs which challenge perhaps long-held and certainly reinforced stereotypes, should more focused competency-based training be delivered.

However, there are wider issues for both clinicians and their support staff in relation to the interventions of choice in particular units/teams:

■   Why specific strategies are important
■   The need for reflective practice and supervision as discussed in Chapter 6
■   The importance of an organised, team-coordinated approach
■   The absolute essential of open communication
■   Issues of understanding and managing boundaries while still working in partnership with patients and their carers

This list is not exhaustive, but the principles and issues of working in a different kind of therapeutic alliance, whether in a forensic setting or not, need to be clearly explored with all members of the team, not just those who have undertaken a programme of advanced therapeutic skills.

Recent trends towards short, flexible skills-based modules or courses, preferably delivered in the workplace, indicate the funding preferences of managers and employers, who work within considerable fiscal pressures. Evidence (NHS Education for Scotland, 2004) of the reduction in support for Specialist Practitioner Qualifications, comprising up to three years and based in Higher Education, and the proliferation of short, snappy skills-based and 'on the job' work-based learning are examples of this. In addition, skills-based courses can be more clearly linked to the clinical effectiveness agenda (i.e. using the current evidence base to provide a rationale for a specific intervention, and then ensuring practitioners undergo accredited training and ongoing supervision in that intervention) than can more broad knowledge-based, and possibly academic, programmes.

Education providers and workforce developers need to consider whether they are utilising an appropriate and effective range of education and training methodologies for developing the complex knowledge and skills required to work effectively and safely with people with personality disorders, and to find ways of demonstrating this. Educationalists and workforce developers also need to investigate the education and training needs not just of practitioners but also of service planners and managers, so that they can understand the range of educational needs of their staff and commission the range of educational methodologies best suited to meeting them.

There is a need for education and training resources which enable staff to explore some of the complex legal, ethical and interpersonal/professional issues involved in understanding the experience of having a personality disorder diagnosis, as well as of providing care and treatment. Elsewhere in this book (see Chapter 4) when discussing the experience of service users, it is clear that somewhere in the educational experience the attitudes and values of staff must be explored and challenged, and different educational methodologies, including exploring these issues jointly with service users and their carers, need to be considered. This should not be confused with supervision. Developing knowledge and understanding of the issues should not be done with one's own patients or clients. Clinicians need a sound theoretical framework within which to work, and this must be delivered outside of the practice arena to enable practitioners to engage fully with the issues and to test out strategies for fit with their own therapeutic style.

Working with people with personality disorders (in fact with a range of individuals cared for in secure environments) fundamentally challenges what clinicians may have learned about the therapeutic alliance (Swinton and Boyd, 2000). Changing an individual's model of caring and working therapeutically with clients needs careful exploration theoretically, practically and emotionally in a safe and supportive environment. This type of learning is essential prior to testing this out in practice, particularly with a very challenging client group, and is based on the principles of adult learning (see for example Kolb, 1976; Knowles, 1984). This would also enable an exploration of the range of different personality disorders, and the various degrees and types of risks and dangerousness within that range. This would be an alternative to learning in the clinical context of the specific client group with whom a practitioner is working (even definitions of competence include the ability to apply the skills in a range of settings and with clients with varying degrees of acute and chronic conditions (Benner and Wrubel, 1989). Psycho-education, both for service users and their families, is an area which needs much development, and education needs to focus on enabling practitioners at all levels to be able to articulate and communicate the concepts, issues and dilemmas of personality disorders in language that is not loaded or judgemental.

It is important though, not to lose some of the basic elements of good mental health care which need to be learned by everyone. The Sainsbury Centre for Mental Health's (2001) Ten Essential Shared Capabilities are as relevant to this client group as to any other, but how they are used and the issues they may raise needs to be explored. Equally, the forensic competencies developed in Scotland (National Board for Nursing Midwifery and Health Visiting for Scotland, 2000); NBS is now part of NHS Education for Scotland) were not designed to exclude the care and treatment of people with a diagnosis of personality disorder. Changes to legislation in the different countries of the UK mean that the legislative as well as the policy context of care and treatment may be significantly different; certainly within the Scottish context, The Mental Health (Care and Treatment) (Scotland) Act 2003, with its underpinning principles (see Box 7.1) fundamentally challenge how mental health care is delivered, and extensive education and training is under way across health and social care services to prepare practitioners to understand not just the Act itself but the impact of the principles on their practice. At the time of writing it is unclear how the Act will appear in English Law, but given that it must articulate with Human Rights legislation, it will therefore be significantly different from current legislation, and practitioners and service users alike will expect changes in practice.

Box 7.1: Guiding principles underpinning The Mental Health (Care and Treatment) (Scotland) Act 2003.

These help to set the tone of the Act and guide its interpretation. As a general rule, anyone who takes any action under the Act has to take account of the principles.

1. **Non-discrimination**: People with mental disorder should, wherever possible, retain the same rights and entitlements as those with other health needs.
2. **Equality**: All powers under the Act should be exercised without any direct or indirect discrimination on the grounds of physical disability, age, gender, sexual orientation, language, religion or national, ethnic or social origin.
3. **Respect for diversity**: Service users should receive care, treatment and support in a manner that affords respect for their individual qualities, abilities and diverse backgrounds, and properly takes into account their age, gender, sexual orientation, ethnic group and social, cultural and religious background.
4. **Reciprocity**: Where society imposes an obligation on an individual to comply with a programme of treatment or care, it should impose a parallel obligation on the health and social care authorities to provide safe and appropriate services, including ongoing care following discharge from compulsion.
5. **Informal care**: Wherever possible, care, treatment and support should be provided to people with mental disorder without the use of compulsory powers.
6. **Participation**: Service users should be fully involved, so far as they are able to be, in all aspects of their assessment, care, treatment and support. Their past and present wishes should be taken into account. They should be provided with all the information and support necessary to enable them to participate fully. Information should be presented in an understandable format.
7. **Respect for carers**: Those who provide care to service users on an informal basis should be respected for their role and experience, receive appropriate information and advice, and have their views and needs taken into account.
8. **Least restrictive alternative**: Service users should be provided with any necessary care, treatment and support in the least invasive manner and in the least restrictive manner and environment compatible with the delivery of safe and effective care, taking account, where appropriate, of the safety of others.
9. **Benefit**: Any intervention under the Act should be likely to produce for the service user a benefit that cannot reasonably be achieved other than by the intervention.
10. **Child welfare**: The welfare of a child with mental disorder should be paramount in any interventions imposed on the child under the Act.

Supervision and support

Education and training have elements which may be understood or experienced as discrete activities, yet they are also described as a continuing process. Guidance and feedback are core elements of ongoing learning and contribute also to support and supervision. A range of supervision models which may be most effective are discussed earlier (in Chapter 6). However, as stated at the beginning of this chapter, caring for patients with a diagnosis of personality disorder is a challenge, and stress, burnout and low morale are always a risk when practitioners are working with patients and clients who may not respond quickly or easily, or indeed predictably, to therapeutic approaches, and learning must also include strategies for self-maintenance (Gournay and Carson, 2000). The development of these strategies will also require support and supervision, probably involving both group and individual models of supervision. The investment in time in relation to supporting staff, in helping them learn how to be effective, strong, fair and consistent, specifically within the treatment/intervention protocol, and maintain positive and realistic expectations of their patients and clients, will be an essential element in the effectiveness of any service.

Conclusion

Education and training in relation to personality disorder does not exist (National Institute for Mental Health in England, 2003) or has been marginalised within current courses and cannot be delivered within a paradigm vacuum; practice-based and theoretical models for working with individuals who may have a personality disorder are an essential element of professional preparation to work with this group.

Within this foundation level it is important to view personality disorders from a wider perspective than health care delivery. If we are to fulfil a public health education role in relation to mental health and well-being, then personality disorder must be integrated into the wider mental health promotion and prevention agenda. The Scottish Needs Assessment Programme on Child and Adolescent Mental Health Services structured its recommendations for service development around three elements: Promotion, Prevention and Care. The subsequent draft service framework (Scottish Executive Health Department, 2004) and a competency development framework (NHS Education Scotland, 2004) followed the same structure.

The Report from the National Programme on Forensic Mental Health R&D Seminar on Preventing Personality Disorder by Intervening in Adolescence (Harrington and Bailey, 2003) also stressed the need for better early recognition of children and young people at significant risk of antisocial personality disorder. These recommendations have wide-ranging implications for the educational preparation and development of professionals in primary and secondary education, as well as health, social care and the criminal justice system.

Only by looking at the education and training needs across agencies and public sector services, and taking an integrated and partnership approach with patients, clients and their carers, will progress be made in both preventing the development of significant health and social problems for vulnerable and at risk individuals, and promoting mental health and well-being. This in turn may help those of us in forensic services to develop and sustain more positive beliefs and expectations about those in receipt of our care.

References

American Psychiatric Association (1994) *Diagnostic and Statistical Manual of Mental Disorders*, 4th edn (DSM-IV). American Psychiatric Association, Washington.

Bedford, H., Philips, T., Robinson, J. and Schostak, J. (1993) *Assessing Competencies in Nursing and Midwifery Education. Final Report*. English National Board, London.

Benner, P. and Wrubel, J. (1989) *The Primacy of Caring*. Addison-Wesley, Menlo Park, California.

Bowers, L. (2002) *Dangerous and Severe Personality Disorder: Response and Role of the Psychiatric Team*. Routledge, London.

Carlisle, C., Luker, K., Davies, C., Stilwell, J. and Wilson, R. (1999) Skills competency in nurse education: nurse managers' perceptions of diploma level preparation. *Nurse Education Today*, **17**, 128–134.

Crisp, A. (2003) *Every Family in the Land: Understanding Prejudice and Discrimination Against People with Mental Illness*. RSM Press, London.

Department of Health (2001) *Mind Out for Mental Health Anti-Stigma Campaign*. Department of Health, London.

Gournay, K. and Carson, J. (2000) Staff stress, coping skills and job satisfaction in forensic nursing. In: Robinson, D. and Kettles, A. (eds.) *Forensic Nursing and Multidisciplinary Care of the Mentally Disordered Offender*, Chapter 12. Jessica Kingsley, London.

Harrington, R. and Bailey, S. (2003) *Preventing Personality Disorder by Intervening in Adolescence*. The National Programme on Forensic Mental Health Research and Development, Liverpool.

Knowles, M. S. (1984) *Andragogy in Action*. Jossey-Bass Publishers, San Francisco.

Kolb, D. A. (1976) *A Learning Style Inventory*. McBer, Boston.

McMurran, M. (2001) *Expert Paper on Personality Disorders*. The National Programme on Forensic Mental Health Research and Development, Liverpool.

National Board for Nursing Midwifery and Health Visiting for Scotland (2000) *A Route to Enhanced Competence in Forensic Mental Health Nursing*. National Board for Nursing Midwifery and Health Visiting for Scotland, Edinburgh.

National Institute for Mental Health in England (2003) *Personality Disorder: No Longer a Diagnosis of Exclusion. Policy Implementation Guidance for the Development of Services for People with Personality Disorder*. National Institute for Mental Health in England, London.

NBS (2000) [PLEASE SUPPLY]

NHS Education for Scotland (2004) *Themes and Issues 2002–2004: Quality Assurance and Professional Regulation: Programme Approval & Monitoring*. NES, Edinburgh.

Peach, L. (1999) *Fitness for Practice: The UKCC Commission for Nursing and Midwifery Education*. United Kingdom Central Council for Nursing, Midwifery and Health Visiting, London.

Sainsbury Centre for Mental Health (2001) *The Capable Practitioner: A Framework and List of Practitioner Capabilities Required to Implement the National Service Framework For Mental Health*. Sainsbury Centre for Mental Health, London.

Schafer, P. (2002) Nursing interventions and future directions with patients who constantly break rules and test boundaries. In: Kettles, A. M., Woods, P. and Collins, M. (eds.) *Therapeutic Interventions for Forensic Mental Health Nurses*, Chapter 4. Jessica Kingsley, London.

Scottish Executive Health Department (2002) *See Me: Scotland's National Anti-Stigma Campaign – The National Programme to Improve the Mental Health and Wellbeing of Scotland's Population*. Scottish Executive Health Department, Edinburgh.

Scottish Executive Health Department (2004) *Children and Young People's Mental Health: A Framework for Promotion Prevention and Care – Draft for Consultation*. Scottish Executive Health Department, Edinburgh.

Shimmin, H. and Storey, L. (2000) Social therapy: a case study developing a staffing model for work with personality disordered offenders. In: Mercer, D., Mason, T., McKeown, M. and MacCann, G. (eds.) *Forensic Mental Health Care: a Case Study Approach*. Churchill Livingstone, Edinburgh.

Singleton, N., Bumpstead, R., O'Brien, M., Lee, A. and Meltzer, H. (2000) *Psychiatric Morbidity Among Adults Living in Private Households*. The Stationery Office, London.

Swinton, J. and Boyd, J. (2000) Autonomy and personhood: the forensic nurse as moral agent. In: Robinson, D. and Kettles, A. (eds.) *Forensic Nursing and Multidisciplinary Care of the Mentally Disordered Offender*. Jessica Kingsley, London.

WHO (2002) *WHO Guide to Mental and Neurological Health in Primary Care*, 2nd edn. Royal Society of Medicine Press, London.

CHAPTER 8

Gender and sexuality issues

Anne Aiyegbusi and Richard Byrt

Introduction

This chapter is concerned with gender, sexuality, sexual orientation and gender identity, and the relevance of these issues for nursing interventions for individuals with 'personality disorders'.

Women with personality disorder: introduction

Any reference to women with personality disorder must take into account the complex clinical presentation that corresponds with the clinical diagnosis of borderline personality disorder. Many women presenting to mental health services diagnosed with personality disorder do so with symptoms corresponding to borderline personality disorder. There is a view within the literature that this is because borderline personality disorder is, in fact, an adult clinical syndrome arising from extensive traumatic experience, which has often occurred during childhood (Herman, 1992). The reasons why more women than men present to mental health services with diagnoses of borderline personality disorder is not clear. However, it has been suggested that girls and women are more vulnerable to certain types of abusive experience than are boys and men, and also that women are more likely to internalise their distress than are men. As core symptoms of borderline personality disorder include a number that are indicative of self-directed anger and violence, such as affective instability and self-injurious and suicidal behaviour, it may make sense that women are more likely to present with this clinical picture.

Borderline personality disorder and psychological trauma

Despite people diagnosed with borderline personality disorder often presenting with histories of extensive psychological trauma, this negative and damaging experience is not amongst the criteria for diagnosing borderline personality disorder. Adshead (1994) notes relatively recent discussions about the possibility of post-traumatic stress disorder and borderline personality disorder constituting overlapping or even synonymous diagnoses. Adshead (1994) suggests that post-traumatic stress disorder is more likely to be diagnosed for victims while borderline personality disorder is more likely to be diagnosed for offenders. Gunderson and Sabo (1993) certainly recognised that sympathy is associated with post-traumatic stress disorder diagnoses while dislike of a patient may be reflected in a clinician's diagnosis of borderline personality disorder. Herman and Van Der Kolk (1987) noted that the significant difference between post-traumatic stress disorder and borderline personality disorder diagnoses lies in the fact that the criteria for diagnosing borderline personality disorder do not include a stress factor in patients' histories. Despite the fact that research has consistently reported severe known or reported trauma in the backgrounds of around 60–80% of people diagnosed with borderline personality disorder, this is not included in the formal diagnostic criteria. Gunderson and Sabo (1993) explored the interface between DSM-IV (American Psychiatric Association, 1994) diagnoses of post-traumatic stress disorder and borderline personality disorder. They conclude that the two disorders are related. They specify that histories of prolonged trauma during childhood join other forms in shaping the enduring personality traits seen in borderline personality disorder. Gunderson and Sabo (1993) also describe borderline personality disorder as typical of a type of personality that has been formed in the context of enduring abusive experience and which is, as a result, particularly sensitive to subsequent traumatic experience. An example of how histories of childhood traumas figure in the clinical presentation of borderline personality disorder is provided by Van Der Kolk (1996), who in linking the borderline personality disordered patients' thinking when under stress with the pre-operational thinking seen in children, regards this as a fallback position of the traumatic fixation point. That is, when under stress, people with borderline personality disorder have a tendency to re-enact prior traumatic experience. Van der Kolk (1996) suggests that understanding the traumatic histories of these patients could assist clinicians in making sense of patients' behaviours that are otherwise difficult to fathom. Traumatic re-enactment may be central to understanding what may otherwise appear gratuitous or 'manipulative' conduct on behalf of the patient with borderline personality disorder. This may apply to self-injury, in particular.

In a pilot study, Adshead (1994) reports evidence of a link between trauma that was experienced during childhood and later violence and self-mutilation in a sample of women referred to a department of forensic psychiatry. Adshead (1994) goes further by identifying the risk these patients pose to caregivers, especially females, on account of their traumatic and disturbed experiences at the hands of earlier carers. She discusses the concept of complex post-traumatic stress disorder and links their histories as victims with their subsequent dangerous and victimising behaviours. Adshead (1994) recommends that current caregivers could better work with these challenging patients if they gain an understanding into how traumatic experiences link with subsequent rage and violence. Van Der Kolk (1996) describes a similar population of patients and advises that it is the task of professionals to understand what trauma is being re-enacted by the patients (or, for that matter, by caregivers).

In essence then, women presenting to mental health services diagnosed with borderline personality disorder may be experiencing a chronically traumatised state, resulting from prolonged childhood maltreatment The criteria laid down in DSM-IV (American Psychiatric Association, 1994) for diagnosis of borderline personality disorder does not include a link between the dysfunctional pattern of behaviours which typify the diagnosis with sufferers' histories of early deprivation and trauma. De Zulueta (1997) identifies two problems with the diagnosis. The first is that it strengthens the patient's own negative, self-damaging and entrenched sense of their own badness. The second problem described by De Zulueta (1997) is that by colluding with this belief in their inherent badness, patients' identification with their abuser is reinforced. This prolongs treatment because it reinforces violence and personality dysfunction.

Herman and van der Kolk (1987) suggest that the negative therapeutic reaction that is generally associated with borderline personality disorder could be avoided by early recognition and validation of trauma in patients' earlier lives. In recognising the need for professionals to understand and validate the traumatic roots of patients' distress, De Zulueta (1997) says:

> To deprive ourselves and our patients of some understanding of what they may be struggling with in terms of the past traumatic experiences and its physiological and cognitive effects, can leave us all groping in the dark.

The specific need to view the problems experienced by these patients through a paradigm other than, or in fact additional to, that of borderline personality diagnoses can be most succinctly represented in a comment from Herman (1992, p. 127), which also refers to the diagnoses of dissociative identity disorder and somatoform disorder.

> Understanding the role of childhood trauma in the development of these severe disorders also informs every aspect of treatment. This understanding provides the basis for a proper therapeutic alliance that normalises and validates the survivor's emotional reaction to past events, with recognition that these reactions may be maladaptive in the present. (De Zulueta, 1997)

Additionally, Herman (1992) points out that understanding the relationship disturbances which characterise these disorders from the perspective of trauma protects against unwitting re-enactments within current therapeutic relationships. It may be added that re-enactments can occur within all manner of relationships that people associated with the services have. Focusing on patients' traumatic psychopathology may be a helpful way to make sense of the pervasive disturbance that can often be a forbidding presence in services for women diagnosed with personality disorders.

For nurses, working with women suffering from borderline personality disorder is often extremely challenging. In particular, the emotional task is a difficult one as another core symptom of borderline personality disorder is a gross relational disturbance, which is most often manifest in the context of care giving. For the woman with borderline personality disorder, being at the receiving end of care can provoke overwhelming anxiety and fear. This is a consequence of fear-provoking early experience with primary carers that is re-enacted in the transference with current carers.

Case example

Meredith is a 26-year-old woman who was placed in the care of local authorities when she was two years old. Her mother, who was a single parent, suffered from severe depression after Meredith was born. This depression interfered with early bonding, with Meredith's mother being emotionally una-vailable and therefore unable to meet her baby's basic need for an attuned primary caregiver. The depression Meredith's mother suffered from was not responsive to psychiatric medication, so she sup-plemented her prescription with alcohol and illicit hypnotic medication, which were taken in excess. While experiencing severe depression and under the influence of drugs and alcohol, Meredith's mother often behaved in a disinhibited manner, frequently screaming at Meredith in a way that was terrifying for an infant. Additionally, Meredith was emotionally and physically neglected by her mother, who was unable to manage the task of caring for an infant. By the time Meredith was taken into care, she was physically underdeveloped and local authority carers found her difficult to feed and soothe. Bonding was not achieved and Meredith grew up to be socially isolated and prone to being victimised by other children. By adolescence, she was mixing with a gang of older, delinquent youths and at the age of 15 was picked up by police for soliciting. Further exploration established that Meredith had been working as a prostitute since the age of 13, having been introduced to sex work by an older former resident from her children's home. Meredith was handing over most of her earnings to this older girl.

By the time Meredith was in her late teens, she had been using drugs and consuming large amounts of alcohol for a number of years. She had also begun to cut herself. This behaviour occurred following her third violent relationship with a male partner. At the age of 20, she had a child and, for a short while, appeared to function without abusing substances. However, when her son was two years old, Meredith began to suffer marked depression, to misuse alcohol and to abuse other substances. After she took an overdose, her child was taken into care and Meredith was admitted to an acute mental health unit under a section of the Mental Health Act (1983) with a diagnosis of borderline personality disorder. Since then, she has had repeated admissions with brief periods in the community. Her son was adopted at Meredith's request, as she believed herself to be an unfit mother who would only damage her child.

As a psychiatric inpatient, Meredith was considered to be difficult to manage. She was experienced as provocative, often responding to nursing care by seemingly emotionally attacking the nurses who had attempted to help her. For example, one nurse spent one hour counselling Meredith when she had complained of feeling low and isolated. The nurse had expected Meredith to feel less distressed after the input and was very shocked when Meredith was found in her bedroom with a ligature tied tightly around her neck only ten minutes after the counselling had ended. This incident caused the nurse mas-sive anxiety and shock. The nurse also felt incompetent, believing for a while that she had personally produced such distress in her patient. However, through supervision, she was able to understand her feelings as projected from Meredith, who had not been able to communicate how she felt verbally during the one-to-one session but had instead acted out in such a way that she had unconsciously made the nurse feel as distressed and worthless as she herself did. The nurse was also able to understand the origins of these disturbing, unbearable feelings and why they would be provoked by the nurse's efforts to care for Meredith, given her early experience of being vulnerable and in need of care at the hands of her mother, who was unable to meet her needs.

Discussion

Meredith's presentation is in keeping with Hinshelwood's (2002) thesis about the task of provid-ing care for people with severe personality disorders who have histories of abusive early care.

According to Hinshelwood (2002), the central dynamic of caring for personality-disordered individual is that of abusive care. That is, the personality-disordered individual has received abusive early care, which they have identified with. Thereafter, the core of their relationships with other people and also with themselves is abuse. From early adolescence Meredith was caught up in an abusive cycle, abusing herself directly with drugs, alcohol and self-injury, and unconsciously and indirectly through recruiting others who became her bullies, pimps and violent partners. Once detained in hospital, this pattern of abusive relating extended to her caregivers, who often felt overwhelmingly distressed following contact with Meredith.

Conclusion of 'women with personality disorder'

While the experience of early abusive experience is not confined to women with personality disorders, this population does appear to be particularly prone to re-enacting abusive experience through the emotional impact they have on their caregivers while detained in mental health services. The complex clinical presentations and communications that this patient group bring to the clinical arena, can be understood from the perspective of unprocessed psychological trauma, which usually has its origins in interpersonal abuse in the context of failed early care. This paradigm is an important one for nurses, whose roles make them particularly vulnerable to becoming drawn into re-enactments of these abusive scenarios, either as victim or victimiser. Hinshelwood's (2002) paradigm is a particularly useful one, focusing on the importance of caregivers receiving support and supervision in order to process the difficult emotional experiences that are central to working with this patient population and without which good enough care is practically impossible to provide, thus running the risk of further perpetuating the patients' experiences of rejection and failed care.

Introduction to sexuality

The following section will consider issues concerning sexuality, sexual orientation and gender identity in relation to nursing interventions with people with personality disorders.

Sexuality

Sexuality has been described as an essential and significant part of an individual's life (Kessel, 2001), involving his/her 'appearances ... beliefs, behaviours and relationships with others' (Poorman, 2001, p. 548) and includes the following components (Poorman, 2001, p. 548):

- ■ **'Genetic identity'**, which is a person's chromosomal gender.
- ■ **'Gender identity'**: the individual's experience of self as male or female.
- ■ **'Gender role'**, which reflects social and cultural expectations about masculinity and femininity and how the individual should behave, according to his or her gender (Adshead, 2004).
- ■ **'Sexual orientation'**, which refers to attraction to a particular gender.

Several authors outline the need for nurses to be self-aware about their own feelings and views about sexuality, and the ways in which these may affect the care of clients (Irwin, 2002; Ward, 2002). The Nursing and Midwifery Council (NMC) Code of Conduct, Clause 2.2 states:

> You are personally accountable for ensuring that you promote and protect the interests and dignity of patients and clients, irrespective of ... age ... sexuality ... lifestyle ... (Nursing and Midwifery Council 2004, Clause 2.2, p. 5)

Individuals' needs related to gender identity

For most individuals, a vital source of self-esteem is the maintenance of valued activities and modes of self-expression that reinforce their gender identity (Byrt *et al.*, 2001). These may be lost or become less accessible to individuals admitted to mental health services, including people with personality disorders (Ward, 2002). Examples include access to items restricted for safety reasons, but essential for the person's gender presentation, consequent self-esteem and self-image. Items may include razors and cosmetics, access to which is likely to be restricted for individuals considered to be a risk, including those admitted to secure environments (Byrt, 1993; Taylor, 1998). Many individuals with personality disorders lack self-esteem (Motz, 2004), and such restrictions may decrease this further.

Safety reasons may restrict access to activities essential to the individual's identity, self-esteem, and gender expression, including activities and occupations which use sharp instruments, such as gardening, cooking and carpentry. These may be restricted for individuals with personality disorders for reasons of risk, when, ironically, such activities may help to channel and reduce feelings of aggression or depression (Cutcliffe, 2003; see Chapter 10 of this text).

In summary, an important aspect of nursing individuals with personality disorders is to maintain, within parameters of safety, security and risk management, access to all the activities and possessions that help the individual to maintain self-esteem and pride in identity as a man or as a woman.

Access to loving, fulfilling relationships

Visits may need to be supervised for safety reasons, especially in secure settings, and to ensure the welfare of any visiting children, in line with the Children Act, 1989 and the Children Act,

2004 (HM Government, 1989, 2004c). However, it is important to realise that supervision of visits, although sometimes necessary for risk management, may inhibit the expression of love and tenderness when patients need this most. (Would you feel able to kiss a loved one, in the way you wanted to, if observed by a nurse?) The literature appears to lack consideration, on the effects on patients, including those with personality disorders, of years of inpatient treatment in secure services, without opportunities for emotional or sexual relationships. In secure services, where treatment may last several years, the lack of opportunities for affection and intimacy can add to the deprivations of many individuals with personality disorders, who have often experienced adverse early relationships, and may be in particular need of warm human contact (Taylor, 1998). If the individual has started a partnership or marriage before admission, this may be very difficult to maintain, particularly in secure settings. Harner (2004) considers the considerable deprivations experienced by women in prison (many of whom have personality disorders) and their difficulties in forming or sustaining friendships and loving relationships with other inmates; or in maintaining relationships with families and partners outside prison.

The adverse effects of long stays in institutions can be compounded by the particular difficulties that many individuals with personality disorders have in trusting others or in establishing fulfilling relationships (Campling, 1999; Taylor, 1998; see also Chapter 6 of this text). Chapters 6, 14 and 15 of this text consider specialist approaches and nursing interventions to enable individuals to develop more satisfying relationships. Previous experience of being the recipient of physical, sexual or emotional abuse may make it difficult to establish or sustain close relationships, or indeed, friendships (Aiyegbusi, 2002). Individuals with borderline personality disorders may have difficulty in this area, partly because of their very intense needs and tendencies to see others as 'wholly bad' or 'wholly good' (Bateman and Fonagy, 2004). People with obsessive-compulsive or anankastic personality disorders often find it hard to be spontaneous and relaxed in relationships (Joines, 2004). Individuals with antisocial personality disorders may find it difficult to empathise with others, or feel close to them (Bowers, 2002). In conjunction with other factors, this may result in unsatisfying frequently changing relationships and, in some individuals, perpetration of sexual and other offences involving violence (Taylor, 1998). This has obvious implications for the nurse's responsibility in ensuring that, as far as possible, individuals are not harmed from relationships with other patients. Ifill (2002) describes the problems of women residents in a former medium secure therapeutic community that admitted both women who had been abused and men who had committed sexual offences against women (see Chapter 14 of this text).

Institutional processes can also inhibit the development of emotional and sexual relationships between patients (Adshead, 2004; Ward, 2002). Generally, these are not encouraged in inpatient settings because of safety and security (see Table 8.1). Taylor (1998) states that, in high secure hospitals, staff are sometimes more anxious about heterosexual than gay/lesbian relationships, possibly because of concerns about unwanted pregnancies arising from the former. In UK secure environments, individuals are not provided with facilities for private relationships. Several heterosexual high secure hospital patients have married each other, but Taylor reported that legislation did 'not, however, further support conjugal rights' (Taylor, 1998, p. 137). More recently, the Civil Partnerships Act 2004 (HM Government, 2004a) enables gay and lesbian patients, detained under many sections of the Mental Health Act 1983, to enter into civil partnerships.

In contrast to secure and other services in the UK, some secure hospitals in Scandinavia and Holland enable 'conjugal visits' for patients and their spouses/partners when the former are undergoing rehabilitation (Taylor, 1998). This includes the Van der Hoeven Clinic, Utrecht, a secure

Table 8.1: Proposition: sexual relationships between patients with personality disorders should be possible in inpatient settings.

For – Individuals who are inpatients with personality disorders:	But	Against – Individuals who are inpatients with personality disorders:
'Have a right to: loving relationships, sexual fulfilment' (Byrt, 1993), with consequent 'increased self-esteem' (Taylor, 1998)	But	'Have a right to be protected from harm: e.g. sexual assault, sexually transmitted disease, unwanted pregnancy'
Have free will, and 'are encouraged to make choices, and to take responsibility for their lives' within various therapeutic frameworks	But	'Staff have professional responsibility and accountability'. In addition, individuals with some personality disorders may find it harder to exercise certain choices or responsibilities
'Have a right to decide what is morally right and acceptable in their relationships'	But	The Department of Health, Trust managers, 'the public and the media may have different views about what constitutes moral behaviour'
'Need opportunities to form more creative and close relationships'	But	'Such relationships can interfere with other aspects of treatment: e.g. the effective use of therapeutic groups'
Have the capacity to help each other in the establishment of relationships, in relation to shared experiences of physical, sexual and emotional abuse (Taylor 1998).	But	Some services admit individuals with histories of perpetration of such abuse

Based on: Byrt, R. (1993) and Taylor (1998, Table 12.1, p. 148). Unless otherwise stated, quotations are from Byrt (1993).

unit for individuals with personality disorders, which has a rehabilitation flat for patients to spend time with spouses or partners. One Canadian hospital provides a space for:

> Sexual intimacy in a private and dignified setting where [patients] are as safe from harm as is reasonably possible. Sexually active patients are safer from harm when sexual activity occurs in a privacy suite than when it occurs elsewhere in the Hospital or grounds (Riverview Hospital, 1998, quoted in Grant, 2003, p. 519).

Table 8.1 includes various factors, which, it is suggested, nurses need to consider in relation to sexual relationships between individuals with personality disorders. Whilst consideration of patients' safety needs to be paramount (Chapter 11), it is essential to enable individuals to express aspects of their sexuality. This includes expression of the individual's identity as a heterosexual or gay/lesbian or bisexual man or woman, of either fixed or transsexual gender identity. It involves, also, privacy, within safety parameters, for masturbation or other safe ways of achieving sexual satisfaction or release. It is suggested that lack of privacy, especially during intensive observation, may make this difficult for individuals to achieve and compounds individuals' despair, aggression and frustration.

Addressing needs related to individuals' sexuality: an example

The following account is based on the author's experience, but names and details have been changed to ensure confidentiality and anonymity.

This example illustrates the inextricable links between individuals' psychosexual and other needs.

'Mr Abe Jones' and 'Mr Baz Smith', both in their twenties, were inpatients in separate wards (because of differing treatment and rehabilitation needs) in a low secure mental health service. They had several shared interests, particularly listening to rap music and going to the gym. Abe was often visited by his family, but Baz had few contacts with relatives. Both Abe and Baz had a diagnosis of personality disorder.

Soon after Abe met Baz at a Unit-wide social event, they told other patients and staff that they were boyfriends. At their request, senior nursing staff enabled Abe to visit Baz a few times a week on Baz's ward. Views amongst staff polarised, with a few nurses emphasising the needs and rights of Abe and Baz as gay men, and others stating that their relationship 'shouldn't be encouraged', and that their holding hands and kissing was 'going too far'.

However, there was limited discussion about these differing views and feelings, with no related staff training on gay issues. Crucially, there was also little discussion about the safety, risk assessment and risk management issues involved. There was a lack of consistency in staff reactions to Abe and Baz as a couple, and the extent that their time together was supervised for safety reasons. The low secure unit offered few specialist interventions (such as those outlined in Chapters 6, 14 and 15). Both Abe and Baz were seen individually by a psychologist, but there was little feedback to other staff from these sessions.

About three months after they first met, and following a disagreement, Baz attempted to hit Abe, and made threats to seriously harm him. Staff then realised that these were similar to threats that Baz had made, before admission, towards two other gay men. Baz and Abe decided to discontinue their relationship. Understandably, both of them felt very sad, and Abe's self-harming behaviours, which had existed for many years, initially increased considerably. Both men needed considerable support from staff.

What could have been done differently?

Could this situation have been avoided? Whilst there were some positive aspects of practice, it is argued that nursing practice should have been informed by the following:

- **Risk assessment, using valid and reliable tools, and risk management** (see Chapter 10). This would include addressing factors involved in Baz's threatening behaviours and Abe's self-harm.
- **Specialist interventions, based on a therapeutic framework**, which addressed the specific problems of Abe and Baz (see Chapters 14 and 15).
- **A philosophy that respects diversity, and takes account of patients' individual needs**, including those related to sexual orientation and gender identity (Thompson, 2003).

Risk assessment, risk management, specialist interventions and a Unit philosophy that respects diversity could have been used to:

- Inform decisions about *safety* issues related to the relationship of Abe and Baz, visits and their supervision; and bearing in mind Baz's history of threats towards other gay men.
- Enable Abe and Baz to safely express and resolve anger and other feelings.
- Provide opportunities for Abe and Baz to discuss issues concerning their sexuality, as they wished, with staff with whom they had established trust.
- Ensure that relevant information related to sexuality, including sexual orientation, was accessible to *all* patients.
- Address issues of early abuse experienced by both Abe and Baz, and Abe's resultant self-harm.
- Ensure consistency of approach by all staff, with good inter-professional communication, rather than staff working in isolation.
- Ensure that staff received appropriate clinical supervision and education in relation to these areas.
- Ensure an organisational climate that enabled staff self-awareness and open discussion and resolution of issues that staff found difficult.

Lesbians, gay men, bisexual individuals and people who are transsexual: some definitions

What does it mean to be lesbian, gay, bisexual or transsexual? The first three terms involve both:

- **Sexual orientation**: i.e. emotional and sexual attraction to individuals of the same sex (lesbians and gay men) and to both sexes (individuals who are bisexual) (Wilton, 2000).
- In addition, for many individuals, a positive feeling of **identity** as a lesbian, a gay man or a bisexual individual is particularly important. Sexual identity has been defined as 'a consistent, enduring self-recognition of the meaning that sexual orientation and sexual behaviour have for oneself' (Savin-Williams, 1990, p. 3, quoted in Davies, 1996, p. 31). However, not all people who have sex with partners of the same sex see themselves as lesbian, gay or bisexual. Identity is considered later in this chapter.
- Work by Kinsey (1947) and others suggests that, whilst some people are exclusively heterosexual or lesbian/gay during all or most of their lives, this may vary over time (Davies and Neal, 1996a).

Identity is also crucial in individuals who are **transsexual**. Transsexualism is known, also, as 'gender dysphoria, gender identity disorder and transgenderism' (Murjan *et al.*, 2002, p. 210). An individual who is transsexual, although brought up as a boy or a girl, has a strong identity as an individual of the other sex, and feels unhappy and uncomfortable with both their anatomical gender and the gender that others ascribe to them. Transsexual people usually wish to live as a member of their identified gender (that is, the gender that they perceive themselves to be, 'inside' their body). These individuals generally request hormonal and surgical treatments to enable gender change (Murjan *et al.*, 2002; The Gender Trust, 2004). Individuals who are transsexual can be heterosexual, lesbian, gay or bisexual.

Lesbians, gay men, bisexuals and transgendered individuals are sometimes referred to in the literature by the abbreviation 'LGBT'. For convenience, this will be used in the rest of this chapter, with 'LGB' being used to refer to lesbians, gay men and bisexual individuals. These abbreviations are used as convenient shorthand, and are not intended to deny the great diversity amongst people so described.

Attitudes in wider society

Attitudes of nurses and other health professionals are likely to reflect those in wider society (Godfrey, 2003). Many LGBT individuals still face stigma and discrimination. This will have affected the lives and the level of distress of many who both have a personality disorder and are lesbian, gay, bisexual or transsexual. Nurses need to be aware of the adverse experiences of many of these individuals. Many will have become aware, from attitudes expressed in their families, at school and at work, that same sex attraction and doubts about gender identity are seen as deviant and regarded with disgust and contempt. Until recently, young people, in particular, had few positive role models of people who were 'out' (i.e. open about their sexual orientation or gender identity) and leading fulfilling lives as LGBT. The isolation of many such individuals has been compounded by widespread heterosexism. The latter includes taken-for-granted beliefs that only heterosexual relationships and fixed gender identity are acceptable and 'natural'. Such beliefs are *institutionalised*: i.e. bolstered by powerful social institutions, such as Parliament, the law, some religions and the media (Godfrey, 2003). However, for the first time, the Civil Partnership Act 2004 gives legal status to lesbian and gay partnerships in the UK (HM Government, 2004a). The Employment Equality (Sexual Orientation) Regulations 2003 (HM Government, 2003b) makes it illegal to discriminate in employment on the grounds of sexual orientation; and the Criminal Justice Act, 2003 (HM Government, 2003a) explicitly states the illegality of homophobically motivated offences (Stonewall, 2005).

Homophobia

Weinberg (1972, p. 4) defined *homophobia* as 'the dread of being in close quarters with homosexuals'. Homophobia can include 'anxiety, disgust, aversion, anger, discomfort and fear' (Davies, 1996b, p. 41, quoting Weinberg, 1972, and citing Hudson and Ricketts, 1980).

Internalised homophobia is a term referring to the individual's self-hatred, shame and other negative feelings about himself/herself and his/her sexuality (Davies, 1996b; Tate and Longo, 2004). Internalised homophobia can further low self-esteem in individuals with personality disorders, and needs to be taken into consideration in nursing/multidisciplinary assessments and interventions.

'Homosexuality' as a 'mental disorder'

Psychiatry has been criticised for taking for granted attitudes in wider society, and allowing these to influence decisions that homosexuality is a mental disorder. Homosexuality was included in the Diagnostic and Statistical Manual (DSM) until 1973 and in the World Health Organization International Classification of Diseases (ICD-10) until 1992 (Davies and Neal, 1996; Taylor, 2000), which is one reason that many lesbians and gay men dislike the term 'homosexuality'. (DSM and ICD classifications are considered in Chapter 2 of this text). In the 1960s and 70s, gay men were treated with psychoanalysis and other psychodynamic psychotherapy, or with behaviour therapy. The latter involved the administration of electric shocks or other aversive stimuli to coincide with pictures of naked men. Such 'treatments' were unsuccessful in changing individuals' sexual orientations (King *et al.*, 2004; Smith *et al.*, 2004). Prior to 1967, it was illegal for adult men to have sex with other consenting men; and some gay men were referred by courts for such treatment as an alternative to imprisonment. Smith *et al.* (2004) conclude:

> The definition of same sex attraction as an illness and the development of treatments to eradicate such attraction have had a negative long-term impact on individuals ... our study shows the negative consequences of defining same sex attraction as a mental illness and devising treatments to eradicate it. It serves as a warning against the use of mental health services to change aspects of human behaviour that are disapproved of on social, political, moral or religious grounds (Smith *et al.*, 2004, pp. 427 and 429).

Many transsexual individuals have criticised DSM-IV for including 'gender identity disorder' in this classification system and argued that such inclusion is stigmatising (Ettner, 1999). There have been varied findings as to whether there is a link between transsexualism and mental health problems, including personality disorders. One study found that transsexual individuals had similar problems to individuals with borderline personality disorders (Ettner, 1999, citing Murray, 1985). However, a detailed study of 435 individuals found no link between transsexualism and personality disorders and other types of mental health problem (Ettner, 1999, citing Bodlund *et al.*, 1993).

Transsexual individuals have often been misunderstood, stigmatised and discriminated against. For the first time in the UK, 'acquired gender', with appropriate 'rights and responsibilities' (Gender Recognition Panel, 2005) can now be legally recognised, under the Gender Recognition Act 2004 (HM Government 2004b). The Sex Discrimination (Gender Reassignment) Regulations 1999 make it illegal to discriminate in employment (The Gender Trust, 2004). Transsexual individuals do not always receive appropriate health services. One survey found that, although 82%

of service providers arranged some form of treatment for transsexual individuals, this was often inappropriate and not delivered locally (Murjan *et al.*, 2002).

The mental health of LGBT individuals

An important aspect of nursing interventions with LGBT individuals with personality disorders is to appreciate the possible effects of social stigmatisation and discrimination. However, it needs to be recognised that individuals' experience of this will vary considerably. Some LGBT individuals have experienced few negative responses from others to their sexual orientation or gender identity. For example, Berger (1982) found in his study that the majority of older gay men reported leading fulfilled lives, often with little homophobia from others. In contrast, many individuals, including some people with personality disorders, have experienced internalised homophobia in response to rejection, and sometimes, hostility from family, friends, peers at school or work and strangers. Such reactions may make it difficult for people to 'come out' and be open about their sexuality (Coyle and Kitzinger, 2002). Some individuals experience strain from 'passing': i.e. hiding the secret of their sexual orientation or gender identity, and hoping that it will not be discovered (Godfrey, 2003). Internalised homophobia involves acceptance of negative images in wider society, with consequent low self-esteem and poor self-image. This appears to be one factor responsible for high suicide rates in gay men, in particular, although they have not been included as a high-risk group in the Department of Health's (2002) National Suicide Prevention Strategy for England (McAndrew and Warne 2004). (Indeed, Godfrey (2003) argues that the health needs of LGBT individuals are often marginalised and ignored). The effects of homophobia on depression, self-harm and suicide in LGBT individuals with personality disorders have implications for nursing and multidisciplinary assessment and interventions (see Chapters 9, 10, 14 and 15).

Research has found that gay men, lesbians and bisexual individuals have, in general, higher 'levels of psychological distress', and are more likely to use mental health services, compared with the rest of the population (King *et al.*, 2003, p. 552). They have higher rates of harmful use of alcohol and other drugs (Taylor, 2000) (see Chapter 13 of this text); and this has implications for nursing and other interventions for some people with personality disorders. Gay men are more likely to develop anorexia nervosa compared with other men. Research found that, in contrast to an estimated 5% in the general population, '12% of 118 men with borderline personality disorder ... had features of homosexual orientation ... and problems with gender identity' (Dowson, 1995, p. 181). An Australian study discovered that the incidence of mental health problems was much higher in bisexual individuals, compared with gay men and lesbians. The authors conclude that this may be partly because having an orientation that is not clearly heterosexual or lesbian/gay is particularly stressful. The bisexual individuals in this study were found to have more stressful current and past life events and less support from relatives and friends (Jorm *et al.*, 2002). Another study found that gay men and lesbians were more likely than bisexuals to be 'out' to others and to be more self-accepting about their sexuality (King and McKeown with Warner *et al.*, 2003).

Transsexual individuals have often felt unhappy about expectations that they should adopt what are seen by others to be gender-appropriate roles, activities, attitudes and clothing. They often learn to keep secret their gender identity, and their wish to live as a member of the gender they know themselves to be. However, wider social attitudes may make it difficult for them to be open about their gender identity. In addition, media accounts of transsexual individuals tend to sensationalise and emphasise difference (The Gender Trust, 2004). These and related findings are relevant to an understanding of the varied experiences of LGBT individuals with personality disorders.

Nurses' attitudes and communication as a crucial part of LGBT individuals' care

Research suggests that nurses' attitudes and communication are crucial to the care of LGBT people with personality disorders. Although good practice has been reported, there is evidence that nurses and other health professionals are not always sensitive to the needs of lesbians and gay men and their partners, and sometimes have negative attitudes towards them (Godfrey, 2003; Golding, 1997; King and McKeown with Warner *et al.*, 2003). Gay men living with HIV positive status have been blamed and stigmatised by some nurses (Rondahl *et al.*, 2003, 2004). Godfrey (1999) reports that:

> ... The reported attitudes of health care staff [towards lesbian and gay clients and carers] include a wide range of behaviours. Most commonly identified responses tend to be negative and discriminatory. This is, perhaps, not surprising, as we are all affected by socialisation processes, but it does highlight the need for awareness of prejudice in health care workers. Prejudicial responses can disempower individuals, particularly when they originate from people in professional and respected positions (Godfrey, 1999, p. 180).

Golding (1997), in a survey for Mind, found that, despite some good practice, many lesbians and gay men had experienced negative discrimination in mental health services. This was reported by 73% of people who took part in the survey. One respondent commented:

> We are as diverse as anyone else, but we need high quality, non-judgemental counselling and sensitivity. We need to describe our experiences and need validation and support – not silence or embarrassment ... (Golding, 1997, p. 41).

A more recent survey found that 'up to a third of gay men, one quarter of bisexual men and over 49% of lesbians recounted negative or mixed reactions from mental health professionals when being open about their sexuality'. Reported problems included 'instances of overt homophobia and discrimination, [and professionals'] perceived lack of empathy around sexuality issues ... ' (King and McKeown with Warner *et al.*, 2003, p. 5).

Given findings on nurses' attitudes, a fundamental aspect of good practice in nursing interventions with LGBT clients and patients, including those with personality disorders, relates to nurses' awareness of their own attitudes towards, and beliefs about, these individuals. Godfrey (1999, p. 181) reports the importance of 'good communication skills, warmth and sensitivity, compassion .... Lesbians and gay men need to feel accepted and valued, rather than pathologised by their sexuality'.

Gay affirmative therapy

Davies and Neil (1996, 2000) refer to 'gay affirmative therapy', which has the characteristics listed below. These can inform nursing interventions with individuals with personality disorders who are lesbian, gay or bisexual. Many of these principles also appear to be relevant to individuals who are transsexual (Davies and Neal 1996, 2000):

Gay affirmative therapy:

■ 'Affirms a lesbian, gay or bisexual identity as an equally positive human experience and expression to heterosexual identity' (Davies 1996a, p. 25).
■ Enables the individual to question and reduce guilt related to others' homophobia and negative evaluations.
■ Sees homophobia, rather than sexual orientation or gender identity, as pathological.
■ Enables people to creatively, and safely express anger related to their experiences of homophobia.
■ Establishes a relationship of trust, bearing in mind that the individual may have experienced negative attitudes in health services, as well as in wider society.
■ Treats the individual, and his/her 'culture and lifestyle' (Davies, 1996a, p. 27) with respect.
■ Is based on awareness that widespread societal homophobia is likely to affect one's own attitudes and beliefs as a professional.
■ Involves staff who feel reasonably comfortable about their own sexuality.
■ Involves a readiness to listen to the individual, without being judgemental.
■ Attempts to empathise, and to validate (i.e. to positively confirm the individual, and appreciate his/her perspectives and experiences) and to successfully convey this appreciation to him/her (Boggs, 2003).
■ Includes a readiness to learn from the individual and to increase one's own understanding.
■ Involves preparedness to be aware of the diversity of experiences and lifestyles amongst LGBT individuals, rather than assuming similarities.
■ Attempts to collaborate with the individual and to enable his/her active participation in nursing and other professional interventions.

Empowerment and increased self-esteem and self-efficacy

In addition, gay affirmative therapy and nursing interventions informed by this approach enable the individual to find ways to become empowered and to increase self-esteem and self-efficacy. (The latter term 'refers to an individual's belief that he/she is able to achieve specific goals': Byrt and Dooher, 2003, p. 9, citing Tones and Green, 2002). For some individuals (but by no means all), this may include developing pride in identity as lesbian, gay, bisexual or transsexual (and for the latter, pride as an individual of the identified gender). LGBT pride often includes a coming out to others, and a *raising of consciousness* of social oppression. For some individuals, political action is a means to both challenge discrimination and increase self-esteem and self-efficacy and

> **Box 8.1. An example of good practice: health services for lesbians and gay men in North Warwickshire.**
>
> Fitzgerald (2003) describes the development of health services which are sensitive to the needs of lesbians, gay men and transsexual individuals. One client commented:
>
> > ... I wasn't particularly self-confident about my sexuality, and was still quite worried about how people would react to my being gay. Coming to 'SPACE' [a health service] helped me to change that. By meeting other people who felt the same as me, I really felt a sense of belonging. Having a space to talk about any problems ... SPACE has really changed my outlook to life and to myself ...
>
> (Fitzgerald, 2003, quoting Kevin (aged 17))

is achieved individually and through groups such as Outrage (2005), Stonewall (2005) and The Gender Trust (2005).

Coming out may include the development of supportive networks with others outside the mental health service, e.g. meeting socially with other LGBT individuals. Local gay and lesbian switchboards and the Beaumont Society (2005) (which includes a membership of transsexual individuals) have details of various social and support groups, clubs and other meeting places.

In some services, creating a space where LGBT individuals can meet is helpful in positively affirming their experiences and identities, facilitating mutual support and enabling people to have fun (see Box 8.1). One example is the Rainbow Club at Rampton (Unison and Royal College of Nursing, 2004), a high secure hospital which includes services for individuals with personality disorder. This club was facilitated by Rampton Hospital patients and staff, with the help of the Lesbian and Gay Foundation (2005).

Some criticisms of approaches using gay affirmative therapy

It has been argued that interventions should be neutral, rather than positively affirming the individual's sexual orientation or gender identity (Pett, 2000). However, Davies's approach is one of accepting the individual, rather than 'promoting homosexuality' or transsexualism. Gay affirmative therapy has been criticised, also, for being prescriptive about the individual's development of a gay identity, rather than enabling the individual to discover, and make choices about, this (Pett, 2000, citing du Plock, 1997). Whilst gay affirmative therapy emphasises the importance of validating LGBT individuals and their experiences, this also needs to include the possibility that some people may wish to change their sexual orientation, which they may not wish to be affirmed: an issue considered by Davies (1996a).

The therapeutic use of touch?

Davies (1996a) suggests that the careful use of touch can be therapeutic, but gives little considera-tion to the contra-indications. Great care needs to be exercised in the use of touch with individuals with personality disorders, many of whom are likely to see this as intrusive. Therapeutic touch could be particularly threatening for people with doubts or uncertainties about their sexual ori-entation or gender identity. It could also be misunderstood as an indication that the nurse wished to enter into a friendship or close emotional or sexual relationship. In addition, therapeutic touch may be problematic because of difficulties, related to early experiences, in trusting people (Hunter and Struve, 1998). There are also issues related to individuals' experiences of abuse. In some instances, therapeutic touch and control and restraint may induce 'flashbacks' of abuse experi-ences (Gallop, 1998; Stafford, 1999).

The partners and friends of LGBT individuals and their involvement in care

Research findings suggest that nurses and other professionals fail to recognise the importance to LGBT clients/patients of their partners and friends, and their wish for them to be involved in their care, given information in relation to this, and contacted in an emergency (Godfrey, 2003; Unison and Royal College of Nursing, 2004). Good practice in these areas is important in nursing inter-ventions with people with personality disorders. In one study, lesbians expressed a wish 'to be treated in a way in which their sexual orientation was taken calmly, and as a matter of fact, their partners being included without challenge. Such responses from health care workers show support and respect ...' (Godfrey, 1999, p. 181, citing Stevens and Hall, 1988).

There have been reports of conflicts between blood relatives and LGBT individuals' partners and friends; and nurses' mistaken assumptions that only blood relatives can be counted as 'next of kin' and given information (Godfrey, 2003; Unison and RCN 2004). The report by Unison and RCN (2004) gives guidance on the need for health professionals to recognise that some clients/ patients identify partners of the same gender (including civil partners) as the person closest to them. When the individual requests that this person is given information about his/her care, there is no legal reason for professionals not to do so (Unison and Royal College of Nursing, 2004).

Assessment

Several authors refer to heterosexist assumptions that all patients are heterosexual. This is some-times reflected in assessment forms, with terms such as 'marital status' and questions that assume fixed gender identity or a heterosexual orientation. 'Next of kin', although often used as a term in health services, mainly in relation to blood relatives, has little basis in law, except in relation to the disposal of property. Rather than being asked his or her next of kin, it has been suggested that patients be asked about their 'chosen contacts', without having to state their sexual orientation (Unison and Royal College of Nursing, 2004, p. 7). In relation to the Mental Health Act 1983, it has been difficult for lesbians and gay men to achieve recognition as formally admitted patients' nearest relative (Unison and Royal College of Nursing, 2004). However, if proposals in the Mental Health Bill for England and Wales (Department of Health, 2004) are adopted, same sex partners may receive more formal recognition as carers (Unison and Royal College of Nursing, 2004).

In the admission of transsexual individuals who are in the early stages of living as a member of their identified gender, care needs to be taken to establish what the individual likes to be called, and preference for being referred to as 'he' or 'she'. These details may be different from those recorded in the individual's multidisciplinary records (The Gender Trust, 2004). If the individual is in an early stage of transition towards their identified gender, care should be taken not to make assumptions about the sexual orientation of him/her and his/her partner. Confidentiality related to transsexual status may be particularly important to the individual (The Gender Trust, 2004), and it is crucial that this is discussed with him/her in relation to the sharing of information.

Transsexual individuals' transitions to their identified gender

During assessment, it is important to establish the transsexual individual's stage of transition towards their identified gender. Commonly, he/she spends childhood, and perhaps teenage years and earlier adulthood, feeling very troubled and ill at ease with the gender identity assigned by others. At this stage, the individual may be very certain, or may have some doubts about their identified gender. Once the individual is referred for specialist intervention, there follows a period of assessment to evaluate whether he/she is transsexual, as well as the presence of personality disorder or mental illness (Murjan et al., 2002). These would need to be treated to ensure that the individual's further decisions about gender realignment were not affected by specific mental health problems. At the assessment stage, information is given about treatment available (Murjan et al., 2002). There is a full evaluation of physical health, 'psychosexual development ... sexual behaviour and sexual orientation ... body image ... intellectual and emotional coping mechanisms' (Irwin, 2002, p. 152), and of whether the individual prefers to dress in the clothing of the identified gender.

Following the period of assessment, if it is evident that the individual still wishes to live his/her life in the identified gender, he/she would undertake a 'real-life test' (Wilson, 2000, cited in Irwin, 2002). This involves living in the identified gender for two years in his/her relationships, family and work or study life. Unfortunately, many transsexual people are the recipients of considerable abuse and discrimination, and need particular support as a result (The Gender Trust, 2004). Treatment with hormones of the identified gender commences during or after these two years, sometimes with referral for genital reconstruction surgery and other procedures to develop secondary sex characteristics (Irwin, 2002; Murjan et al., 2002), following the completion of the 'real-life test'.

There appears to be little literature on interventions for transsexual individuals with personality disorders. It is likely that interventions for the personality disorder would be completed before commencing the 'real-life test' and other treatments related to transsexualism. An important role of nursing and other staff is recognition of, and responding to, the considerable upheaval which transsexuals undergo immediately before and during assessment, the 'real-life test' and subsequent treatment (Irwin, 2002).

Patients are sometimes required to undergo psychotherapy before these treatments (Irwin, 2002), although some transsexuals and professionals would question the need for this (Ettner, 1999). Certain specialist interventions for transsexual individuals with personality disorders might be relevant (see Chapters 14 and 15 of this text). For example, cognitive behavioural therapy could be used to identify and find structured solutions to particular problems encountered during the 'real-life test'. A therapeutic community could provide a relatively safe, supportive environment for individuals to try new roles. However, great care would be needed to liaise carefully with staff specialising in gender reassignment and to ensure consistency in approach (The Gender Trust, 2004).

Accessibility and availability of relevant information

Information about LGBT issues should be accessible and available to clients/patients who are uncertain about their sexual orientation/gender identity and people who identify as heterosexual, but who have sex, at times, with people of the same gender. For example, leaflets on safer sex needs to have different content and presentation for gay men and for men who identify as heterosexual, but who sometimes have sex with other men. The visibility of LGBT literature also reflects a message that a health service values the needs and rights of a diverse range of clients.

Self-disclosure

Finally, little has been written about the extent to which LGBT nurses and other professionals should disclose their sexual orientation or gender identity to patients/clients, although research has explored this in relation to LGBT health care staff in general (Riordan, 2004). The main considerations in decisions about self-disclosure would be whether or not this adversely affected safety, and was for the benefit of the patient/client (Stuart, 2001). In relation to the former, some individuals might use information about the nurse in unsafe ways. Much would also depend on the specific therapeutic framework and related interventions used. A unit using psychodynamic psychotherapy, for example, might view self-disclosure as adversely affecting the transference process (see Chapter 15). One of the most compelling reasons for nurses self-disclosing as LGBT is the argument that this renders LGBT issues as visible. Clients, especially those who are uncertain about their sexuality, may feel less isolated and more empowered (Davies, 1996a). On the other hand, this could be achieved, also, through contacts with individuals in local LGBT organisations. Anonymous (2002) makes it clear that, as a gay service user, information about the sexual orientation of health professionals has been irrelevant and unwelcome to him.

Conclusion

This section has considered issues of sexuality, sexual orientation and gender identity in relation to nursing interventions with individuals with personality disorders. Both personality disorders and aspects of inpatient care may affect the individual's expression of his/her sexuality, including aspects of identity and self-esteem as a man or a woman. Issues concerning sexuality are closely linked with individuals' other needs; and with appropriate nursing and multidisciplinary interventions to ensure safety, assess and manage risk, ensure respect for the individual and his/her diversity; and affirm his/her experiences and perspectives. It is argued that it is crucial for nurses and other professionals to understand the individual's possible experience of discrimination and stigmatisation and their effects on his/her self-esteem. Viewing 'homosexuality' or 'gender dysphoria' as 'mental disorders' has negative consequences for individuals. However, high incidences of mental health problems in LGB individuals (e.g. resulting in high suicide rates in gay men) has consequences for nursing and other professional interventions for some patients with personality disorders. Also important are issues concerning assessment, the involvement of partners in LGBT patients' care and staff self-disclosure.

Acknowledgement

Richard Byrt would like to thank Kate Harding for drawing some sources to his attention.

References

Adshead, G. (1994) Damage: trauma and violence in a sample of women referred to a forensic service. *Behavioural Sciences and the Law*, **12**, 235–249.

Adshead, G. (2004) More alike than different: gender and forensic mental health. In: Jeffcote, N. and Watson, T. (eds.) *Working Therapeutically with Women in Secure Mental Health Settings*, Chapter 6. Jessica Kingsley, London.

Aiyegbusi, A. (2002) Nursing interventions and future directions with women in secure services. In: Kettles, A. M., Woods, P. and Collins, M. (eds.) *Therapeutic Interventions for Mental Health Nurses*, Chapter 9. Jessica Kingsley, London.

American Psychiatric Association (1994) *Diagnostic and Statistical Manual of Mental Disorders*, 4th edn (DSM-IV) American Psychiatric Association, Washington.

Anonymous (2002) If you prick us, do we not bleed? In: Ramsay, R., Page, A., Goodman, T. and Hart, D. (eds.) *Changing Minds: Our Lives and Mental Illness*, (pp. 77–79). Gaskell, London.

Bateman, A. and Fonagy, P. (2004) *Psychotherapy for Borderline Personality Disorder*. Oxford University Press, Oxford.

The Beaumont Society (2005) Website: `http://www.beaumontsociety.org.uk/`.

Berger, R. M. (1982) *Gay and Grey: The Older Homosexual Man*. University of Illinois Press, Urbana.

Boggs, K. U. (2003) Bridges and barriers in the therapeutic relationship. In: Arnold, E. and Boggs, K. U. (eds.) *Interpersonal Relationships: Professional Communication Skills for Nurses*, 4th edn, Chapter 6. W. B. Saunders, Philadelphia.

Bowers, L. (2002) *Dangerous and Severe Personality Disorder: Response and Role of the Psychiatric Team*. Routledge, London.

Byrt, R. (1993) Moral minefield. *Nursing Times*, **89**(8), 63–66.

Byrt, R. and Dooher, J. (2003) 'Service users' and 'Carers' and their desire for empowerment and participation. In: Dooher, J. and Byrt, R. (eds.) *Empowerment and the Health Service User*, Chapter 1. Quay Books, Mark Allen Publishing, Dinton, Salisbury.

Byrt, R., Lomas, C., Gardiner, J. and Lewis, D. (2001) Working with women in secure environments. *Journal of Psychosocial Nursing and Mental Health Services*, **39**(9), 42–50.

Campling, P. (1999) Chaotic personalities: maintaining the therapeutic alliance: In: Campling, P. and Haigh, R. (eds.) *Therapeutic Communities: Past, Present and Future*, Chapter 11. Jessica Kingsley, London.

Castillo, H. (2003) *Personality Disorder: Temperament or Trauma?* Jessica Kingsley, London.

Coyle, A. and Kitzinger, C. (eds.) (2000) *Lesbian and Gay Psychology: New Perspectives*. British Psychological Society/Blackwell, Oxford.

Cutcliffe, J. (2003) Engagement and observation of people at risk. In: Barker, P. (ed.) *Psychiatric and Mental Health Nursing: The Craft of Caring*, Chapter 53. Arnold, London.

Davies, D. (1996a) Towards a model of gay affirmative therapy. In: Davies, D. and Neal, C. (eds.) *Pink Therapy: A Guide for Counsellors and Therapists Working with Lesbian, Gay and Bisexual Clients*, Chapter 2. Open University Press, Buckingham.

Davies, D. (1996b) Homophobia and heterosexism. In: Davies, D. and Neal, C. (eds.) *Pink Therapy: A Guide for Counsellors and Therapists Working with Lesbian, Gay and Bisexual Clients*, Chapter 3. Open University Press, Buckingham.

Davies, D. and Neal, C. (1996) Homophobia and heterosexism. In: Davies, D. and Neal, C. (eds.) *Pink Therapy: A Guide for Counsellors and Therapists Working with Lesbian, Gay and Bisexual Clients*, Chapter 1. Open University Press, Buckingham.

Davies, D. and Neal, C. (2000) (eds.) *Pink Therapy*, Vol. 2. *Therapeutic Perspectives in Working with Lesbian, Gay and Bisexual Clients*. Open University Press, Buckingham.

Department of Health (2004) *Draft Mental Health Bill*. Cm 6305. The Stationery Office, London.

Department of Health (1983) *The Mental Health Act For England And Wales*. HMSO, London.

Department of Health (2005) Website: `http://www.doh.gov.uk/`.

De Zulueta, F. (1997) Working on the borderline: can we continue to turn a blind eye? In: Welldon, E. V. and Van Velsen, C. (eds.) *A Practical Guide To Forensic Psychotherapy*, Chapter 32, pp. 223–227. Jessica Kingsley, London.

Dowson, J. H. (1995) Longitudinal aspects of personality disorders. In: Dowson, J. H. and Grounds, A. T. (eds.) *Personality Disorders: Recognition and Clinical Management*, Chapter 4. Cambridge University Press, Cambridge.

Ettner, R. (1999) *Gender Loving Care: A Guide to Counselling Gender-Variant Clients*. W. W. Norton and Company, New York.

Fitzgerald, P. (2003) A question of 'choices and space': gay, lesbian and transgendered services in North Warwickshire. In: Dooher, J. and Byrt, R. (eds.) *Empowerment: and the Health Service User*, Chapter 6. Quay Books, Mark Allen Publishing, Dinton, Salisbury.

Gallop, R. (1999) Personality disorder: finding a way. In: Clinton, M. and Nelson, S. (eds.) *Advanced Practice in Mental Health Nursing*, Chapter 9. Blackwell Science, Oxford.

Gender Recognition Panel (2005) Website: http://www.grp.gov.uk/.

Gender Trust, The (2004) Transsexualism. *Nurse2Nurse*, **4**(1), 25–27.

Golding, J. (1997) *Without Prejudice: Mind Lesbian, Gay and Bisexual Mental Health Awareness Research*. Mind Publications, London.

Godfrey, J. (1999) Empowerment through sexuality. In: Wilkinson, G. and Miers, M. (eds.) (1999) *Power and Nursing Practice*, Chapter 12. Macmillan, Basingstoke.

Godfrey, J. (2003) The lesbian, gay man and transgendered experience as users of healthcare services. In: Dooher, J. and Byrt, R. (eds.) *Empowerment and the Health Service User*, Chapter 6. Quay Books, Mark Allen Publishing, Dinton, Salisbury.

Grant, A. (2003) Sexuality and gender. In: Barker, P. (ed.) *Psychiatric and Mental Health Nursing: The Craft of Caring*, Chapter 56. Arnold, London.

Gunderson, J. G. and Sabo, A. N. (1993) The phenomenological and conceptual interface between borderline personality disorder and PTSD. *American Journal of Psychiatry*, **150**(1), 19–27.

Harner, H. M. (2004) Relationships between incarcerated women: moving beyond stereotypes. *Journal of Psychosocial Nursing and Mental Health Services*, **42**(1), 38–46.

Herman, J. L. (1992) *Trauma and Recovery: From Domestic Violence to Political Terror*. Basic Books, London.

Herman, J. and Van Der Kolk, B. A. (1987) Traumatic antecedents of borderline personality disorder. In: Van Der Kolk, B. A. (ed.) *Psychological Trauma*, Chapter 5, pp. 111–126. American Psychiatric Press, Washington.

HM Government (1989) *The Children Act*. HMSO, London.

HM Government (1999) *Sex Discrimination (Gender Reassignment) Regulations*. HMSO, London.

HM Government (2003a) *Criminal Justice Act*. The Stationery Office, London.

HM Government (2003b) *Employment Equality (Sexual Orientation) Regulations*. The Stationery Office, London.

HM Government (2003c) *The Sexual Offences Act*. The Stationery Office, London.

HM Government (2004a) *The Civil Partnership Act*. The Stationery Office, London.

HM Government (2004b) *Gender Recognition Act*. The Stationery Office, London.

HM Government (2004c). *The Children Act, 2004*. The Stationery Office, London.

Hinshelwood, R. D. (2002) Abusive help-helping abuse: the psychodynamic impact of severe personality disorder on caring institutions. *Criminal Behaviour and Mental Health*, **12**, S20–30.

Hunter, M. and Struve, J. (1998) *The Ethical Use of Touch in Psychotherapy*. Sage, Thousand Oaks.

Ifill, W. (2002) Therapeutic communities. *The Joint Newsletter of the Association of Therapeutic Communities, the Charterhouse Group of Therapeutic Communities, and the Planned Environment Trust*, **6**, 4.

Irwin, R. (2002) *Psychosexual Nursing*. Whurr, London.

Joines, V. S. (2004) The treatment of personality adaptations using redecision therapy. In: Magnavita, J. J. (ed.) *Handbook of Personality Disorders: Theory and Practice*, Chapter 10. John Wiley & Sons, Hoboken, New Jersey.

Jorm, A. F., Korten, A. E., Rodgers, B., Jacomb, P. A. and Christensen, H. (2002) Sexual orientation and mental health: results from a community survey of young and middle-aged adults. *British Journal of Psychiatry*, **180**, 423–427.

Kessel, B. (2001) Sexuality in the older person. *Age and Ageing* **30**, 121–124.

King, M., McKeown, E., Warner, J., Ramsay, A., Johnson, K., Cort, C., Wright, L., Blizard, R. and Davidson, O. (2003) Mental health and quality of life of gay men and lesbians in England and Wales. *British Journal of Psychiatry*, **182**, 552–558.

King, M. and McKeown, E. with Warner, J., Ramsay, A., Johnson, K., Cort, C., Davidson, O. and Wright, L. (2003) *Mental Health and Social Wellbeing of Gay Men, Lesbians and Bisexuals in England and Wales*. Mind/University College London, London.

King, M., Smith, G. and Bartlett, A. (2004) Treatments of homosexuality in Britain since the nineteen fifties: an oral history: the experience of professionals. *British Medical Journal*, **328**(7437), 429–432.

Lesbian and Gay Foundation (2005) Website: http://www.lgf.org.uk/.

McAndrew, S. and Warne, T. (2004) Ignoring the evidence dictating the practice: sexual orientation, suicidality and the dichotomy of the mental health nurse. *Journal of Psychiatric and Mental Health Nursing*, **11**, 428–434.

Mason, T., Carlisle, C., Watkins, C. and Whitehead, E. (eds.) (2001) *Stigma and Social Exclusion in Healthcare*. Routledge, London.

Motz, A. (2004) Hiding and being lost: the experience of female patients and staff on a mixed sex ward. In: Jeffcote, N. and Watson, T. (eds.) *Working Therapeutically with Women in Secure Mental Health Settings*, Chapter 6. Jessica Kingsley, London.

Murjan, S., Shepherd, M. and Ferguson, B. G. (2002) What services are available for the treatment of transsexuals in Great Britain? *Psychiatric Bulletin*, **26**, 210–212.

Nursing and Midwifery Council (2004) *The NMC Code of Professional Conduct: Standards for Conduct, Performance and Ethics*. Nursing and Midwifery Council, London.

Outrage (2005) Website: http://outrage.nabumedia.com/.

Pett, J. (2000) Gay, lesbian and bisexual therapy and its supervision. In: Davies, D. and Neal, C. (eds.) *Therapeutic Perspectives on Working with Lesbian, Gay and Bisexual Clients*, Chapter 4. Open University Press, Buckingham.

Poorman, S. G. (2001) Sexual responses and sexual disorders. In: Stuart, G. W. and Laraia, M. T. (eds.) *Principles and Practice of Psychiatric Nursing*, 7th edn, Chapter 27. Mosby, St Louis.

Riordan, D. C. (2004) Interaction strategies of lesbian, gay and bisexual healthcare practitioners in the clinical examination of patients: qualitative study. *British Medical Journal*, **328**, 1227–1229.

Rondahl, G., Innala, S. and Carlsson, M. (2003) Attitudes to gay HIV positive patients. *Journal of Advanced Nursing*, **41**(5), 454–461.

Rondahl, G., Innala, D. and Carlsson, M. (2004) Nurses' attitudes towards lesbians and gay men. *Journal of Advanced Nursing*, **47**(4), 386–392.

Smith, G., Bartlett, A. and King, M. (2004) Treatments of homosexuality in Britain since the nineteen fifties: an oral history: the experience of patients. *British Medical Journal*, **328**(7437), 427–429.

Stafford, P. (1999) *Defining Gender Issues. Redefining Women's Services*. WISH, London.

Stonewall (2005) Website: `http://www.stonewall.org.uk/`.

Stuart, G. W. (2001) Therapeutic nurse–patient relationship. Chapter 2 in: Stuart, G. W. and Laraia, M. T. (eds.) *Principles and Practice of Psychiatric Nursing*, 7th edn. Mosby, St Louis.

Tate, F. B., Longo, D. A. (2004) Homophobia: a challenge for psychosocial nursing. *Journal of Psychosocial Nursing and Mental Health Services*, **42**(8), 26–33.

Taylor, G. (2000) Psychopathology and the social and historical construction of gay male identities. In: Coyle, A. and Kitzinger, C. (eds.) *Lesbian and Gay Psychology: New Perspectives*, Chapter 9. British Psychological Society/Blackwell, Oxford.

Taylor, P. (1998) Patients as intimate partners: resolving a policy crisis. In: Kaye, C. and Franey, A. (eds.) *Managing High Security Psychiatric Care*, Chapter 12. Jessica Kingsley, London.

Thompson, N. (2003) *Promoting Equality: Challenging Discrimination and Oppression*, 2nd edn. Palgrave Macmillan, Basingstoke.

Tones, K. and Green, J. (2002) The empowerment imperative in health promotion. In: Dooher, J. and Byrt, R. (eds.) *Empowerment and Participation: Power, Influence and Control in Contemporary Health Care*, Chapter 5. Quay Books, Mark Allen Publishing, Dinton, Salisbury.

Unison and Royal College of Nursing (2004) *Not Just a Friend: Best Practice Guidance on Health Care for Lesbian, Gay and Bisexual Service Users and Their Families*. UNISON, London.

Van Der Kolk, B. A. (1987) *Psychological Trauma*. American Psychiatric Press, Washington.

Van Der Kolk, B. A. (1996) The complexity and adaptation to trauma: self regulation, stimulus discrimination, and characterological development. In: Van Der Kolk, B. A., McFarlane, A. C. and Weisaeth, L. (eds.) *Traumatic Stress: The Effects of Overwhelming Experience on Body, Mind and Society*, Chapter 9, pp. 182–213. Guilford Press, New York.

Ward, M. (2002) Sexuality and people with mental health needs. In: Heath, H. and White, I. (eds.) *The Challenge of Sexuality in Health Care*, Chapter 11. Blackwell Science, Oxford.

Wilton, T. (2000) *Sexualities in Health and Social Care: A Textbook*. Open University Press, Buckingham.

Community interventions

Michael Coffey

Introduction

Working with people diagnosed with personality disorder in the community presents numerous challenges to mental health nurses. For the most part, mental health nurses have traditionally been neither educated nor trained in understanding and intervening in helpful ways with this particular group of service users. In fact, the prevailing attitudes of many professionals has been one of negative and pejorative labelling of people with this diagnosis, to the extent that many nurses will have limited positive work experiences in this field. Mental health services themselves have in effect operated in such a way as to mirror the type of social exclusionary practices that we frequently accuse others of perpetrating on those with other types of mental health problems. However, it is now becoming increasingly likely that new mental health legislation will remove the remaining formal excuses for denying services to people with these diagnoses in the future.

Community mental health nurses as the largest group of professional qualified mental health professionals working in the community will be at the forefront of working with people diagnosed with personality disorder. The extent to which this may be actively psychotherapeutic (that is, focused upon treatment and resolution of the personality problem) or perhaps more realistically focused on maintenance, is as yet to be determined. What is clear, however, is that concepts of recovery as applied to general mental health problems have currency when considering how to support and help people diagnosed with personality disorder. It is also clear that services must be intensive, long-term and based upon a collaborative negotiated therapeutic relationship between the nurse and the person.

This chapter is based upon a number of assumptions. First, with the exception of densely populated areas, most community services for people with a diagnosis of personality disorder will be offered in primary care or by community mental health teams providing services more generally to those with enduring and serious mental illness. It is, I believe, unlikely and unrealistic to believe that specialist personality disorder services can be provided in a comprehensively national manner given the neglect the topic has received from mainstream mental health services, the lack of education and training and the consequent paucity of adequately prepared staff. Given this assumption it leads me to my second assumption, which is that in such circumstances most community mental health nurses will be required not to offer treatment for the personality disorder but rather to provide the basis for a consistent, mature and engaged interaction with the person so that crises can be managed safely to prevent harm to the person or others. This is not to deny that this form of working may have its own therapeutic benefit. My third assumption is that many people with personality disorder will have co-occurring mental health and or substance misuse problems. As such, the complexity of the challenges faced by individuals and the services providing for them suggest that a multidisciplinary approach to their care is warranted. It is on this basis that this chapter is offered and as such the focus will be on engagement, social support, liaison and crisis resolution within the community context. What limited evidence there is for efficacy in the care and treatment of people with mental health problems appears to centre on those with serious mental illness. This chapter approaches the topic of community interventions in personality disorder from the perspective that those interventions that have been found to be effective in the care and treatment of mentally ill people in the community could be successfully applied to the care of people with personality disorder. There is limited evidence for such a claim and significant research in this area would be a welcome development.

Community support for people diagnosed with personality disorder

Traditionally people with a diagnosis of personality disorder have had a very mixed response from community mental health services. They have often been rejected by, or themselves rejected services. Mental health services have been able to reject people with this diagnosis because there is an established belief that personality disorder is not treatable, at least not within the current parameters of community mental health services. This belief is formally enshrined within the Mental Health Act (1983). However, many services already have people with primary or secondary diagnoses of personality disorder on their caseloads. They may be seen as the difficult or unpopular patient by staff (Stockwell, 1972) or can be characterized as Breeze and Repper (1998) suggest as being in a constant struggle for control with staff. Mental health nurses may struggle to understand what it is they should be doing when working with this group of service users and the rationale for this work. This section of the chapter will focus in turn upon engagement with the person, social support, and liaison with other services, particularly primary care and crises management.

Engagement

The process of engagement with service users must form a clear and coherent element of providing services so that detailed assessment can occur and appropriate services can be offered. The tasks of engagement may more closely be determined with reference to their intention, i.e. to engage rather than being seen as engagement interventions in their own right. Perhaps one of the most crucial tasks of working with the person is establishing and sustaining meaningful contact to facilitate later work. Many people diagnosed with personality disorder will want help only when they are particularly distressed and may be difficult to engage. They may reject the nurse and the service only to present in crisis within a few days or weeks. The nurse must attempt to understand this behaviour within the context of the person's life, which may be characterized by inconsistent and/or abusive relationships.

Watkins (2001, p. 87) outlines what he sees as the fundamental requirements that will allow mental health nurses to develop lasting collaborative relationships with users of mental health services. These include:

- Meet people with humanity and humility so that the alliance is one of equals.
- Acknowledge that as helpers we are both resourceful and fallible, as is the client.
- Recognise that power can be shared, discovered and generated within the helping alliance.
- Make the helping process participative rather than directive.
- Share our knowledge of the helping process so that people can become more resourceful and self-supporting.

Principles such as these are at the very heart of mental health nursing, and many mental health nurses will be familiar with them and have applied similar principles to working with other groups of clientèle. For people diagnosed with a personality disorder these principles are equally applicable, with the caveat that consistency in adherence to these principles is an important added element.

Frank and Gunderson (1990) have offered evidence that good quality therapeutic alliances predict better clinical outcomes in people with schizophrenia. This suggests that there are real benefits to be gained for the service user by what is considered a fundamental of mental health nursing – that is, interpersonal relationships with therapeutic intent. When working with service users diagnosed with personality disorder we must strive to facilitate and sustain these therapeutic relationships in the context of pressures to resort to legal compulsion, which essentially removes choice from the person and potentially relegates their involvement to a token contribution.

The Sainsbury Centre document *Community Support for Mental Health* (Sainsbury Centre for Mental Health, 1995) suggests that trust is an essential and fundamental component of establishing relationships with service users – we should not expect trust, but we must establish it.

Engaging people who have rejected services or who may reject formal services requires a trust based on mutual respect. This suggests that nurses must respect the person's views and rights, and services must be based on this principle rather than one of coercion. This does not mean, however, that the person cannot be presented with alternative views.

Onyett (1992) makes the point that the person needs to place the nurse in context, and mental health nurses need to make themselves real people when approaching the person. It can therefore be important to make contact through an established source. This can smooth the path for mental health nurses to establish a relationship with the person without the antagonism that often occurs when people are approached 'cold'.

Repper *et al.* (1994) investigated the strategies used by mental health nurses who worked as case managers, in establishing relationships with serious mentally ill people. A number of areas were felt to be important in the initial stages of the relationship with the person. Case managers referred to the effectiveness of being able to demonstrate their usefulness to the person. It was felt that this area was particularly important when people were wary of the case manager.

Repper *et al.* (1994) found that the emphasis in the early stages of the relationship was aimed at achieving practical tasks, and this served both to clarify the worker's role and to provide the foundations for the relationship. Engagement with the person requires persistence, skill and imagination (Holloway *et al.*, 1996). As such, both Onyett (1992) and Holloway *et al.* (1996) emphasise the importance of a respectful approach to the person. Repper *et al.* (1994) suggest that the first principle of working with the seriously mentally ill is to establish realistic expectations from the outset. This enables the person and the worker to reduce the feelings of frustration and failure, which can envelop the process when working in this area. A cooperative approach is appreciated by people and can help in establishing, the relationship as indicated by Watkins (2001). Central to this and emphasised by Repper *et al.* (1994) is the importance of empathic understanding to establishing a relationship with the patient. Placing yourself in the person's situation enables understanding, and this, once communicated to the person, may help in establishing the relationship.

Engagement is not only about the initial linking with the person but also about maintaining the person in contact with the service. Case management approaches, for instance, involve assertively following the person into the community and linking with him in whatever venue is appropriate. There are issues for many service users about the concept inherent within assertive outreach. This may mean for instance that 'assertive' is seen as 'aggressive' or indeed 'intrusive'. In the context of working with people with personality disorder in the community it may be seen as a positive step to engage with people who would otherwise not be offered the service they might need. Assertiveness therefore means giving proper opportunities to engage and information upon which to make an informed choice. Adopting a passive approach will tend to increase the likelihood of people losing contact with and not receiving appropriate services.

It is important to note that the engagement process may continue for some time. Repper *et al.* (1994) note that a case management role allows for consistent and persistent contact over a long period of time. Engagement with the person while primarily involving establishing a relationship also involves the process of assessment. The assessment forms an important part of the engagement process and should be preceded by the development of a collaborative helping relationship which may centre on practical help/tasks (e.g. benefits).

Burns and Firn (2002) suggest a much more controversial approach to engagement and one that may account for the perception of assertive outreach by service users as aggressive outreach. They conceptualise engagement under three broad areas, which they feel provide a spectrum of engagement. These are:

1. Constructive approach (relationship building)
2. Informative approach (monitoring)
3. Restrictive approach (legal sanction)

Burns and Firn suggest that engagement should follow the three strands in turn and will graduate from a constructive approach to a more restrictive approach depending on the success of the former. Both the constructive and informative strands are very similar to that suggested above. It is the restrictive approach that differs markedly and involves the use of formal legislative controls to ensure the person remains in contact with the service. The efficacy of such an approach has not been clearly demonstrated in mental health services and the likely impact upon the relationship with someone with a personality disorder is not clear. What is clear is that work with people with personality disorder has to a large extent focused upon the person developing a sense of responsibility and control over their lives and their responses to life events. Compulsion through legal sanction will have to be judged carefully so that it does not reinforce a sense of life being subject to external controls for the person.

Social support

Traditional approaches to mental illness have tended to locate the causes of mental ill health within the individual, suggesting a biochemical rationale as the source of mental illness. One failure of this rationale is that it ignores the social world of people, and therefore offers an incomplete understanding of the person and their condition. We are social beings and are influenced by our social world and by the people in it. We too have influence over our social worlds and the people we have contact with. To consider mental illness without recognising that other people and their actions and interactions have an impact upon the experience and the development and presentation of illness is ignoring a major source of real influence and potential for intervention. This is not to suggest that either model has predominance in any real sense over the other, but rather that we should make efforts to recognise the broader picture and incorporate into our understanding of personality disorder and our responses to it, a view of the world that allows for the recognition of all factors influencing mental health. Stress vulnerability models are one way of considering multi-modal influences upon the creation and maintenance of mental ill health (see, for example, Zubin and Spring, 1977).

Two concepts are relevant here; they are social support and social networks. Having access to a social network does not necessarily mean that you can access social support.

Much of what is called social support theory seems to have arisen as a result of a consideration of attachment theory as fundamental to human development (Bowlby, 1969). Essentially we need security (or a sense of attachment), practical help and reciprocity as part of our support systems. Social support is therefore necessary to meet both basic and higher order needs. Social support is assumed to be a moderator of stress, although there is evidence of certain types of social contact being seen to exacerbate social stress – for example as seen in expressed emotion.

Thoits (1982, p. 147) defines social support as 'the degree to which a person's basic social needs are gratified through interaction with others'. Basic social needs include affection, esteem or approval, belonging, identity and security. These may be met by either the provision of socio-emotional aid (affection, sympathy, understanding, acceptance and esteem from a significant other) or the provision of instrumental aid (advice, information, help with family or work responsibilities, financial assistance).

Perkins and Repper (1996) have likened the social support needs of the seriously mentally ill to the needs of the physically disabled in that both groups require assistance to negotiate the able-bodied world. This essentially advocates a social disability and access model. That is, the consequences of mental illness create social disabilities, and as a result the person experiences social exclusion and requires help to facilitate access to the broader social world. People diagnosed with personality disorder may struggle to develop relationships that assist them to function socially. As such they may require help to access and benefit from services. It has to be recognised too that they may initially reject such help.

The types of support needed by us all in the community have been identified, and Gottlieb (1981) suggests helping behaviours to be found in socially supportive relationships and as such provides a clear outline of how mental health nurses can be helpful to those they work with:

- Emotionally sustaining behaviours, including providing reassurance, encouragement, listening and understanding, trust, respect and companionship
- Problem-solving behaviours, including focused talking, suggesting and directing, sheltering the individual from the problem, material aid and distraction
- Being available if needed – this perhaps would also include the sense of knowing that someone is available, that is perceived availability of support
- Direct intervention to diminish the source of stress

Support should therefore be an inclusive term that incorporates assistance with money management, advice about daytime activities and emotional support, as well as working with people to achieve their treatment goals. There is some data which suggests that social supports may help in reducing violent behaviour among those mentally ill persons who can be a danger to others (Estroff *et al.*, 1994). Clearly for people diagnosed with a personality disorder the challenge is to engage them with services so that they may benefit from socially supportive interventions. The challenge for services is to start to construct such intervention strategies as a means of offering hope to people who find themselves in this distressing predicament.

The social support networks of the mentally ill have been researched in depth (see Cresswell *et al.* (1992) for useful references). What we know about these social networks is that as the career of mental illness progresses the social networks of service users decrease. Primary networks often consist of only seven people, three of whom are only seen regularly. In some cases these include professionals, and in most cases the networks are made up of other mentally ill individuals or relatives. Many service users will have (or have had) close acquaintances that have attempted or completed suicide and this may have a significant impact upon the mental health of the individual. Imagine, if you will, our own social network being made up entirely of people who want to, and who often attempt to, kill themselves. These may be people who you see as being like you in many ways and this may create threats to your personal identity (Estroff, 1989). The presence therefore of a consistent, supportive professional relationship with a community mental health nurse can be crucial in sustaining the person while they engage in treatment or until they are ready to participate in treatment.

Helping people build social networks, however, may not be sufficient. As Lazarus and Folkman (1984) have pointed out, the ability to draw on social support is a coping skill and as such poor social skills or illness related symptoms may reduce this ability.

Suls (1982) identifies a number of negative consequences of social support on health:

- Creating uncertainty and worry
- Setting a bad example
- Negative labelling
- Giving misleading information (the focus of much family work is correcting erroneous information)
- Discouraging compliance (can give rise to particular problems in mental illness)
- Negative social comparisons
- Creating dependence (awareness of institutional type behaviours)

The giving of social support can place an intolerable burden of care on families and we must take account of this in providing community-based services and not expect that families will make up for the shortfall in services. Community mental health nurses must be aware of family and carers' needs, as they may require information and support to help relieve the burden of care and sense of loss they may have experienced.

Social support can reduce personal control and the sense of self-efficacy and can induce dependence. In such cases this type of social support will reduce the likelihood of the person being able to manage their illness, for example in planning for crises.

Social support can, however, enhance personal control, sense of self-efficacy and self-esteem so that service users have real control over their illness, feel supported to try out new ways of living with their illness and can rebuild their sense of personal and social identity.

Liaison work

Much more effort in supporting primary care to work with people diagnosed with personality disorder is needed from community mental health services. Moran *et al.* (2000) have indicated that the prevalence of personality disorder in primary care is as high as 24%. Many of these attendees are likely to have other psychological problems and often attend primary care services in crisis. Primary care services have some difficulty in addressing most enduring mental health problems and personality disorder is no exception. Specialist mental health services at the very least have the benefit of training and experience in working with people with enduring and complex mental health needs. Primary care is the first point of contact for many and it is clear that the majority of people diagnosed with personality disorder will be treated there, and only those suffering the most difficulty will be referred on to secondary services. As such, there is an immediate need for specialist mental health services to provide consultation and support to primary care professionals in this aspect of their work. Liaison work in mental health is a model of collaboration which allows psychiatric knowledge and skills to be accessible to the wider health care team (see Box 9.1). The term is used to refer to the provision of consultation services and brief therapeutic interventions within general medical settings with the aim of facilitating onward referral. Tunmore (1994, p. 4) defines it as 'the care, treatment, study and prevention of mental health problems in clients from non-psychiatric health-care settings'.

Box 9.1: Rationale for liaison in mental health.

- Smooth paths between and within services.
- Improve communication and integration of service provision – the concept of joined-up services – no falling through the net of care!
- Ensure that those in mental distress get a service response.
- Addresses NSF standards for improvements in access to mental health services.
- Crises management.

Theoretically, liaison mental health care has been based upon the work of Caplan (1964). This primarily focuses on crisis resolution, with the aim of resolving current problems and helping the person, staff or system to develop their coping abilities so that they can better deal with future problems. As such, in its pure form it has a 'hands-off' approach that may not always be appreciated by those seeking the consultation.

Other theories appear to be relevant. The interest in holistic care is a frequent rhetoric in nursing (Clarke, 1999). Holism aims to see the person as a whole entity, recognising all aspects of the person and their relationship to their environment. It is therefore seen as integrative, combining many aspects of the person and recognising many influencing factors. This makes holistic assessment a complex process and many professionals struggle to perform such assessments and tend to opt for a less complex reductionism, i.e. see the illness, treat it, cure it or discharge it! Theories of stress, systems, and personality development are also implicated in a mental health nursing approach to liaison care (Roberts, 1997).

Nelson and Schilke (1976) outline what they see as the fundamental requirements of liaison mental health nursing. These include consultation, education (of the person, the carer/relative and the system), direct specialised psychological care, expertise in psychiatric problems (responses to illness and adaptation), awareness of the interrelationship between the physical and the psychological, knowledge of systems theory and group processes and liaison between disciplines. Community mental health nurses or specialist primary care liaison nurses are in a prime position to offer such services to people with a diagnosis of personality disorder. If they provide little else other than regular support and communication between disciplines working with those with this diagnosis then this will still be an enormous improvement upon the status quo. There is the potential to do a lot more however.

Education, training and supervision

Staff may not be adequately prepared for working with service users diagnosed with personality disorders. The treatability issue has for years allowed services to reject and exclude people with personality disorders from services on the basis that the condition was not treatable. As such mental health nurses have reduced opportunities for working with people with personality disorder. More than this, however, when mental health nurses actually encounter someone with a personality disorder the service response is one that is typified by confrontation, to the extent that the clinical experience of working constructively with people with personality disorder may actually be rare. This therefore suggests that for many mental health nurses there is a need for formal education and training in this aspect of clinical practice. Education and training can be directed toward fundamental skills such as engagement and relationship maintenance skills, and progress toward advanced therapy skills with the aim of employing evidence-orientated intervention such as dialectic behaviour therapy (Linehan, 1993). Most mental health nurses will not have covered this in their initial training and will require further professional development to enable them to work effectively with people with a personality disorder diagnosis. This much is recognized in central government guidance on personality disorder and the National Institute for Mental Health in England has now produced further guidance on the required capabilities of practitioners working with those with personality disorder diagnoses (National Institute for Mental Health in England, 2003). Education and training must commence by developing an understanding of personality disorder and its effects upon the person, the family and the community in which the person resides. In tandem with this fundamental knowledge community mental health nurses must examine their own attitudes and values about who is deserving of mental health care and any exclusionary practices they may be adopting and enacting.

Working with people who are frequently in distress and crisis, often seeking help only to reject it, can have its toll upon staff. Bassuk and Gerson (1980) have intimated that a discrete group of people they term 'chronic crises patients' have significant impact on staff morale and their subsequent occupational burnout. It has been demonstrated previously that community mental health nurses experience significant amounts of occupational stress and burnout both in generic services (Carson *et al.*, 1995) and in forensic services (Coffey and Coleman, 2001). In many cases the effects of organizational pressures are frequently implicated rather than specific types of patient behaviours. There is little evidence to support any one particular response to such negative occupational outcomes; however, clinical supervision with formal guided reflection on aspects of patient interaction appears to be valued by clinicians regardless of profession. The opportunity to discuss and seek advice on relationships and interventions with this group of service users from an experienced senior clinician is an important aspect of staff support and development. It should not be overlooked when developing services and mental health nurses should demand such support as a right and not as a luxury.

Nursing interventions at times of crisis

Diagnoses of personality disorder are implicated in both completed suicides and acts of deliberate self-harm (Moran, 2002). Such events will often be a result of increased distress and crises. A crisis can be defined as a situation where a person experiencing overwhelming stress due to a significant life event, such as relationship breakdown or job loss, finds that their usual coping mechanisms for everyday life no longer work (Caplan, 1964). People with diagnosed personality disorder often have poor coping mechanisms. If exposed to excessive stress, these coping mechanisms can break down and this can then lead to increased distress and self-harming behaviour for which crisis resolution techniques may be used.

Hospital admission is sometimes indicated either due to self-harming behaviour or as a result of brief psychotic episodes that can occur in crisis. The aim, however, is to maintain the person in the community as much as possible and to keep hospital admissions as short as possible. This is because general adult acute admission wards are not structured in ways that can successfully contain and address the often difficult behaviour of people with personality disorder. It seems indeed that such units exacerbate the presentation.

The assessment of potential risk to self and others and its severity must form the initial response to crises. Once satisfied that risk behaviours can be managed without recourse to hospitalisation then the nurse should address the resolution of the crisis with the person. The nurse should focus on solving the person's 'here-and-now' problems, despite the person wishing to avoid reality-oriented problem-solving. The nurses should determine the problem with the person, define the goals to be achieved to resolve the problem, work with the person to achieve this resolution and finally ensure follow-up with the person. The emphasis is on collaborating with the person so they have ownership of the crisis and its resolution, the rationale being that the person may then be better able to cope themselves with future crises. It is useful to determine the range of resources available to the person and to review how these resources can be accessed for support. Crisis management plans may be one way of providing tangible responses that the person can use to help themselves. Crisis intervention work is seen as short term, usually a two- to three-week period. During this time services must be accessible 24 hours a day, in some cases this can include telephone support and the team should be available to respond rapidly should the need arise.

It is important to note at this point that *crisis* does not mean *emergency*. An emergency may be defined as a life-threatening situation demanding an immediate response from services (Rosen, 1997). Crises can lead to emergencies, but not in all circumstances. Should a crisis appear to be turning into an emergency then it is incumbent upon the nurse to seek assistance from the most appropriate source and not to attempt to manage the situation alone.

Conclusion

Working with people diagnosed with personality disorder in the community is a challenging task. Nurses may find they lack an informed knowledge base to provide much of the care they are asked to provide. Overcoming long-established negative stereotypes of people with personality disorder will also be a significant hurdle. Most people with personality disorder reside in the community and many will be in contact with health service personnel. They often experience significant mental distress themselves and this has consequences for their families and the community as a whole. Mental health nurses, as the largest professional mental health workforce, should develop their expertise to offer help and advice to those with this diagnosis, their families and other health professionals who work with them.

References

Bassuk, E. and Gerson, S. (1980) Chronic crisis patients: a discrete clinical group. *American Journal of Psychiatry*, **137**, 1513–1517.

Breeze, J. A. and Repper, J. (1998) Struggling for control: the care experiences of 'difficult' patients in mental health services. *Journal of Advanced Nursing*, **28**, 1301–1311.

Burns, T. and Firn, M. (2002) *Assertive Outreach in Mental Health – a Manual for Practitioners*. Oxford University Press, Oxford.

Bowlby, J. (1969) *Attachment and Loss*. Hogarth Press, London.

Caplan, G. K. (1964) *Principles of preventive psychiatry*. Basic Books, New York.

Carson, J., Fagin, L. and Ritter, S. (eds.) (1995) *Stress and Coping in Mental Health Nursing.* Chapman & Hall, London.

Clarke, L. (1999) *Challenging Ideas in Psychiatric Nursing.* Routledge, London.

Coffey, M. and Coleman, M. (2001) The relationship between support and stress in forensic community mental health nursing. *Journal of Advanced Nursing*, **34**, 397–407.

Cresswell, C. M., Kuipers, L. and Power, M. J. (1992) Social networks and support in long-term psychiatric patients. *Psychological Medicine*, **22**, 1019–1026.

Estroff, S. E. (1989) Self, identity, and subjective experiences of schizophrenia: in search of the subject. *Schizophrenia Bulletin*, **15**, 189–196.

Estroff, S. E., Zimmer, C., Lachicotte, W. S. and Benoit, J. (1994) The influence of social networks and social support on violence by persons with serious mental illness. *Hospital and Community Psychiatry*, **45**, 669–679.

Frank, A. F. and Gunderson, J. G. (1990) The role of the therapeutic alliance in the treatment of schizophrenia: relationship to course and outcome. *Archives of General Psychiatry*, **47**, 228–236.

Gottlieb, B. H. (1981) *Social Networks and Social Support.* Sage, California.

Holloway, F., Murray, M., Squire, C. and Carson, J. (1996) Intensive case management: putting it into practice. *Psychiatric Bulletin*, **20**, 395–397.

Lazarus, R. S. and Folkman, S. (1984) *Stress, Appraisal and Coping.* Springer, New York.

Linehan, M. (1993) *Cognitive Behavioral Treatment of Borderline Personality Disorder.* Guilford Press, New York.

Moran, P. (2002) *The Epidemiology of Personality Disorders.* Available at http://www.NIMHE.org.uk/.

Moran, P., Jenkins, R., Tylee, A. *et al.* (2000) The prevalence of personality disorder among UK primary care attenders. *Acta Psychiatrica Scandinavica*, **102**, 52–57.

Nelson, J. K. N. and Schilke, D. A. (1976) The evolution of psychiatric liaison nursing. *Perspectives in Psychiatric Care*, **14**(2), 60–65.

National Institute for Mental Health in England (2003) *Breaking the Cycle of Rejection: the Personality Disorder Capabilities Framework.* Department of Health, London.

Onyett, S. (1992) *Case Management in Mental Health.* Chapman & Hall, London.

Perkins, R. and Repper, J. (1996) *Working Alongside People with Long-Term Mental Health Problems.* Chapman & Hall, London.

Repper, J., Ford, R. and Cooke, A. (1994) How can nurses build trusting relationships with people who have severe and long-term mental health problems? Experiences of case managers and their clients. *Journal of Advanced Nursing*, **19**, 1096–1104.

Roberts, D. (1997) Liaison mental health nursing: origins, definition and prospects. *Journal of Advanced Nursing*, **25**, 101–108.

Rosen, A. (1997) Crisis management in the community. *Medical Journal of Australia*, **167**, 633–638.

Sainsbury Centre for Mental Health (1995) *Community Support for Mental Health.* Sainsbury Centre for Mental Health, London.

Stockwell, F. (1972) *The Unpopular Patient*. Royal College of Nursing, London.

Suls, J. (1982) Social support, interpersonal relations and health: benefits and liabilities. In: Sanders, G. S. and Suls, J. (eds.) *Social Psychology of Health and Illness*, pp. 255–277. Lawrence Erlbaum Associates, New Jersey.

Thoits, P. A. (1982) Conceptual, methodological and theoretical problems in studying social support as a buffer against life stress. *Journal of Health and Social Behaviour*, **23**, 145–159.

Tunmore, R. (1994) Encouraging collaboration. *Nursing Times*, **90**(20), 66–67.

Watkins, P. (2001) *Mental Health Nursing: the Art of Compassionate Care*. Butterworth-Heinemann, Oxford.

Zubin, J. and Spring, B. (1977) Vulnerability: a new view of schizophrenia. *Journal of Abnormal Psychology*, **86**, 103–126.

CHAPTER 10

Assessing and managing risk to self and others

Michael Doyle and David Duffy

Introduction

Assessing and managing risk to self and others has long been a key task for clinicians working in mental health services. Although the majority of users of mental health services are not violent, it is clear that a small yet significant minority are violent in inpatient settings and the community (Swanson *et al.*, 1990; Monahan, 1992; Hidáy, 1997). People with personality disorder have been identified as a diagnostic group more likely to be violent in psychiatric populations (Litwack and Schlesinger, 1987; Monahan *et al.*, 2000) and up to 78% of male remand prisoners in England and Wales are thought to suffer from at least one personality disorder (Singleton *et al.*, 1997). It has been suggested that violence is endemic in health care (United Kingdom Central Council for Nursing, Midwifery and Health Visiting, 2001). This is reinforced by the finding that nurses are the occupational group most at risk of violence (Gallagher, 1999) and staff working in NHS Mental Health Service Trusts are up to eight times more likely to be assaulted than staff working in non-Mental Health Trusts (NHS Executive, 1999, p. 8). Despite the association between personality disorders and violence to others, people with personality disorder who come into contact with services usually have a multiplicity of problems that may also place them at risk to themselves. Furthermore, it has been found that people with personality disorder are at much greater risk of harming themselves than of harming others (Department of Health, 2001). In mental health services clinical decisions on risk are made at all stages of the patient care process. For Mental Health Nurses (MHNs) risk assessment and management are key components of clinical practice. As a strong association exists between personality disorders and risk it is important that MHNs have a clear structured approach to risk assessment and management when working with people with personality disorder. This is reinforced by the fact that the National Institute for Mental Health in England (2003) identified eight capabilities for professionals in relation to assessing and managing risk when working with people with personality disorder (Table 10.1). In this chapter the link between personality disorders, violence risk and risk to self will be considered, and a systematic

Table 10.1: Personality disorder capabilities framework: professional capabilities for assessing and managing risk to self and others.

Capability required following professional training

1. Capable of undertaking actuarial risk assessment paying attention to the risk of offending and of harm to self or others.

2. Capable of undertaking a dynamic risk needs assessment paying particular attention to cognitive and inter-personal factors, substance abuse and life style indicators.

3. Capable of understanding and supporting criminogenic needs assessment paying particular attention to cognitive and interpersonal factors, substance abuse and life style indicators under direction.

4. Capable of undertaking a family and community risk needs assessment.

5. Capable of planning and delivering interventions based on case formulation addressing specific risk factors, providing proposals for risk management and for motivating individuals.

6. Capable of applying an understanding of legal and ethical issues in the context of risk assessment and management.

7. Capable of collaborating with multi-disciplinary and multisectoral risk management plans

8. Capable of reflective practice

Source: National Institute of Mental Health (2003)

approach to assessing, formulating and managing risk will be described that should prove useful for MHNs when working with people with personality disorders.

Understanding the link between personality disorder and risk

Looking at the diagnostic criteria for personality disorders it's not surprising that the presence of a personality disorder diagnosis alone is seen by some as sufficient to assume a high risk of violence. Nevertheless, it is not exactly clear why personality disorder is such a significant factor when assessing and managing risk to self or others. A number of theories have been suggested. It is likely that individuals with personality disorder have cognitive schemas that predispose them to perceive hostile and critical intent in the actions of others (Young, 2003; Beck *et al.*, 1990). It is also possible that they may be prone to violence and self-harm due to a general pattern of impulsivity (Linehan, 1993). Hiday (1997) highlighted the link between antisocial personality disorder, social disorganisation and poverty to explain the pathway to violent behaviour. In relation to antisocial, sociopathic and psychopathic personality disorders it has been noted that they tend to have a generalised emotional deficit that prevents them from experiencing empathy, fear, guilt and so on, which normally inhibit the expression of violent impulses (Hart and Hare, 1996). Of the 10 personality disorder categories listed in the *Diagnostic and Statistical Manual*

Table 10.2: Characteristics of antisocial, borderline, narcissistic and paranoid personality disorders associated with risk.

Personality disorder	Diagnostic criteria linked to risk (APA, 1994)	View of self	View of others	Main beliefs	Risk behaviour
Antisocial	*Since age 15* Repeatedly performing antisocial acts/fights Impulsive Reckless Irresponsible as a parent *Under age 15* Irresponsible and antisocial behaviour beginning in childhood Often initiated fights Used a weapon in more than I fight Forced someone to have sex Physically cruel to animals/peopleFire setting Destroyed others' property	Loner Autonomous Strong	Vulnerable Exploitative	Entitled to break rules Others are wimps Others are there to be taken/exploited	Attack Rob Deceive Manipulate
Borderline	*Pervasive pattern from childhood or early adolescence* Impulsiveness Affective instability Irritability Poor anger control Suicidal threats Self injurious behaviour Feelings of emptiness	Uncertain self-image Vulnerable Hopeless Miserable	Treacherous Unreliable Undependable	People who get close to me will abandon me Nobody can be relied upon Future is gloomy Poor self-control	Impulsive acts against self/others Extreme anger Aggression Irritable Frantic efforts to avoid abandonment
Narcissistic	Lack of empathy Rage against criticism Exploitative of others Sense of entitlement	Special Unique Deserve special rules Superior	Inferior Admirers Servants	I'm special I deserve special rules I'm better than others	Use others Coerce Manipulate Competitive Transcend rules
Paranoid	Interprets actions of others as demeaning or threatening Bears grudges Unforgiving Easily slighted and explosive Questions fidelity of partner	Righteous Innocent Noble Vulnerable	Interfering Malicious Discriminatory Hostile	Motives are suspect Be on guard Don't trust If you trust then you'll be sorry	Wary Suspicious Accuse Take pre-emptive action Counterattack

of Mental Disorders (American Psychiatric Association, 1994) Antisocial, Borderline, Narcissistic and Paranoid appear to be more closely linked to risk behaviour. The diagnostic, cognitive
and behavioural characteristics of these personality disorders are illustrated in Table 10.2. These
characteristics may be particularly useful in helping clinicians understand the origin and maintenance of risk behaviour while also providing treatment and management targets. Indeed, some
therapeutic approaches designed to help people with personality disorder attempt to elicit these
characteristics as a means of conceptualising individual's problems and needs before applying
interventions (Beck *et al.*, 1990; Linehan, 1993; Young, 2003).

Violence and personality disorder

Antagonistic and hostile traits are evident in virtually all the personality disorders (Widiger and
Trull, 1994). Very often MHNs will be involved in the care and treatment of people where problems and needs arise due to these personality disorders. Violent behaviour is a defining feature of
two personality disorders: borderline (impulsive) and anti-social personality disorder (American
Psychiatric Association, 1994). There is considerable interest in the relationship between these
particular disorders and violence risk. This is particularly true in light of recent advances in our
understanding of psychopathy, where antisocial and impulsive personality traits (associated with
borderline and antisocial personality disorder), have been found to be highly predictive of future
violence (Hart, 1998).

Psychopathy

The term 'psychopathy' originated in the late nineteenth century and was used to embrace all disorders of personality. In England and Wales the term 'psychopathic disorder' became incorporated
into the Mental Health Act 1959 to replace previous terms 'moral insanity' and 'moral defect'
and was a generic term to cover all types of personality disorder. Personality disorder itself was
defined as a chronic disturbance of emotion or volition, or a disturbance of their integration with
intellectual functions that was distinct from both psychotic and neurotic illness and that resulted
in socially disruptive behaviour (Hart and Dempster, 1997). Psychopathic disorder was retained in
the Mental Health Act 1983. The legal term 'Psychopathic Disorder' was not intended as a single
entity – rather it is a generic term adopted for the purpose of legal categorisation and capable
of covering a number of specific diagnoses (Home Office and Department of Health and Social
Security, 1975). Antisocial and other personality disorders are strongly correlated with the 'clinical' psychopath, as described by Hare (1991); see Table 10.3. Whereas the clinical aspects of the
Hare Psychopath are likely to encapsulate the specific personality traits that are linked to violent
behaviour in other personality and mental disorders, it is important to note that psychopathy is a
specific diagnostic category typified by cognitive, affective and behavioural symptoms. Interpersonally, psychopaths are grandiose, arrogant, callous, superficial and manipulative. Affectively,
they are short-tempered, unable to form strong emotional bonds with others and lacking in guilt or

anxiety. Behaviourally they are irresponsible, impulsive and prone to delinquency and criminality. Given these characteristics it is hardly surprising that the disorder is linked with an increased risk of violence. Often anti-social behaviour can be clearly recognised, although this will probably not indicate that a person has an antisocial personality disorder or suffer from psychopathy. The challenge for clinicians is how to reliably assess and measure such a complex concept. Instruments designed to measure psychopathy have been developed and tested in violence prediction research and some of these will be now be discussed briefly.

Psychopathy Checklist – Revised (PCL-R)

Over the past 20 years much progress has been made in developing a reliable scale to measure psychopathy. The *Hare Psychopathy Checklist* (PCL), *Hare Psychopathy Checklist: Revised* (PCL-R) (Hare, 1991) and more recently the *Psychopathy Checklist: Screening Version* (PCL:SV) (Hart *et al.*, 1995) have been used in past and present research in mentally ill and non-mentally ill populations in an attempt to predict violent behaviour. The PCL was based on global ratings from Cleckley's *Mask of Sanity* checklist and it was developed to provide a more reliable measure of psychopathy. Later the original 22-item PCL symptom construct rating scale was revised to the 20-item PCL-R (Hare, 1991). The 20 PCL-R items are listed in Table 10.3. Each item is scored on a three-point scale: 0 = 'item does not apply'; 1= 'item applies somewhat'; 2 = 'item definitely applies'. Total scores can range from 0–40 and scores of 30 or more are considered diagnostic of psychopathy. Cross-cultural comparisons in North American and European samples have found the underlying core of the disorder essentially the same and there appears to be good cross-cultural generalisability of the construct. However, due to possible suppression/facilitation of psychopathic features, it has been suggested that a cut-off score of greater than 25 on the PCL-R, rather than 30, is more appropriate for European and UK samples (Cooke and Michie, 1999). The PCL-R has a stable internal structure comprising of two oblique factors. Factor 1 reflects 'callous and remorseless use of others', whereas Factor 2 reflects a 'chronically unstable and anti-social lifestyle'. More recently, however, research by Cooke and Michie (2001) revealed that the construct of psychopathy as measured by the PCL-R items was in fact underpinned by three factors: arrogant and deceitful interpersonal style, deficient affective experience, and impulsive and irresponsible behavioural style.

Psychopathy Checklist – Screening Version (PCL:SV)

Researchers and clinicians identified the need for a screening instrument for psychopathy that required less time to administer and score than the PCL-R, which could predict PCL-R diagnosis of psychopathy with a reasonable degree of accuracy. The screening version of the PCL-R was designed with several key requirements in mind. It needed to be conceptually and empirically related to the PCL-R, psychometrically sound, based on a symptom construct scale, sensitive to non-forensic samples and shorter than the PCL-R. The 12 items (Table 10.3) are divided into Part 1 – interpersonal and affective symptoms – and Part 2 – social deviance symptoms – in accordance with Factor 1 and 2 of the 20-item PCL-R. The scale is scored in the same way as the PCL-R. Overall the PCL:SV is conceptually and empirically related to the PCL-R, psychometrically sound, based on a symptom construct scale and sensitive to non-forensic samples.

Validity of the Hare psychopathy scales in predicting violent behaviour

Although the PCL-R was intended as a diagnostic instrument, it continues to receive recognition among clinicians and researchers for its ability to predict violent and non-violent recidivism. Numerous studies using the PCL, PCL-R and PCL:SV have found them highly predictive of future violent behaviour and treatment outcome in criminal, forensic psychiatric and civil psychiatric settings. Dolan and Doyle (2000) reviewed the evidence for the PCL scales as predictors of violence and found that psychopathy significantly predicted criminal and violent recidivism in forensic and psychiatric samples. The impressive predictive validity of psychopathy is reinforced by findings from the largest violence prediction prospective study of its type. The MacArthur Violence Risk Assessment Study (MacVRAS) considered the predictive validity of 134 risk factors for community violence in a civil psychiatric sample in the USA. They found that a score >12 on the PCL: SV was the best predictor of community violence by non-forensic patients in the first 20 weeks, and one year after discharge (Monahan *et al.*, 2000). The impressive research findings to date mean that the PCL scales are being integrated into contemporary risk management programmes designed for personality disordered offenders (e.g. Dangerous & Severe Personality Disorder Programme, 2004).

Violence risk assessment tools

In addition to the PCL scales, various systematic tools have shown promise in improving predictive accuracy in mental health services. Three of these that may be of practical use when assessing violence risk in people with personality disorder will be briefly described (Table 10.3). The *Violence Risk Appraisal Guide* (VRAG: Webster *et al.*, 1994) is a pure actuarial instrument and was developed in a maximum-security facility in Canada. It contains 12 variables, each of which are attributed numerical weight ranging from –5 to +12 (Table 10.3). A score on the PCL-R is included as the highest weighted item. Previous research indicates that the VRAG predicts violent recidivism moderately well (Grann *et al.*, 1999; Rice, 1997; Rice and Harris, 1995). Three item scores require the participant to have committed an index offence to rate and therefore the VRAG may not be appropriate for non-forensic settings. The *Historical Clinical Risk Management 20 Items* (HCR-20: Webster *et al.*, 1997) is a broad-band violence risk assessment instrument with potential applicability to a variety of settings. The conceptual scheme of the HCR-20 aligns risk markers into past, present, and future. Its ten historical factors concern the past. The HCR-20 also contains five clinical items that are meant to reflect current, dynamic (changeable) correlates of violence. The future is recognised in the five risk management items, which focus attention on situational post-assessment factors that may aggravate or mitigate risk. The HCR-20 takes it name from these three scales – Historical, Clinical, Risk Management – and from the number of items,

20 (Table 10.3). The items are scored in a similar manner to the PCL:SV: 0, 1, and 2. Scores range from 0–40. In a review by Dolan and Doyle (2000) the HCR-20 demonstrated significant predictive accuracy in civil and forensic settings and evidence suggests that the HCR-20 demonstrates good predictive validity in North American and European samples. It has also been found to have superior predictive validity relative to the screening version of Hare's psychopathy checklist and it is valid in males and females and in patients diagnosed with schizophrenia and personality disorder. Unlike the PCL scales or the VRAG, the HCR-20 is sensitive to change, as the Clinical and Risk Management items are rated dependent on current functioning and context and can act as a risk barometer. The *Violence Risk Scale* (VRS: Wong and Gordon, 2000) is a scale specifically designed to assess the risk of violent recidivism in forensic patients. The VRS was developed based on the conception that to provide a comprehensive evaluation of an individual's risk for violent recidivism it is necessary to assess both the static and dynamic factors that are empirically or theoretically related to violent recidivism. The VRS-Version 2 consists of six static or historical factors and 20 dynamic or changeable factors (Table 10.3). Each item is rated on a four-point scale, 0–3, against descriptive criteria. It has been used effectively to evaluate the effect of treatment on risk in a violence prevention programme in Canada and the authors report that research to date indicates that the VRS has demonstrated strong predictive validity for violent recidivism over a two-year follow up period. As yet, there is little published data to support the VRS as a valid instrument for violence risk assessment. Its promise lies in its comprehensive evidence-based background, its practical format and its link in measuring treatment impact.

Risk of self-harm and personality disorder

The term *self-harm* is subject to much debate. Behaviour intended to take one's own life and non-lethal self-harming behaviour are not necessarily considered to be the same phenomenon. There is evidence to suggest that they occur in largely different populations, but there is also data to suggest considerable overlap (MacLeod *et al.*, 1992). All categories of mental disorder carry an increased risk of self-harm. Self-mutilation and self-injurious behaviour are very common problems in mental health services. Non-fatal self-harm, the strongest single indicator of future suicide, is also known to occur more frequently among those with mental health problems. Self-harming behaviour is common in people with personality disorder and is one of the main diagnostic features of borderline personality disorder (American Psychiatric Association, 1994). A significant proportion of persons who self-injure are at a greatly increased risk of committing suicide at some later date. Misuse of both drugs and alcohol is common in people with personality disorder and strongly associated with suicidal behaviour. The National Confidential Inquiry into Suicide and Homicide (Department of Health, 2001) showed that 10% of the people who committed suicide who were in contact with mental health services in the 12 months before death had a primary diagnosis of personality disorder. Miles (1977) estimated that 15% of alcohol misusers ultimately kill themselves and most of the rise in young male suicide has been related to higher levels of substance misuse (Needleman and Farrell, 1997).

Table 10.3: Items in violence risk assessment tools

PCL-R (Hare, 1991)	PCL-SV (Hart et al., 1995)	HCR-20 (V2) (Webster et al., 1997)	VRAG (Webster et al., 1994)	Violence Risk Scale (Wong and Gordon, 2000)	
				Static	Dynamic
1 Glibness/ superficial charm (1)	1 Superficial (1)	H1 Previous violence	1 PCL-R score	1. Current Age	1. Violent lifestyle
2 Grandiose sense of self-worth (1)	2 Grandiose (1)	H2 Young age at first violent incident	2 Elementary school maladjustment	2. Age at first violent conviction	2. Criminal personality
3 Need for stimulation/ proneness to boredom (2)	3 Manipulative (1)	H3 Relationship instability	3 DSM-III diagnosis of personality disorder	3. No. of young offender convictions	3. Criminal attitudes
4 Pathological lying (1)	4 Lacks remorse (1)	H4 Employment problems		4. Violence throughout lifespan	4. Work ethic
5 Conning/ manipulative (1)	5 Lacks empathy (1)	H5 Substance misuse problems	4 Age at index offence	5. Prior release failures or escapes	5. Criminal peers
6 Lack of remorse or guilt (1)	6 Does not accept responsibility (1)	H6 Major mental illness	5 Lived with both parents to age 16	6. Stability of family upbringing	6. Interpersonal aggression
7 Shallow affect (1)		H7 Psychopathy (PCL-R/PCL-SV)	6 Failure on prior conditional release		7. Emotional control
8 Callous/lack of sympathy (1)	7 Impulsive (2)	H8 Early maladjustment	7 Non-violent offence score		8. Violence in institution
9 Parasitic lifestyle (2)	8 Poor behaviour controls (2)	H9 Personality disorder	8 Marital status		9. Weapon use
10 Poor behavioural controls (2)	9 Lacks (goals) (2)	H10 Prior supervision failure	9 DSM-III diagnosis of schizophrenia		10. Insight into cause of violence
11 Promiscuous sexual behaviour	10 Irresponsible (2)	C1 Lack of insight			11. Mental disorder
12 Early behavioural problems (2)	11 Adolescent antisocial behaviour (2)	C2 Negative attitudes	10 Victim injury (index offence)		12. Substance use
13 Lack of realistic long-term goals (2)		C3 Active symptoms of major mental illness	11 History of alcohol misuse		13. Stability of relationships
14 Impulsivity (2)	12 Adult antisocial behaviour (2)		12 Female victim (index offence)		14. Community support

Table 10.3: Items in violence risk assessment tools (*continued*)

PCL-R (Hare, 1991)	PCL-SV (Hart et al., 1995)	HCR-20 (V2) (Webster et al., 1997)	VRAG (Webster et al., 1994)	Violence Risk Scale (Wong and Gordon, 2000)	
				Static	Dynamic
15 Irresponsibility (2)		C4 Impulsivity			15. Release to high risk situations
16 Failure to accept responsibility		C5 Unresponsive to treatment			16. Violence cycle
17 Many short-term marital relationships		R1 Plans lack feasibility			17. Impulsivity
18 Juvenile delinquency (2)		R2 Exposure to destabilisers			18. Cognitive distortion
19 Revocation of conditional release (2)		R3 Lack of personal support			19. Compliance with community supervision
20 Criminal versatility		R4 Non-compliance with remediation attempts			20. Security level of institution
		R5 Stress			

PCL-R, Psychopathy Checklist (Revised); PCL-SV, Psychopathy Checklist; Screening Version; HCR-20 (V2), Historical/Clinical/Risk Management 20-item scale, Version 2; VRAG, Violence Risk Appraisal Guide.
1. H1-10 relate to history, C1-5 to clinical and R1-5 to risk.
(1), factor 1 loading; (2), factor 2 loading.

Assessing risk of self-harm

Self-harm is defined by the National Institute for Clinical Excellence (NICE) (2004) as self-poisoning or injury, irrespective of the apparent purpose of the act. In forensic mental health settings, self-harming behaviour may take many forms, including cutting, overdoses, burning, scalding, inserting, hair-pulling, swallowing and other acts. The individual may or may not be aware of either the behaviour or the underlying distress. Yet self-harm is an expression of personal distress, not an illness. Babiker and Arnold (1997) describe it as 'a language that we as helpers are called upon to comprehend in all its meanings'. It is essential that assessment of self-harm risk begins from the understanding that self-harm is a personal, individual act, and that there are many varied reasons for a person to harm him- or herself.

Because self-harm is both a personal act and a multi-factorial behaviour, its assessment must form part of an overall, comprehensive assessment of the person's needs. As such, it is crucial that in addition to accessing all available clinical records and the views of others, the assessment is person-centred, seeking to understand the potential for self-harm from the individual's own perspective. The aim should be to arrive at a clear formulation of self-harm risk that can be shared with the individual if possible and be communicated to others such as carers and relevant professional staff.

A comprehensive assessment will identify both socio-demographic and individual clinical risk factors. In the general population, self-harm is more common in females than males, though the gender ratio has declined in recent years. Self-harm is also more common in areas of socioeconomic deprivation and poor social integration (Hawton, 2004). The most typical problems associated with self-harm are relationship difficulties and mental health disorders, particularly depression, alcohol and drug abuse, anxiety and eating disorders. Self-harm is one of the clinical features linked with a diagnosis of Borderline Personality Disorder. Borderline personality disorder is defined by DSM-IV as 'a pervasive pattern of instability of interpersonal relationships, self-image, and affects, and marked impulsivity that begins by early adulthood and is present in a variety of contexts' as indicated by five or more symptoms including, among others, identity disturbance, impulsivity, recurrent suicidal behaviour, affective instability, inappropriate and intense anger. Borderline personality disorder, like other forms of personality disorder, is usually seen in the literature as caused by a combination of in-born biological traits, psychological factors such as traumatic childhood experiences, and social factors such as the lack of a supportive childhood environment. Repetition is common after self-harm, while there is a high risk of suicide, particularly during the first year.

Van der Kolk et al. (1991) conducted a study of patients who engaged in cutting behaviour and suicidality. They found that exposure to physical or sexual abuse, physical or emotional neglect, and chaotic family conditions during childhood and adolescence were reliable predictors of the amount and severity of cutting. The earlier the abuse began, the more likely the subjects were to cut and the more severe their cutting was. Sexual abuse victims were the most likely of all to cut. According to Linehan (1993), many self-harming people come from 'invalidating' backgrounds, where the expression of private experiences is not validated; instead it is often punished and/or trivialized. The experience of painful emotions is disregarded. The individual's interpretations of her own behaviour, including the experience of the intents and motivations of the behaviour, are dismissed. Self-harming behaviour then becomes a language in which to express distress where more overt expression has been disallowed.

In addition to identifying the risk factors associated with self-harm, it is essential to seek to clarify the meaning of self-harming behaviour for the individual person. Haines et al. (1995) found that reduction of psychophysiological tension may be the primary purpose of self-injury such as cutting. It is possible that when a particular degree of physiological calm is reached, the person no longer feels an urgent need to inflict harm on his or her body. It is also possible that the person who self-injures is attempting to mediate levels of sensory arousal. Self-injury, such as cutting, can increase or decrease sensory arousal by masking sensory input. In some ways this can be even more distressing than the self-harm. Behavioural explanations of self-harm include the view that individuals who self-injure are positively reinforced by getting attention and thus tend to repeat the self-harming acts. The sensory stimulation associated with self-harm could serve as a positive reinforcer and thus a stimulus for further self-harm. Another behavioural explanation is that self-harm is a way to escape otherwise intolerable emotional pain. Only by engaging with the person as an individual can the meaning of self-harming behaviour for them be explored and understood. Cooper and Kapur (2004), discussing the assessment of the suicidal person, note that skills of the interviewer should include a number of interpersonal and observational competencies (Table 10.4). By employing such interpersonal skills, trust and rapport can be promoted and the person will be encouraged to confide more detailed information. Further, such an approach can

Table 10.4: Interpersonal skills and important issues to consider when assessing risk of self-harm.

Interpersonal skills	Important issues
■ Adopt an appropriate manner (genuine, warm, respectful, professional) ■ Demonstrating empathy (acknowledging feelings and problems) ■ Observation ■ Clarifying, reflecting, summarising ■ Probing (feeling and events) ■ Asking clear concise questions (avoid directive and double questions) *(Cooper and Kapur, 2004)*	■ Has the individual attempted suicide in the past? ■ Do voices command the individual to harm himself or herself? (What exactly are the voices saying?) ■ Is the individual unable to resist the commands at present? ■ Is it likely that the individual will continue to be unable to resist the commands? ■ Is the individual extremely depressed or expressing suicidal ideation? ■ Was the individual recently diagnosed or recently discharged from hospital? ■ Does the individual live alone or unsupervised? ■ Is the individual also using illegal drugs? ■ Does the individual have a plan of action? ■ Does the individual have the skills or weapons to carry out this plan? ■ Is there evidence of impulsive behaviour? *(National Electronic Library for Mental Health)*

foster the development of a therapeutic alliance that can become the basis for an effective plan of care and treatment. In addition, the *National Electronic Library for Mental Health* provides a list of key issues to be addressed within the context of an assessment interview (Table 10.4). By addressing these key issues, the interviewer will be in a position to gauge the likelihood of self-harming behaviour and also its potential form and severity, bearing in mind that around half of people who end their own lives have a previous history of self-harm and are at high lifetime risk of suicide. Services need to develop appropriate training for staff working with people who self-harm and this should be informed by service users and promote positive attitudes amongst staff (National Institute for Clinical Excellence, 2004). Mental health nurses need to ensure that they have regular training in risk assessment/management and there is a need for clinical audit to ensure good standards of risk assessment and translation of assessments into care plans.

Systematic approach to assessing, formulating and managing risk in clinical practice

The stages of clinical risk assessment and management may be conceptualised as an ongoing process. This process has been described as a Risk Management Cycle (Doyle, 1998) and is usually implicit to the provision of good quality health care and integrated into the Care Programme Approach. The basis of the any assessment relies on the accumulation of reliable information and consideration of risk factors. The debate as to whether the clinical, 'subjective', or actuarial – 'statistical/objective' – approach is most relevant to clinical practice is complex and beyond the scope of this chapter (see Buchanan, 1999, for discussion). The reality of clinical practice is that tests and scales can help to inform clinical judgement, not replace it, as ultimately it is people, not tests, who make decisions. There is evidence to suggest that a combination of the clinical and actuarial approach is warranted to structure clinicians' risk judgements and this may be superior to unaided clinical judgement (Borum, 1996; Douglas *et al.*, 1999; McNiel and Binder, 1994). The Structured Professional Approach attempts to bridge the gap between the scientific (actuarial) approach and the clinical practice of risk assessment. This approach emphasises the need to take account of past history, objective measures, current presentation, context/environment and protective factors; and recognises the reality that the process of clinical risk assessment is a dynamic and continuous process which is mediated by changing conditions (see Doyle, 2000; Dolan and Doyle, 2000).

A number of instruments (see Table 10.3) and systematic approaches have been developed to facilitate a Structured Professional approach to Risk Management in clinical mental health services (for example Hart *et al.*, 2003). Recently, Doyle (2004) proposed a sequential five-step approach to risk management in mental health services (Table 10.5) designed to (1) structure professional risk judgements and foster an evidence-based approach; (2) enhance understanding of origins, development and maintenance of risk behaviour; (3) involve the person being assessed; (4) identify targets for intervention; and (5) facilitate defensible decision making and positive risk taking.

The first step is concerned with accumulating information about the individual, being mindful of the need for multiple assessment methods and the use of different sources of information. *Step 2* involves identifying historical and current risk factors relating to the outcome of concern, e.g. self-harm and violence. *Step 3* supplements step 2 by identifying past and present protective factors associated with a decreased risk. Protective factors could include compliance with treatment, good support from friends, family and services or restrictions on movements. *Step 4* is the stage where the risk information already collected in steps 1–3 is analysed in an attempt to gain a

---

Table 10.5: Five-step Structured Professional Approach to risk management

Step 1: Case information

History, Mental State, Substance Use

Step 2: Presence of risk factors

Historical, Current, Contextual

Step 3: Presence of protective factors

Historical, Current, Contextual

Step 4: Risk formulation

Nature, Severity, Imminence, Likelihood, Risk Reducing/Enhancing

Step 5: Management plan

Treatment, Management, Monitoring, Supervision, Victim Safety Planning

---

better understanding and formulation of the person's current risk. This stage resembles attempts to conceptualise risk behaviours for treatment purposes (for example Novaco, 1994; Linehan, 1993). Recently, Huessman (1998) developed a unified social information processing model which similarly linked events, schemas and emotional states to provide an information processing framework which explained the role of cognition in aggression. An idiosyncratic, personalised risk formulation should inform *Step 5*, where management interventions are developed into a risk management plan. The five-step approach is meant to be broad in its applicability to different service settings. The approach is practice-based in that it attempts to both reflect existing clinical practice while enhancing the utility of a structured evidence-based approach to risk management.

Summary

Assessing and managing risk to self and others has long been a key task for clinicians working in mental health services. Despite the association between some personality disorders and violence to others, people with personality disorder who come into contact with services usually have a multiplicity of problems that may also place them at risk to themselves. As a strong association exists between personality disorders and risk, it is important that mental health nurses have a clear structured approach to risk assessment and management when working with people with personality disorder. Understanding the link between personality disorder, risk to self and violence to others is crucial for successful assessment and management of risk. The interaction between the characteristics of personality disorder and risk behaviour is important when trying to gain an understanding of the origins and maintenance of risk behaviour. Evidence-based tools and systematic approaches need to be considered to help structure professional risk judements. A five-step approach to aid clinical risk management is proposed. This approach should assist MHNs in structuring informed judgements about this complex and often difficult client group.

References

American Psychiatric Association (1994) *Diagnostic and Statistical Manual of Mental Disorders*, 4th edn (DSM-IV). American Psychiatric Association, Washington.

Babiker, G. and Arnold, L. (1997) *The Language of Injury*. Blackwell, London.

Beck, A. T., Freeman, A. and Associates (1990) *Cognitive Therapy of Personality Disorders*. Guilford Press, New York.

Borum, R. (1996) Improving the clinical practice of violence risk assessment. *American Psychologist*, **51**(9), 945–956.

Buchanan, A. (1999) Risk and dangerousness. *Psychological Medicine*, **29**(2), 465–473.

Cooke, D. J. and Michie, C. (2001) Refining the construct of psychopathy: Towards a hierarchical model. *Psychological Assessment*, **13**(2), 171–188.

Cooke, D. J. and Michie, C. (1999) Psychopathy across cultures: North America and Scotland compared. *Journal of Abnormal Psychology*, **108**, 58–68.

Cooper, J. and Kapur, N. (2004) Assessing suicide risk. In: Duffy, D. and Ryan, T. (eds.) *New Approaches to Preventing Suicide*, pp. 20–38. Jessica Kingsley, London.

Department of Health (2001) *Safety First: Five-Year Report of the National Confidential Inquiry into Suicide and Homicide by People with Mental Illness*. Department of Health, London.

Dolan, M. and Doyle, M. (2000) Violence risk prediction: clinical and actuarial measures and the role of the psychopathy checklist. *British Journal of Psychiatry*, **177**, 303–311.

Douglas, K., Cox, D. and Webster, C. (1999) Violence risk assessment: science and practice. *Legal and Criminological Psychology*, **4**, 149–184.

Doyle, M. (1998) Clinical risk assessment for mental health nurses. *Nursing Times*, **94**(17), 47–49.

Doyle, M. (2000) Risk assessment and management. In: Chaloner, C. and Coffey, M. (eds.) *Forensic Mental Health Nursing: Current Approaches*, pp. 140–170. Blackwell Science, London.

Doyle, M. (2004) *Systematic Approaches to Assessing, Formulating and Managing Risk*. Keynote Paper Presented at Annual NW Forensic Network Conference: 'Seeing Red: Current Perspectives on Violence'. Lowry Centre, Salford Quays, 25 November.

Dangerous & Severe Personality Disorder Programme (2004) *Dangerous and Severe Personality Disorder (DSPD) High Secure Services. Planning & Delivery Guide*. Home Office, London.

Gallagher, J. (1999) *Violent Times: TUC Report on Preventing Violence at Work*. Trade Union Congress Health and Safety Unit, London.

Grann, M., Langstrom, N., Tengstrom, A. and Kullgren, G. (1999) Psychopathy (PCL-R) predicts violent recidivism among criminal offenders with personality disorders in Sweden. *Law and Human Behavior*, **23**(2), 205–217.

Haines, J., Williams, C. L., Brain, K. L. and Wilson, G. V. (1995) The psychobiology of self-mutilation. *Journal of Abnormal Psychology*, **104**(3), 471–489.

Hare, R. D. (1991) *The Hare Psychopathy Checklist-Revised*. Multi-Health Systems, Toronto.

Harris, G. and Rice, M. (1997) Risk appraisal and management of violent behaviour. *Psychiatric Services*, **48**(9), 1168–1176.

Hart, S. D. (1998) The role of psychopathy in assessing risk for violence: conceptual and methodological issues. *Legal and Criminological Psychology*, **3**, 121–137.

Hart, S. D. and Dempster, R. J. (1997) Impulsivity and psychopathy. In: Webster, C. D. and Jackson, M. A. (eds.) *Impulsivity, Theory, Assessment and Treatment*, pp. 212–232. Guilford Press, New York.

Hart, S. and Hare R. (1996) Psychopathy and risk assessment. *Current Opinion in Psychiatry*, **9**, 380–383.

Hart, S. D., Kropp, R., Klaver, J., Logan, C. and Watt, K. (2003) *The Risk for Sexual Violence Protocol (RSVP)*. Pacific Psychological Assessment Corporation, Canada.

Hart, S., Cox, D. and Hare, R. (1995) *The Hare PCL: SV: Psychopathy Checklist: Screening Version*. Multi-Health Systems Incorporated, New York.

Hawton, K. (2004) Deliberate self-harm. *Medicine*, **32**(8), 38–41.

Hiday, V. (1997) Understanding the connection between mental illness and violence. *International Journal of Law and Psychiatry*, **20**(4), 399–417.

Home Office and Department of Health and Social Security (1975) *Report of the Committee on Mentally Abnormal Offenders (Butler Report)*. HMSO, London.

Huessmann, L. R. (1998) The role of social information processing and cognitive schema in the acquisition and maintenance of habitual aggressive behavior. In: Geen, R. and Donnerstein, E. (eds.) *Human Aggression: Theories, Research and Implications for Social Policy*. Academic Press, London.

Linehan, M. M. (1993) *Cognitive Behavioural Treatment of Borderline Personality Disorder*. Guilford Press, New York.

Litwack, T. R. and Schlesinger, L. B. (1987) Assessing and predicting violence: research, law and applications. In: Weiner, I. B. and Hess, A. K. (eds.) *Handbook of Forensic Psychology*, pp. 205–257. Wiley, New York.

MacLeod, A., Williams, J. and Linehan, M. (1992) New developments in the understanding and treatment of suicidal behaviour. *Behavioural Psychotherapy*, **20**, 193–218.

McNiel, D. E. and Binder, R. L. (1994) Screening for risk of inpatient violence. *Law and Human Behavior*, **18**, 579–586.

Miles, C. (1977) Conditions predisposing to suicide: a review. *Journal of Nervous and Mental Disease*, **164**, 231–246.

Monahan, J. (1992) Mental disorder and violent behaviour: perceptions and evidence. *American Psychologist*, **47**, 511–521.

Monahan, J., Steadman, H. J., Appelbaum, P. S., Robbins, P. C., Mulvey, E. P., Silver, E., Roth, L. H. and Grisso, T. (2000) Developing a clinically useful actuarial tool for assessing violence risk. *British Journal of Psychiatry*, **176**, 312–319.

National Institute for Clinical Excellence (2004) *Clinical Guideline: Self-Harm*. National Institute for Clinical Excellence, London.

National Institute for Mental Health in England (2003) *Personality Disorder Capabilities Framework: Breaking the Cycle of Rejection*. NHS, 15 November. (Available on http://www.nimhe.org/uk/)

NHS Executive (1999) *Campaign to Stop Violence Against Staff Working in the NHS*. Press Release 1999/0615.

Novaco, R. (1994) Anger as a risk factor for violence among the mentally disordered. In: Monahan, J. and Steadman, H. (eds.) *Violence and Mental Disorder: Development in Risk Assessment*, pp. 21–59. University of Chicago Press, USA.

Rice, M. (1997) Violent offender research and implications for the criminal justice system. *American Psychologist*, **52**, 414–423.

Rice, M. E. and Harris, G. T. (1995) Violent recidivism: assessing predictive validity. *Journal of Consulting and Clinical Psychology*, **53**, 737–748.

Singleton, N., Meltzer, H., Gatward, R., Coid, J. and Deasy, D. (1998) *Psychiatric Morbidity Amongst Prisoners*. Office of National Statistics, London.

Swanson, J., Holzer, C., Ganju, V. and Jono, R. (1990) Violence and psychiatric disorder in the community: evidence from the Epidemiological Catchment Area Surveys. *Hospital and Community Psychiatry*, **41**, 761–770.

United Kingdom Central Council for Nursing Midwifery & Health Visiting (2001) *The Recognition, Prevention and Therapeutic Management of Violence in Mental Health Care*. Health Services Research Department, Institute of Psychiatry, London.

Van der Kolk, B. A., Perry, C. and Herman, J. L. (1991) Childhood origins of self-destructive behavior. *American Journal of Psychiatry*, **148**, 1665–1671.

Webster, C., Harris, G., Rice, M., Cormier, C. and Quinsey, V. (1994) *Violence Prediction Scheme: Assessing Dangerousness in High Risk Men*. Centre of Criminology, University of Toronto.

Webster, C. D., Douglas, K., Eaves, D. and Hart, S. (1997) *HCR-20: Assessing Risk for Violence – Version 2*. Simon Fraser University, British Columbia.

Widiger, T. A. and Trull, T. J. (1994) Personality disorders and violence. In: Monahan, J. and Steadman, H. (eds.) *Violence and Mental Disorder: Developments in Risk Assessment*, pp. 203–226. University of Chicago Press, Chicago.

Wong, S. and Gordon, A. (2000) *Violence Reduction Programme: Phases of Treatment and Content Overview*. Regional Psychiatric Centre, Saskatoon, Saskatchewan.

Young, J. E. (2003) *Cognitive Therapy for Personality Disorders: A Schema-Focused Approach*. Professional Resources Press, Sarasota.

CHAPTER 11

The assessment of security need

Mick Collins, Steffan Davies and Chris Ashwell

Introduction

This chapter is not about a specific nursing intervention; instead it provides a detailed description of the multidimensional aspects of patient security needs and methods of assessing these. Providing appropriate security for patients with a personality disorder can be a challenging and complex task requiring considerable experience and skill. If the security needs of patients are met appropriately then other individualised nursing interventions can flourish, if they are not met the maintenance of a safe environment can become an overriding concern, to the detriment of treatment. When we refer to security we are considering those patients with a personality disorder who are subject to detention in secure settings, in the UK described as low, medium and high security. We therefore make numerous references to offending behaviour; this is not meant to imply that all people suffering from a personality disorder are either offenders or that they need to be detained (see Department of Health (2003) for a description of the wide range of issues). Some of the concepts we cover are also relevant to open and community settings, but, for the purposes of this chapter, we concentrate on secure settings.

The relationship between the various clinical constructs of personality disorder and the Mental Health Act (1983) legal classification of psychopathic disorder can cause confusion. Many patients with a personality disorder will be detained under the legal classification of psychopathic disorder within secure settings, but some may be detained with a mental illness or mental impairment classification also. The utility of the legal classification is subject to much debate, as is the clinical construct of the 'psychopath' (for a fuller discussion see Dolan and Coid, 1993). However, some clinical studies have found that this legal classification does have certain discriminant properties. For example in a study of patients detained in secure services, McCartney *et al.* (2001) found that patients classified with psychopathic disorder scored more highly on scales of Dominance, Coercion, Nurturance and Gregariousness when using the CIRCLE (Chart of Interpersonal Reactions in Closed Living Environments) (Blackburn and Renwick, 1996). Further complication arises from proposals for Dangerous and Severe Personality Disorder in the UK (Department of Health and Home Office, 2000).

It is impossible to make generalisations about the range of clinical presentations that 'personality disorder' covers, or issues of co-morbidity. Issues of diagnosis and classification are discussed more fully in Chapter 2. This chapter describes the background to secure services in the UK, definitional constructs and a framework for assessing and managing security needs of patients with a personality disorder. Given the wide range of clinical presentations of personality disorder, this framework can be applied and varied depending on the individual needs of the patient no matter the level of complexity they present. This system is applicable to the whole range of clinical diagnoses encountered within secure services.

Background to secure provision in the UK

Patients with a personality disorder are detained and treated under differing levels of security. If a patient requires care under conditions of security, the purpose of security is to provide a level of risk management and physical containment commensurate with the risks the patient poses. UK secure services are traditionally categorised as high, medium and low, yet widely accepted and detailed definitions of these services, outside of high security, are lacking. Describing a patient as needing 'medium security', for example, may not reflect the complexity of differing security needs. Furthermore, there can be considerable variation in security provision between units that provide the same theoretical level of security; for example, differing fence height and construction type across medium secure units in England. This is changing – for example, there has been standardisation of the security provided by the English High Security Hospitals following a recent review of security (Tilt, 2000). Low secure environments may also become more uniform following recent Department of Health (2002) guidance. The lack of any widely accepted definitions of security provision or ability to provide a reliable fine-grained assessment of security need exacerbates problems of inappropriate patient placement (other factors like bed availability must also be considered). It is within the secure environment that therapeutic interventions are delivered, and inappropriate placement can in itself be a barrier to the effectiveness of such interventions and progress.

There is a history in the UK of patients being detained under conditions of security greater than is necessary, most notably in high security. Various studies have highlighted these problems (for example, Bartlett *et al.*, 1996; Pierzchniak *et al.*, 1999). In response to such studies and government policy there have been reductions in patient numbers detained in high security. The phenomenon of 'creaming off' is described by Abbott (2002), whereby reductions in the high-security hospitals over the last 10 years may be a result of the least complex cases being dealt with first. A result of this is that the high-security hospitals may now be left with smaller numbers of patients, but these will represent more complex clinical presentations. This is probably a feature of all secure services and a significant proportion of these complex cases will be represented by patients with a personality disorder. This makes the notion of detailed attention to security needs even more important. To further add to the complexity there is an acknowledged group of patients who require different services than are currently sufficiently available, long-term medium security being one example. Getting aspects of security right for this group of patients will be equally important, and once again a significant proportion of this group will be patients with a personality disorder.

UK national policy aims for the detention of patients under conditions of security proportionate to the risk that they present. Emphasis was placed upon this in the NHS National Service Framework for Mental Health (Department of Health, 1999, 2004). Part II of the White Paper Reforming the Mental Health Act 1983 (Department of Health and Home Office, 2000) states: 'Where individuals are detained as a result of their mental disorder, they must be held in a therapeutic environment which is designed to address their needs effectively' (paragraph 6.23). The Mental Health (Care and Treatment) (Scotland) Act (2003) gives patients a right to appeal to be transferred to conditions of lower security.

Security

In the UK nursing staff predominantly provide and administer security, as well as individualised programmes of treatment. The difficulty of this task is easily underestimated.

Parker (1985) identified four factors of security: physical security; quality of nursing care; the control of patients; and patient motivation. Later, into the 1990s, some of the first extended policy definitions for high security were described by Kinsley (1992). This was in terms of the importance of a combination of good basic physical security and related systems to enable the provision of more relaxed regimes and appropriate progress through different levels of security restriction. The idea of security and therapy as complementary rather than adversarial factors has continued to expand, and there is a growing forensic nursing literature that describes these issues and deals with the complexities (e.g. Burrow, 1994; Collins, 1999; Woods *et al.*, 2002). Security has become to be regarded as having a theoretical separation into three domains (see for example, Kinsley, 1998).

Physical

Most people are familiar with the physical aspects of security; indeed it is probably where differences between services can be most easily identified (varying heights of fence or types of locks for example). The physical elements are the most obvious aspect of security. These can include: perimeter fences of differing height and construction materials; electronic intrusion alarms; locks (including electronic locking mechanisms); doors; and CCTV cameras.

Procedural

This domain encompasses the wide range of procedures that are practised within the boundaries of the physical elements to prevent breaches of security and minimise risk of harm to others. Examples include: the restriction of certain potentially dangerous items within a secure unit; proactive and reactive searching of patients and the physical environment; frequency of patient observation; staff to patient ratio; and supervision/restriction of visitors. It is here that we can begin to highlight the complexity of the nursing task, involving nurses in what can be intrusive procedures whilst concurrently building/maintaining a therapeutic relationship that will allow more traditional nursing interventions.

Relational

Chapter 2 has described the wide range of clinical features associated with personality disorder. Examples may include patients who are extremely vulnerable to exploitation and harm from others (e.g. dependent personality disorders), impulsive and unpredictable (e.g. emotionally unstable personality disorder) or, at the opposite end of the spectrum, patients who may present a high risk of harm to others (e.g. antisocial personality disorder). All patient groups may exhibit a range of offending behaviours and require high levels of relational nursing skills. The idea of relational security is more complex than physical and procedural security.

At its heart lies the building and maintenance of a therapeutic relationship between the clinician and patient. This is an in-depth understanding of patients receiving secure care and a comprehensive knowledge of individual patient management strategies. An experienced forensic nurse (indeed any nurse) will have an extensive knowledge of a patient under their care. However, within the security context this will include knowledge of potential risk behaviours and a nurse/patient relationship that openly acknowledges these behaviours and their potential for harm. This relational knowledge allows the nurse to constantly assess behavioural presentations and changes in mental state that have a direct relationship to breaches of security or harm. As an additional security element the forensic nurse will also be aware of similarities in behaviour to any offending history. For example, a patient with a history of sexual offending may have exhibited a pattern of subtle and progressive 'grooming' of potential and actual victims.

To be aware of this kind of behaviour within the secure environment requires considerable relational skill. Such behaviour unchecked or unobserved is potentially very dangerous, and a threat to the security of individuals, but when noted and addressed safely can become part of a therapeutic interventional package. Interventional strategies will be tailored towards addressing the behaviour, but also procedural security may need to alter, in addition to any physical security elements to minimise harm. Most of these judgements will be made initially by the nurse.

When examining the 'vulnerable' end of the spectrum similar levels of relational skill will be required to observe for and manage behaviours that may place the patient at risk: for example, impulsivity or manipulation from others (such behaviours may have led to previous offences). This demonstrates both the therapeutic and clinically effective importance of appropriate security. Relational skills such as these can contribute to care delivery in an environment where levels of restriction and supervision can vary (where practicable) according to the needs of the patient while maintaining the protection of others. This helps to prevent blanket approaches to security. A feature of such approaches is that security is applied according to the worst-case scenario despite any number of individuals who may not need such high levels. Groups of staff who care exclusively for patients with a personality disorder will often have extensive specialist training and be in receipt of rigorous programmes of clinical supervision.

These three domains are sometimes referred to collectively as therapeutic security (therapeutic in the sense that the domains are tailored as far as is practical to the individual patient's need). It would of course be unrealistic to suggest that certain elements would be free to vary. For example, the perimeter fence of a secure unit could hardly be varied to suit differing needs, but certain elements of security within the perimeter can quite realistically be varied for individual patients. This theoretical separation can only be regarded as just that – theoretical – because good secure care will involve a combination of all three domains. It is, however, useful to make theoretical distinctions for both illustrative and assessment purposes.

The assessment challenge

As we have described, conventional concepts of security can often be restricted to those elements which are more easily definable, perimeter fences being one example. In addition, the familiar terms such as low, medium and high security lack finer definition. Over a decade ago Reed (1994) called for 'a patient focused definition of what high security connotes' (p. 21). This is equally, if not more, relevant to other levels of security.

When a patient with a personality disorder is described as needing 'medium security', what is actually meant by 'medium security'? Perimeter fence type and staffing ratios may be relatively easy to define, but other elements are more difficult to quantify. Assessing security need is complex, yet the part that such assessment has to play in the overall nursing intervention package cannot be underestimated. Maden *et al.* (1993) described how the security needs of most patients had more of a relationship with nursing care and the internal hospital environment, as opposed to the perimeter fence. Of course, security is only one aspect of a patient's needs within secure services, but we would argue that providing appropriate security is a prerequisite to the successful care, management and treatment of patients with a personality disorder. If we are able to describe fine-grained differences, particularly in procedural and relational security needs, then this offers greater scope for differentiating between regimes (for example between low and medium security), a consequence of which will be more appropriate patient placement.

Issues of definition in studies have long been identified as problematic. Williams *et al.* (1999) in a review of academic literature described how 'few of the studies define 'high' or 'medium' security, or differentiate between physical and observational security measures' (p. 307). Researchers in the field of forensic psychiatry have begun to develop measures that address security needs. Shaw *et al.* (2001) developed a measure of the security, dependency and treatment needs of patients (SDTP). Coid and Kahtan (2000) developed a measure designed for use within medium security. They describe the need for accurate definitions of security need and a lack of agreement on definitions and methods currently available to allocate patients to the correct levels of security.

The fine-grained assessment of security need is underdeveloped when compared to more traditional measures of need, dependency and risk. It is worth comparing dependency and security, as there is some overlap between them. Taking nursing supervision as an example, if we consider a patient requiring extensive help with self care, the patient would be described as dependent. However, if supervision is provided as part of a security management package, for example the management and treatment of some of the 'risky' behaviours exhibited by those with a diagnosis of antisocial personality disorder, then this could more accurately be categorised as a security need. Nursing staff are usually responsible for 24-hour direct care, and the staffing ratio in a unit is regarded as an important security measure. However, numbers alone are no guarantee of appropriate security. Poorly trained and unfamiliar staff can compound security problems rather than resolve them (for example, Fallon, 1999). It is important here that we return to the concept of relational security. Experienced staff with high levels of relational skill will be able to provide appropriate care for difficult behaviours associated with personality disorder (for example, manipulation and splitting of a staff team). However, the term 'personality disorder' (and other terms such as 'psychopath') can conjure up fearful images for unfamiliar staff and lead to a tendency to opt for more restrictive approaches than may be necessary which will ultimately interfere with programs of nursing and other professional care. Rigorous risk management strategies will be entirely appropriate at times. but should always be related to the skills of the care team.

The Security Needs Assessment Profile

The Security Needs Assessment Profile (S.N.A.P.) was developed by Collins and Davies as part of a larger study (Davies *et al.*, 2001). An awareness of the detailed nature of security practice offered by direct carers, and in particular nursing interventions, guided much of the original thinking behind the instrument structure. The instrument items were initially derived from the perspective of high security as this was where the most extensive range of security needs, and the systems in place to meet them existed. Twenty-two security items were formulated after extensive consultation with multidisciplinary colleagues. Each of the 22 items was categorized into physical, procedural or relational security (see Box 11.1).

Following further consultation with colleagues in medium, low and open forensic services, the criteria were carefully defined and an ordinal scale of zero to three developed. Zero represented the absence of security need and three represented the highest level. Whilst these broadly correspond to the traditional nomenclature of open, low, medium and high security, they do not relate directly to current levels of security for each item. It may seem unusual to include an 'open' option in an assessment that is related to security; however, the logic for the inclusion is that patients in secure services should progress through levels of security until they return to the community (although they may still require supervision there). Also, the absence of need indicated by a zero score is important because not all patients being assessed will have an identified need in each of the 22 items. Each ordinal level was criterion-referenced. This involves attaching a detailed description to each ordinal scalar item and potentially improves inter-rater reliability. It offers marked advantages over other scale types that avoid detailed definition of scalar items. This approach to measurement in forensic psychiatry has established validity (e.g. The Behavioural Status Index, Reed and Woods, 2000). See Box 11.2 for an example of a S.N.A.P. item and its ordinal rating scale.

The S.N.A.P. has been subject to extensive studies and validation (see for example, Collins and Davies, 2005). In studies using S.N.A.P. we found that it helped discriminate between different levels of security and also showed good levels of agreement between raters (when two clinicians rated the same patient). Detailed analysis of the instrument showed an underlying factor structure distinct from our theoretical categorisations into physical, procedural and relational. This makes

Box 11.1: Security Needs Assessment Profile items.

Domain 1 – Physical security items

1. **Perimeter**: A perimeter of some type represents one of the primary physical security measures. Perimeter fences or walls vary in height and type depending on security level.

2. **Internal**: Internal building quality and general layout vary according to security level and need. Examples include the resilience of doors, and windows to breakage.

3. **Entry**: Control over what comes in and out of the secure area. For example, limited numbers of entry and exit points with facilities to scrutinise both people and goods.

4. **Facilities**: Varying ranges of on-site recreational, occupational and treatment facilities exist, largely dependent on unit size, to minimise the need for patients to leave the secure area.

Domain 2 – Procedural security items

5. **Patient supervision**: Varying levels of regular patient supervision such as checking location hourly.

6. **Treatment environment**: Certain diagnostic profiles may require specialist treatment environments, gender, diagnosis and staff skills, for example a female personality disorder service.

7. **Searching**: A range of reactive and routine search procedures to control access to prohibited or dangerous items.

8. **Access to potential weapons and fire setting materials**: Restriction of access to obvious and potential weapons, sources of ignition and items which may be used to breach security.

9. **Internal movement**: Movement of patients within a secure perimeter may be subject to various restriction or escorting requirements.

10. **Leave**: Restrictive or flexible leave arrangements, from multiple escorts to unescorted leave.

11. **External communications**: Differing requirements for the monitoring of phone calls or postal communication.

12. **Visitors**: Flexible or highly supervised visiting arrangements which may include prior visitor approval or refusal of certain individuals.

13. **Visiting children**: Varying levels of restriction, supervision or prohibition of visiting children.

14. **Media exposure**: Systems of varying sophistication to detect and manage media interest in individual patients.

15. **Detecting illicit or restricted substances**: A range of measures to detect these substances.

16. **Access to alcohol**: Measures for controlling, supervising or preventing access.

17. **Access to pornographic materials**: Measures for controlling, supervising or preventing access. Also monitoring for sources other than those which are obvious.

18. **Access to information technology**: Restriction or supervision of access, particularly to the internet, internal networks and external media.

> **Domain 3 – Relational skills items**
>
> 19. **Management of violence and aggression**: Varying levels of specialist training and staff ability to manage and prevent incidents; from verbal de-escalation to use of protective equipment.
> 20. **Relational skills**: Different levels of sophisticated training related to the effect of behaviours on security and the safety of others and detailed application to individual patients.
> 21. **Response to nursing interventions and treatment**: Active avoidance and attempts to subvert programmes of treatment have serious implications for other security items.
> 22. **Security intelligence**: Certain patients may require sophisticated and long-term security intelligence/liaison around risk factors, potential victims, and criminal associates.

clinical sense; as we stated earlier, it is a combination of items from the three theoretical domains that will produce the most appropriate management strategy for a patient. The three emerging factors were:

1. **Internal management and protection of others**: this contained items related to the management of the patient within the secure environment and strategies in place to maximise the protection of others from possible harm; for example, appropriate levels of patient supervision.
2. **Management of external influence**: this contained items strongly related to controlling external influence that may increase security risk or risk of harm either to those within or outside of the secure environment; for example, appropriate monitoring of visitors.
3. **Notoriety**: this contained items related to media interest and security intelligence, distinctly separate from the other instrument items but nevertheless very important in any security management strategy.

> ## Box 11.2: Example of the ordinal criteria.
>
> Criterion references for item 6, when considering the needs of the patient in terms of the most appropriate treatment environment.
>
> 3: Single sex patient and specialist treatment groups (for example personality disorder). All members of staff with patient contact have received specialist or specific skills training in the care and management of the particular patient group.
> 2: Single sex patient, some restrictions on the necessity for specialist treatment groups. Some members of staff with patient contact have received specialist or specific skills training in the care and management of the particular patient group.
> 1: Some areas may be of mixed gender with greater flexibility on mixing different treatment groups.
> 0: No restrictions.

Case example using the Security Needs Assessment Profile

We provide a brief working example using the Security Needs Assessment Profile. The patient vignette presented is fictitious but draws on the clinical experience of the authors.

Mr A is a young man transferred from prison to a secure unit. He had been on remand following a serious assault on a fellow resident in the hostel he lived at. The hostel staff had often suspected Mr A of encouraging the other man to accompany him on drinking sessions and exploiting him financially. They also suspected him of encouraging other residents to obtain drugs for him. The assault arose from an argument when the victim refused to give Mr A money. Mr A's admission was due to him describing psychotic symptoms, which may have been drug induced, and the possibility of a personality disorder was recognised at the initial assessment. The admission ward caters for a variety of diagnostic groups (mainly mental illness), and all the patients are male. Following admission (his first to secure care) Mr A was pleasant and cooperated with all assessments. His psychotic symptoms resolved quickly without drug treatment. He acknowledged problems with anger and associated acts of physical aggression, telling staff he was too impulsive and didn't like being told what to do. He also admitted to needing to 'grow up' and that this admission would give him a chance to 'get his life in order'. Mr A participated in all treatment offered, including an anger management programme delivered by specialist nurses. Progress seemed good, with nursing staff reporting him exerting more self-control in situations where he was clearly angry and where he felt he would previously have lost control. The high level of supervision associated with new admissions was quickly relaxed due to his cooperation with treatment and general demeanour. He had also formed a close relationship with two other patients and seemed to have a particularly good rapport with a student nurse.

The first indication of any problems was when the student approached the ward manager and described how Mr A had spent a great deal of time offering praise and asking small favours that had been very difficult to refuse (opening the ward kitchen at non-designated times, letting him phone a friend). An elderly patient approached staff complaining that Mr A was regularly pressurising him into giving away his cigarettes. Ward staff noted that Mr A's behaviour had changed, in that he appeared distracted and less cooperative. Two days later Mr A assaulted the elderly patient after an argument over cigarettes. Mr A required restraint and a short period of seclusion. A drug screen revealed that Mr A had been taking cannabis. A room search found cannabis and property belonging to other patients. It was suspected that the cannabis had been brought into the unit by a friend of Mr A (following the phone call he persuaded the student nurse to let him make). A number of less able patients also complained of him exploiting them.

There are a number of factors to consider if Mr A is to remain within the mental health system. We do not have the space to provide full details of an assessment using the Security Needs Assessment Profile, but will concentrate on illustrative items from each domain.

Within physical security, consideration will be required in relation to item 3 (entry) to prevent drugs being brought into the unit. Relevant procedural items include monitoring external communications and visiting (items 11 and 12), again due to drugs being brought in for Mr A. Searching (item 7) will also need to be enhanced: regular room searches might have detected drugs and other patients' property at an earlier stage. Serious consideration needs to be given to item 6 (treatment environment); whilst Mr A seems to be benefiting from aspects of treatment, his exploitation of more vulnerable mentally ill patients and manipulation of the student nurse indicate that he would be better managed in a specialist personality disorder service. The patient group will be less vulnerable and staff skilled at avoiding situations where team members are manipulated (see also item 20 below).

Relational security is extremely important for Mr A both in terms of minimising security risk and enhancing treatment. Firstly he will require a moderate level of skill in the management of violence and aggression (item 19). This includes staff trained in de-escalation techniques (including recognition of signs and symptoms of aggression) as well as physical techniques. High levels of relational skills are required (item 20, working in combination with other items). There is clear evidence that Mr A has been able to manipulate both members of inexperienced staff and patients, high levels of awareness will be required amongst staff to monitor and address this behaviour through the clinician/patient relationship. Inexperienced staff will require appropriate supervision. Heightened awareness will be important when carrying out procedures such as searching (item 7). A further interesting feature in relational terms is the similarity with Mr A's original offence and the incident with the elderly patient. This again indicates the need for relational skills, and presents the opportunity for clinicians to work on this behavioural profile with Mr A to make treatment more successful and reduce the risk of harm to others.

The situation is also compounded by cannabis use. In retrospect warning signs were evident when Mr A's behaviour changed shortly before the incident, probably due to cannabis use. Additional security measures should minimise any future access, but heightened awareness of behavioural changes would be important (relational skills). Security intelligence (item 22) helps to recognise connections between events that in isolation may seem unimportant, but collectively point to significant security/safety risks.

This is a brief analysis of Mr A's security needs. The challenge is to find the most appropriate environment to meet them, or make modifications within the current environment. There is some evidence that interventions have been successful to a degree, but also that security needs require more attention. Mr A requires treatment and interventions which address his anger, physical aggression, interpersonal relationships, and substance misuse. The current situation has allowed certain maladaptive behaviours to go unchecked and if these continue they will be detrimental both to his treatment and the safety of others.

This hopefully demonstrates how an assessment using the Security Needs Assessment Profile can build a comprehensive picture of the security requirements of individual patients. These requirements can then be matched to the most appropriate environment, allowing other therapies to be delivered safely. Again we would emphasise that not all items will be relevant for all patients. Such a detailed assessment of security need can in itself be regarded as therapeutic strategy.

Conclusion

Secure services continue to develop in complexity in terms of both treatment programmes and security regimes. Our primary reason for developing the system presented here is to provide a comprehensive instrument to aid experienced forensic clinicians to assess patients' security needs across a range of security dimensions. The provision of clear and comprehensive definitions of security and related items can, in our opinion, only improve the assessment process, which should lead to more appropriate placement and consequently offer greater scope for tailored interventional packages. In addition, such a system offers possibilities for greater agreement between clinicians when they are examining the security needs of individual patients. Patients in secure services often meet points of transition between services (from high to medium security for example) and this kind of assessment will assist that process. Security needs should form part of a risk management plan which is dynamic and forms part of regular multi-professional reviews. Clinicians now have available to them a comprehensive range of risk assessment tools and strategies, yet one of the main factors used to manage risk (security) has until recently not been the subject of such detailed analysis.

References

Abbott, P. (2002) Reconfiguration of the high-security hospitals: some lessons from the mental hospital retraction and reprovision programme in the United Kingdom 1960–2000. *The Journal of Forensic Psychiatry*, **13**(1), 107–122.

Bartlett, A., Cohen, A., Backhouse, A., Highet, N. and Eastman, N. (1996) Security needs of South West Thames Special Hospital patients: 1992 and 1993. No way out? *Journal of Forensic Psychiatry*, **7**(2), 256–270.

Blackburn, R. and Renwick, S. J. (1996) Rating scales for measuring the interpersonal circle in forensic psychiatric patients. *Psychological Assessment*, **8**, 76–84.

Burrow, S. (1993) The treatment and security needs of special hospital patients: a nursing perspective. *Journal of Advanced Nursing*, **18**, 1267–1278.

Burrow, S. (1994) Therapeutic security and the mentally-disordered offender. *British Journal of Nursing*, **3**, 314–315.

Chandley, M. (2002) Nursing interventions and future directions with severely assaultive patients. In: Kettles, A. M., Woods, P. and Collins, M. (eds.) *Therapeutic Interventions for Forensic Mental Health Nurses*, pp. 102–119. Jessica Kingsley Publishers, London.

Coid, J. and Kahtan, N. (2000) An instrument to measure the security needs of patients in medium security. *The Journal of Forensic Psychiatry*, **11**(1), 119–134.

Collins, M. (2000) The practitioner new to the role of forensic psychiatric nurse. In: Robinson, D. and Kettles, A. (eds.) *Forensic Nursing and the Multidisciplinary Care of the Mentally Disordered Offender*, pp. 39–50. Jessica Kingsley, London.

Collins, M. and Davies, S. (2005) The Security Needs Assessment Profile: a multidimensional approach to measuring security needs. *The International Journal of Forensic Mental Health*, **4**(1), 39–52.

Collins, M., Davies, S. and Ashwell, C. (2004) *The Security Needs Assessment Profile, Version 2.* Rampton Hospital, Nottinghamshire Healthcare NHS Trust.

Davies, S., Collins, M., Hogue, T., Barrs, H. and Eitel-Smith, G. (2001) An audit of the treatment and security needs of Trent patients in secure care with particular reference to the development of long-term medium and low-secure services. *An Audit Report Commissioned by Forensic*

Services Specialist Commissioning Team, pp. 1–18. North Nottinghamshire Health Authority, United Kingdom.

Department of Health (1999) *The National Service Framework for Mental Health*. The Stationery Office, London.

Department of Health (2004) *The National Service Framework for Mental Health – Five Years On*. The Stationery Office, London.

Department of Health (2002) *Mental Health Policy Implementation Guide. National Minimum Standards for General Adult Services in Psychiatric Intensive Care Units (PICU) and Low Secure Environments*. The Stationery Office, London.

Department of Health (2003) *Personality disorder: no longer a diagnosis of exclusion*. The Stationery Office, London.

Department of Health and Home Office (2000) *Reforming the Mental Health Act. Part II – High risk patients, developing specialist services for those who are dangerous and severely personality disordered*. The Stationery Office, London.

Dolan, B. and Coid, J. (1993) *Psychopathic and Antisocial Personality Disorders. Treatment and Research Issues*. Gaskell, London.

Fallon, P. (1999) *The Report of the Committee of Inquiry into the Personality Disorder Unit, Ashworth Special Hospital*, Paragraph 4.7.16. NHS Executive, London.

Gallop, R. (1985) The patient is splitting: everybody knows and nothing changes. *Journal of Psychosocial Nursing*, **23**(4), 7–10.

Gallop, R. (1992) Self-destructive and impulsive behaviour in the patient with a borderline personality disorder: re-thinking hospital treatment and management. *Archives of Psychiatric Nursing*, **1**(3), 178–182.

Kinsley, J. (1992) *Security in the Special Hospitals a special task*. SHSA, London.

Kinsley, J. (1998) Security and therapy. In: Kaye, C. and Franey, A. (eds.) *Managing High Security Psychiatric Care*, pp. 75–84. Jessica Kingsley, London.

Maden, A., Curle, C., Meux, C., Burrow, S. and Gunn, J. (1993) The treatment and security needs of patients in special hospitals. *Criminal Behaviour and Mental Health*, **3**, 290–306.

McCartney, M., Duggan, C., Collins, M. and Larkin, E. (2001) Are perceptions of parenting and interpersonal functioning related in those with personality disorder? Evidence from patients detained in a high security setting. *Clinical Psychology and Psychotherapy*, **8**, 191–197.

Melia, P., Mercer, T. and Mason, T. (1999) Triumvirate nursing of personality disordered patients: crossing boundaries safely. *Journal of Psychiatric and Mental Health Nursing*, **6**, 15–20.

Mental Health (Care and Treatment) (Scotland) Act (2003) Part 17, Chapter 3. The Stationery Office, Edinburgh.

Munroe-Blum, H. and Marziali, E. (1995) A controlled trial of short-term group treatment for borderline personality disorder. *Journal of Personality Disorders*, **9**(3), 190–198.

Parker, E. (1985) The development of secure provision. In: Gostin, L. (ed.) *Secure Provision*, pp. 15–65. Tavistock Publications, London.

Peternelj-Taylor, C. (1998) Care of individuals in correctional facilities. In: Glod, C. A. (ed.) *Contemporary Psychiatric-Mental Health Nursing*. F. A. Davis, Philadelphia.

Pierzchniak, P., Farnham, F., De Taranto, N., Bull, D., Gill, H., Bester, P., McCallum, A. and Kennedy, H. (1999) Assessing the needs of patients in secure settings: a multi-disciplinary approach. *Journal of Forensic Psychiatry*, **10**(2), 343–354.

Reed, J. (1994) *Report of the Working Group on High Security and Related Psychiatric Provision*. The Stationery Office, London.

Reed, V. and Woods, P. (2000) *Behavioural Status Index (Best-index): a Life Skills Assessment for Selecting and Monitoring Therapy in Mental Health Care*. Psychometric Press, United Kingdom.

Sayal, K. and Maden, A. (2002) The treatment and security needs of patients in special hospitals: views of referring and accepting teams. *Criminal Behaviour and Mental Health*, **12**(4), 244–253.

Shaw, J., Davies, J. and Morley, H. (2001) An assessment of the security, dependency and treatment needs of all patients in secure services in a UK health region. *The Journal of Forensic Psychiatry*, **12**(3), 610–637.

Shimmin, H. and Storey, L. (2000) Social therapy: a case study in developing a staffing model of working with personality-disordered offenders. In: Mercer, D., Mason, T., McKeown, M. and McCann, G. (eds.) *Forensic Mental Health Care: A Case Study Approach*. Churchill Livingstone, Edinburgh.

Tilt, R. (2000) *Report of the Review of Security at the High Security Hospitals*. NHS Executive, London.

Williams, P., Badger, D., Nursten, J. and Woodward, M. (1999) A review of recent academic literature on the characteristics of patients in British special hospitals. *Criminal Behaviour and Mental Health*, **9**, 296–314.

Woods, P., Collins, M. and Kettles, A. (2002) Forensic nursing interventions and future directions for forensic mental health practice. In: Kettles, A., Woods, P. and Collins, M. (eds.) *Therapeutic Interventions for Forensic Mental Health Nurses*, pp. 240–245. Jessica Kingsley, London.

CHAPTER 12

Observation and engagement with people with personality disorder

Alyson McGregor Kettles and Jean Woodally

Introduction

Recent discussions about the nature of observations and engagement (Bowles *et al.*, 2002; Cutcliffe and Barker, 2002; Dodds and Bowles, 2001) have suggested that observations are not sufficiently therapeutic to be of value to the patient. However, given recent evidence about the nature of observation (Kettles *et al.* 2004, Porter *et al.* 1998), it is timely to review the value of both observation and engagement in relation to the person with personality disorder who harms self or others.

As with other nursing interventions (Woods and Richards, 2003) there is little in the way of evidence to suggest that either observation or engagement is of more benefit to the individual. However, some evidence may give us pointers to the way in which care can be delivered. This chapter will aim to discuss what is known and practised in this area.

Observation

The traditional view of nurses working with people with personality disorder (PD) has been that they are manipulative people who regularly break rules and test boundaries (Schafer, 2002). This may be characteristic of a more complex problem and therapeutic options leading towards maturation are dealt with later in this book (see Chapter 15).

Norton and Dolan (1995) suggest that the response of an institution (see Box 12.1) to acting out in personality-disordered persons may perpetuate these behaviours. The problem with high-level observation (see Box 12.2) in relation to people with personality disorder is that it does not therapeutically meet the needs of the patient. Rather, it is thought to provoke responses from both the patient and the staff which are detrimental to the person with a personality disorder.

> ## Box 12.1: Differences between institutional responses in general psychiatric hospitals and therapeutic communities (after Norton and Dolan, 1995).
>
> | General psychiatric hospital | Therapeutic communities |
> | --- | --- |
> | Narrow repertoire of immediate/inflexible responses | Wider repertoire of more flexible responses |
> | Custodial/therapeutic function | Therapeutic function |
> | Undemocratic | Democratic |
> | Practical/ritualised | Thinking/feeling |
> | Symptomatic short-term response | Psychological long-term response |

Recent research (Kettles *et al.*, 2004) into the relationship between risk assessment and observation level conducted with both acute and forensic populations suggests that staff may be using some items from risk assessment that are actually not helpful for decision-making about the level of observation. Also, some staff clearly make judgements about observation level regardless of the 'objective' evidence from assessments. Some staff 'play safe' by putting patients on observation levels higher than they need. Patients who do not exhibit the evidence for higher levels of observation are still put on to observation a level higher that they actually require. There is tentative evidence from the Kettles *et al.* (2004) study that it may even be the case that different clinical areas use different assessment profiles. Different areas use different assessment items depending on their client group and it could possibly be the case that there needs to be specific risk assessments developed for this client group that contribute to the observation level.

> ## Box 12.2: Observation levels (NB: It should be noted here that often these levels have other names in different areas, such as 'constant supervision' or 'maximum observation').
>
> | | | |
> | --- | --- | --- |
> | ■ Special | High | ■ Patient at no time left alone by nurses/nursed at arms length at all times. Patient assessed as at risk |
> | ■ Constant | ↑ | ■ Staff can be outside the room but patient must be visible at all times/no locked doors between patient and staff |
> | ■ 15 minute* | | ■ Patient checked at regular intervals (*no longer in use in many hospitals) |
> | ■ General | Low | ■ No nursing action prescribed but whereabouts must be known to staff. Patient not assessed as at risk |

In many ways, what is more important in relation to the personality disordered individual is that the evidence presented from the Kettles *et al.* (2004) exploratory study bears out some of the ideas from Norton and Dolan's (1995) discussion of the institutional response to acting out.

For example, In the Kettles *et al.* (2004) study all the assessments and decisions about observation level were conducted at the point of admission and were written up within eight hours of the patient entering the ward. Norton and Dolan (1995) suggest that the psychiatric system provides for the acting out patient an early, if not immediate, response and that many patients experience high levels of observation, as this provides temporary relief from mental pain and insecurity.

Kettles *et al.* (2004) show that it tends to be relatively junior and inexperienced staff who are carrying out risk assessments and making decisions about observation level. Norton and Dolan (1995) discuss the need for the patient to experience consciously dominant unconscious emotional conflict(s) rather than enact them. For the patient to achieve maturation, the institution must not simply respond to patient behaviour by suppressing or denying the patients' conflicting emotional aspects, as happens when the acting out person is construed as either the victim (in self-harming) or as the perpetrator (in situations of outwardly directed hostility and aggression, when the patient may be sedated) and in either case is closely observed by staff. This response colludes with one or the other side of the patient's internal conflict and creates an interpersonal enactment between staff and patient. The institution should be enabling staff to provide or facilitate a wider range of responses, including honest emotional feedback indicative of both sides of the patient's conflict. Patients are then able to experience themselves more fully (as victims and as perpetrators as well).

Duffy (1995) showed that there are particular issues with special observation of the patient generally, such as the paternalism of staff towards the patient, passing time and the struggle to avoid infantilizing the patient. No matter whether staff were trying to treat the patient in 'adult' or 'parental' terms, Duffy (1995) states that difficulties were encountered and he cites the example of difficulty in preserving an atmosphere of mutual respect with the nurse standing over the patient in the lavatory. Norton and Dolan (1995) suggest that professionals who are involved with personality disorder patients who typically deploy inadequately developed or infantile modes of relating (both to themselves and others), may unwittingly enter into a style of relationship based on power and control rather than on empathy and exploration.

Dodds and Bowles (2001) suggest that there is a lack of engagement with the patient during observation and that staff are not fulfilling their therapeutic function by not using periods of observation appropriately for the patient. This also equates with Norton and Dolan's (1995) view that by providing what they call a symptomatic response (i.e. not exploratory of motive or consequence) the psychiatric system contributes to the maintenance of the status quo, as thoughts and beliefs that feed the behaviour are not challenged.

Staff are also subject to the same fears, guilt and stress as anyone else. Higher level observation procedures have been shown to cause stress to staff in that they find the procedure either boring or at times frightening, and they do not enjoy being away from other staff for lengthy periods of time (Duffy, 1995; Porter *et al.*, 1998). Also, when patients come off observation levels there needs to be a structured environment, so that they are able to have facilitated engagement with the staff caring for them. As there is no longer an official 15 minute observation level (Clinical Resource and Audit Group, 2002) there is a need to enable staff to follow up the patient who has moved from a higher observation level to a general observation level. A structured environment enables staff to do this and keeps the patient safe as a consequence.

> ## Box 12.3: Key features of observation in relation to people with a personality disorder.
>
> - Constant or special observation is not necessarily the right or appropriate response to harming behaviour. It may perpetuate the problem behaviour rather than solving it.
> - A broader range of responses than high level observation is required and should be developed, such as low stimulation environments (Chandley, 2002).
> - Boundary issues will be an aspect of treatment and must be discussed with the patient.
> - Junior/inexperienced staff should not be placed in the position of having to make assessments and decisions about observation level.
> - Staff stress about participating in observation procedures with personality disordered patients must be addressed, either by appropriate supervision or by pre- and post-observation discussion and support.
> - Education and training about the difficulties of observation and how not to infantilise the patient are important.

Staff need to facilitate engagement, whether as a part of the observation process, or outwith any formal observation. The key features of observation with people with a personality disorder are given in Box 12.3.

Engagement

According to Cutcliffe and Barker (2002), engagement is not a single definition in mental health terms. Rather, it comprises more than one human process, including forming a person-to-person relationship which establishes a connection; it conveys acceptance of the person as a person and lets them know that there is tolerance within the relationship and it enables both parties to hear what the other is saying and thus achieve some understanding between them. This is no mean undertaking when working with personality-disordered people.

Engagement begins from the first contact with the person suffering with a personality disorder. Both the nurse and the person begin to assess each other and the situation they find themselves in. The responses of staff can often determine how the person reacts in the future. The depth of experience that the individual staff member has in his or her background will or could enhance the communication between the staff and the person. The life experience of all involved in care of the personality-disordered person will determine the depth of communication between each of the individuals involved in the engagement process.

During the initial welcoming and assessment process people with personality disorders require an area with minimal stimulus to prevent diversion from the topic that the members of the multidisciplinary team wish to address. So, for example, where other patients require a warm, welcoming, pleasant, almost home-like area with pictures and flowers, the personality-disordered person can use these to divert attention from difficult and problematic areas in the therapeutic assessment.

Therefore a blander environment is preferable for establishment of an engaging and therapeutic relationship. The therapeutic use of the environment itself, both the physical and the relational environment, is a part of the process of engagement, especially if there is harm to others.

The experiences and knowledge of the individual person that the team have can enhance the care that can be delivered. Bank nurses and agency staff who do not always have an in-depth knowledge and experience with this patient group should be used in a limited capacity. Managers need to consider carefully the skill mix when using outside staff. Issues such as whether this is the first offence and age at time of first offence, prison and secure environment experiences can all contribute to a greater knowledge and therapeutic baseline to work from.

People with personality disorder exhibit particular difficulties and these are addressed in Box 12.4. Not only are the difficulties addressed, but also some of the nursing responses and appropriate interventions are given. However, across all engagement, intervention and communication with the patient is the most important component: the therapeutic relationship with all that it entails. It must never be forgotten that honesty, trust, acceptance, caring, being as non-judgemental as possible, giving feedback, immediacy, being confidential and being real are the fundamental tools of nursing.

All staff participating in the care of the person with personality disorder have to be open to new attitudes with respect to what is now being categorised as an illness. Staff have to be patient and accepting of mistakes, as there will always be errors at the beginning – the person is not going to get it right the first time. The treatment process will often be long and enduring, as often a lifetime of maladjustment and early trauma requires either psycho-education or to be re-educated.

Engagement requires a degree of formality at times, including designated points of contact. For example, the regular six-monthly case review with patient involvement, so that the person is given honest feedback about their progress, can be a more formal point of contact. Also, the use of assessment and psychometric instruments, such as the Behavioural Status Index (the Best-index) (Reed and Woods, 2000) help to give a clear indication of progress or degress, thus giving individuals the opportunity to take responsibility for themselves and ownership of the treatment contract and intervention programmes. Psycho-educational programmes and psychosocial skills training will enable the person with a personality disorder to ask for help rather than to ask for help through self-harm such as 'cutting.'

There is emerging neuroscience evidence that personality disorder is not a disorder that is stable and cannot change. Rather, there is foundation evidence that there are changes over time (Eisenberger *et al.*, 2003) and that there is even natural relief from symptoms (Zanarini *et al.*, 2003). What this recent evidence gives is a new optimism and a hope that people with personality disorder can be helped and that care and treatment can make a real difference in their lives. For example, Cutcliffe and Barker (2002) suggest that engagement is not just about forming the relationship but is also about inspiring hope. Now there is not just an interpersonal hope that human contact will provide hope and help, but there is also some sound research evidence that there is real hope for the future.

Nursing interventions, such as engagement, can now be based on some scientific evidence. This evidence includes the six major studies about therapist relations during therapy with people with a personality disorder (Bateman and Fonagy, 1999, 2001; Biedel *et al.*, 2000; Koons *et al.*, 2001; Linehan *et al.*, 1991; Linehan *et al.*, 1994; Munroe-Blum and Marziali, 1995; Verheul *et al.*, 2003). It is now even possible to measure the quality of the therapeutic alliance using the Working Alliance Inventory in selected situations.

It must also be borne in mind that other clientèle are around and that the interactions between people provide for either positive or negative peer group influence. Therefore the placement of

Box 12.4: Nursing interventions for personality disorder-specific behaviours/symptoms.

Individual behaviour/ symptom portrayal		Nursing response/intervention
1. Anger/Hostility	THERAPEUTIC RELATIONSHIP	1. Quiet manner, firm, limit social contact Hierarchy of standardised de-escalation (same every time delivered by different staff) Controlled environment Minimising drop-out from group work Minimising exclusion Anger management programmes
2. Acting out		2. Cognitive behavioural therapy or Dialectical behavioural therapy and Contracts with limit setting Allowing for mistakes Patient taking responsibility within a controlled environment Working with resistance
3. Splitting [the team]		3. Named key worker to coordinate care Well structured/tight care plans explicit and easy for all staff to understand Time available to ensure effective communication Safe environment to express any ideas, concerns or anxieties Clinical supervision
4. Manipulation		4. Respond to crisis Clear explicit boundaries Effective communication between all staff Staff with strong personalities who can cope with enforcing boundaries Confident staff Use of peer group pressure Triumvirate nursing Staff resources allocated to cope with particularly difficult patients Robust complaints procedures/staff support throughout
5. Collusion		5. Effective communication

> ## Box 12.5: Key features of observation and engagement with people with personality disorder.
>
> ■ Working with the patient in a controlled, psychologically-based programmed, therapeutic relationship (which does not become the 'warder/incarcerated felon' or 'victim/victimiser' relationship) which has appropriate supervision and boundary maintenance enables the best known therapeutic outcome (Woods and Richards, 2003).
>
> ■ Manipulation should be viewed as a part of treatment needs indicating underlying problems (Norton and Dolan, 1995; Peternelj-Taylor, 1998).
>
> ■ Constant observation leads to 'acting out' in terms of behavioural boundary testing and rule breaking (Norton and Dolan, 1995; Schafer, 2002)
>
> ■ Staff responses need to be calm, consistent and controlled (Chandley, 2002).
>
> ■ Effective communication between staff and consistency avoids manipulation and other problems, such as splitting, therefore decreasing the need for observation (Gallop, 1985, 1992; Melia *et al.*, 1999; Shimmin and Storey, 2000).
>
> ■ Strong management leadership is essential to empower confidence in staff to develop and use both observation and engagement skills (Melia *et al.*, 1999).
>
> ■ Appropriate maintenance of the physical, spatial and relational environment (Collins, 2000; Chandley, 2002) must be maintained
>
> ■ Homogeneity of personality-disordered patient population in any setting is known to be more successful than having a mixed group of clientèle (Norton and Dolan, 1995)
>
> ■ Visitors to the clinical area may require more observation than the patient. Safeguarding both visitors' and patients' rights is essential

people with a personality disorder and for how long must be carefully considered. There have been suggestions that short-term hospitalization should be for crisis or emergency situations only and that the person should be discharged as soon as possible. This does affect how engagement can realistically be instituted and continued, given associated drop-out and exclusion rates (McMurran, 2002).

The role of the nurse, especially in the light of new legislation, is now to give care to people with personality disorder, and like every other patient that nurses give care to, people with personality disorder require both engagement and observation. The key features of observation and engagement, in relation to personality disorder, are given in Box 12.5.

Issues and future directions

From the literature and the arguments about observation versus engagement it is reasonable to suppose that both are still required. However, for this patient group observation needs to be tempered and engagement needs to be more carefully instituted. There is little doubt that research into this area has been a poor relation and that there are many unanswered questions about the care of the person with a personality disorder. More research is urgently needed into what part observation and/or engagement play in care and effective therapeutic outcome, if any. Cost–benefit analysis is also needed, as it would appear from what is already known (McMurran 2002) that there is little difference in care, from a financial point of view, between care delivered at a day hospital and care delivered via therapeutic community. However, this may not be the case when delivering care through the varying levels of observation or delivering care through one-to-one and group engagement.

The therapeutic alliance relates not only to psychiatrist and patient or to psychologist and patient, but also to nurse and patient. Therapeutic engagement through the therapeutic alliance process may be of more value than direct observation, unless that observation is used as a specific part of the therapeutic alliance.

Relatives, family and significant others must not be forgotten in the process of care. Given some of the difficulties that people with personality disorder experience, and that they often have little or no contact with their families, where possible family must be included in the care process.

Issues from the Mental Health Acts of all the United Kingdom countries must include such issues as ethical practice and the use of codes of conduct in relation to people with personality disorder. Prior to the new legislation, when people could be excluded from hospital as they were not classed as suffering from a mental illness, there were no checks on care of the person with a personality disorder. Indeed, they often received care as a result of suffering from associated Axis I disorders such as affective disorder, or other co-morbidity such as substance misuse, with no direct treatment of the personality disorder being given. This will change as a direct result of legislation, the institution of tribunals and the possibility of litigation if care, either observation or engagement, is not provided.

References

Bateman, A. and Fonagy, P. (1999) The effectiveness of partial hospitalization in the treatment of borderline personality disorder – a randomised controlled trial. *American Journal of Psychiatry*, **156**, 1563–1569.

Bateman, A. and Fonagy, P. (2001) Treatment of borderline personality disorder with psychoanalytically oriented partial hospitalization: an 18 month follow-up. *American Journal of Psychiatry*, **158**, 36–42.

Biedel, D. S., Turner, S. M. and Morris, T. L. (2000) Behavioural treatment of childhood social phobia. *Journal of Consulting and Clinical Psychology*, **68**(6), 1072–1080.

Blum, H. M. and Marziali, E. (1995) Time limited group psychotherapy for borderline patients. *Canadian Journal of Psychology*, **33**(5), 364–369.

Bowles, N., Dodds, P., Hackney, D., Sunderland, C. and Thomas, P. (2002) Formal observations and engagement: a discussion paper. *Journal of Psychiatric and Mental Health Nursing*, **9**(3), 255–260.

Clinical Resource and Audit Group (2002) *Engaging People. Observation of People with Acute Mental Health Problems: A Good Practice Statement*. The Stationery Office, Edinburgh.

Cutcliffe, J. and Barker, P. (2002) Considering the care of the suicidal client and the case for 'engagement and inspiring hope' or 'observations'. *Journal of Psychiatric and Mental Health Nursing*, **9**(5), 611–621.

Dodds, P. and Bowles, N. (2001) Dismantling formal observation and refocusing nursing activity in acute inpatient psychiatry: a case study. *Journal of Psychiatric and Mental Health Nursing*, **8**, 183–188.

Duffy, D. (1995) Out of the shadows: a study of the special observation of suicidal psychiatric in-patients. *Journal of Psychiatric and Mental Health Nursing*, **21**(5), 944–950.

Eisenberger, N. I., Lieberman, M. D. and Williams, K. D. (2003) Does rejection hurt? An FMRI study of social exclusion. *Science*, **302**(5643), 290–2.

Kettles, A. M., Moir, E., Woods, P., Porter, S. and Sutherland, E. (2004) Is there a relationship between risk assessment and observation level? *Journal of Psychiatric and Mental Health Nursing*, **11**(2), 156–164.

Koons, C. R., Robins, C. J., Tweed, J. L., Lynch, T. R., Gonzalez, A. M., Morse, J. Q., Bishop, G. K., Butterfield, M. I. and Bastion, L. A. (2001) Efficacy of dialectical behaviour therapy in women veterans with borderline personality disorder. *Behaviour Therapy*, **32**(2), 371–390.

Linehan, M. M., Tuck, D. A., Heard, H. L. and Armstrong, H. E. (1991) A controlled trial of short term group treatment for borderline personality disorder. *Journal of Personality Disorders*, **9**(3), 190–198.

Linehan, M. M., Tuck, D. A., Heard, H. L. and Armstrong, H. E. (1994) Interpersonal outcome of cognitive behaviour therapy for chronically suicidal borderline patients. *American Journal of Psychiatry*, **151**(12), 1771–1776.

McMurran, M. (2002) *Expert Paper: Personality Disorders*. NHS National Programme on Forensic Mental Health Research and Development, Liverpool.

Norton, K. and Dolan, B. (1995) Acting out and the institutional response. *The Journal of Forensic Psychiatry*, **6**(2), 317–332.

Porter, S., McCann, I. and Kettles, A.M. (1998) Auditing suicide observation procedures. *Psychiatric Care*, **5**(1), 17–21.

Reed, V. and Woods, P. (2000) *Behavioural Status Index (Best-index): a Life Skills Assessment for Selecting and Monitoring Therapy in Mental Health Care*. Psychometric Press, United Kingdom.

Schafer, P. (2002) Nursing interventions and future directions with patients who constantly break rules and test boundaries. In: Kettles, A. M., Woods, P. and Collins, M. (eds.) *Therapeutic Interventions for Forensic Mental Health Nurses*, Chapter 4, pp. 56–71. Jessica Kingsley, London.

Verheul, R., van den Bosch, L. M. C., Koeter, M. W. J., de Ridder, M. A. J., Stijnen, T. and van den Brink, W. (2003) Dialectical behaviour therapy for women with borderline personality disorder: 12 month randomised controlled trial in the Netherlands. *British Journal of Psychiatry*, **182**(2), 135–140.

Woods, P. and Richards, D. (2003) Effectiveness of nursing interventions in people with personality disorders. *Journal of Advanced Nursing*, **44**(2), 154–172.

Zanarini, M. C., Frankenburg, F. R., Hennen, J. and Silk, K. R. (2003) The longitudinal course of borderline psychopathology: 6 year prospective follow-up of the phenomenology of borderline personality disorder. *American Journal of Psychiatry*, **160**(2), 274–283.

CHAPTER 13

Dual diagnosis of personality disorder and substance misuse

Alyson McGregor Kettles

Introduction

People with a personality disorder are not easy to work with. Patients with a substance misuse problem are not easy to work with. McMurran (2002) states that:

> Substance misuse and personality disorder commonly co-occur, with a particularly strong relationship with antisocial and borderline personality disorders. Substance misuse and personality disorder are also strongly associated with mood disorders, which may exacerbate the severity of substance misuse.

There is little doubt of the association of personality disorder with substance misuse, but when substance misuse is excluded from such a dual diagnosis personality disorder remains. It appears that both personality disorders and substance misuse are embedded in the same innate personality traits, particularly impulsiveness and aggressiveness (Rounsaville *et al.*, 1998).

This also relates to criminal behaviour, violence and the need for therapeutic interventions when people with co-morbid personality disorder and substance misuse problems enter forensic services. Personality disordered offenders represent a high risk of recidivism, and, given the part substance misuse plays in crime, it is important to treat substance misuse in this group.

Definition of dual diagnosis

The International Classification of Diseases (ICD-10) defines Personality Disorder as:

a severe disturbance in the characterological constitution and behavioural tendencies of the individual, usually involving several areas of the personality, and nearly always associated with considerable personal and social disruption (WHO, 1992).

However, as Dolan and Coid (1993) indicate, there are only five established facts related to personality disorder:

- The diagnosis is unreliable
- Different authors disagree about definition
- It is used as a derogatory term
- It has legal use in some countries
- Doctors have used it to mean that a person is incurable or untreatable

The ICD-10 also identifies the use of psychoactive substances as a wide variety of disorders that differ in severity (from uncomplicated intoxication and harmful use to obvious psychotic disorders and dementia), but that all are due to the use of one or more psychoactive substances (which may or may not have been medically prescribed).

The ICD-10 also includes a section on differential diagnosis including pre-existing mental disorder together with personality disorder as well as co-existing mental disorders with psychoactive substance misuse.

Dual diagnosis has been recognised for some years and as far back as 1989, Carey stated that with dual diagnosis patients, the psychiatric disorders and the substance misuse are separate chronic disorders, each with an independent course, yet each able to influence the properties of the other. Zimberg (1999) defines the term by organising it into three types of co-existing problem:

1. Primary mental health problem with a substance misuse problem which becomes obvious only when the person is experiencing mental illness symptoms such as the use of 'self-medication' alcohol by the client to obliterate or help them to cope with those symptoms.
2. Primary substance misuse with substance-induced mental health problems, such as the amphetamine user who develops a substance-related psychosis.
3. Mental health and substance misuse problems co-existing in the same individual over a long period of time (deemed to be 'true' dual diagnosis).

However, there are also other forms of 'dual diagnosis' such as mental health problems and learning disabilities, but these do not apply here.

Demographic issues

McMurran (2002) identifies that there are high levels of co-morbidity of substance misuse with personality disorders. Verheul *et al.* (1995) in their review of over 50 co-morbidity studies showed that there was a prevalence of just over 60%. The association is stronger between substance misuse and antisocial and borderline personality disorders and illicit drug users show higher personality disorders prevalence than those who abuse alcohol. Substance misuse may make underlying personality traits more evident.

Co-morbidity and crime

Champney-Smith (2002) discusses the forensic importance of dual diagnosis and states that:

> ... only one report mentioned this [substance misuse in violent crime] as a contributory factor to murder. The failure to recognise the role of substance misuse in these cases demonstrates a failure to give sufficient credence to the existence and the potentially dangerous sequelae of dual diagnosis (Ward and Applin, 1998).

There is an increasing agreement that traits of impulsivity and aggressiveness, which are obvious very early on in life, underpin antisocial and borderline personality disorder (McMurran, 2002). These characteristics, along with difficult temperament and hyperactivity, incline to substance misuse and crime, in particular violent crime (Hawkins *et al.*, 1992). Substance-related violence is generally associated with antisocial lifestyle, rather than psychopathic personality traits (McMurran, 2002).

The need for integrated treatment

According to both Dale (2001) and McMurran (2002) the increasing incidence of mentally ill substance misusing individuals is particularly high amongst UK prisoners. However, there is some evidence that despite the situation in prisons the prevalence rates for those hospitalised mentally disordered offenders suffering from dual diagnosis is actually lower than for prisoners (Coid *et al.*, 1999). Authors of studies that give figures on co-morbidity agree that these figures are likely to be an underestimation of the situation. This is probably due to under-reporting by patients or lack of enquiry by the researchers. Therefore it is believed that integrated rather than parallel treatment models are best suited to forensic patients with a dual diagnosis of substance misuse with personality disorder.

Presentation

People presenting with dual diagnosis of substance misuse and personality disorder present a very complex clinical picture with multiple intertwined problems that are difficult to disentangle. Box 13.1 shows some of the presenting problems and associated management difficulties that face the nurse dealing with a person suffering from these types of problems. The course and severity of personality disorders are worsened by substance use.

Box 13.1: Clinical and management problems associated specifically with personality disorder and substance misuse dual diagnosis.

Clinical problems

Depression (Drake, 1995)

Suicidal tendencies (Drake, 1995)

Violence (Drake, 1995)

HIV infection (Drake, 1995)

Associated mental disorder, e.g. schizophrenia (Westereich *et al.*, 1997)

Worsening psychiatric/psychological symptoms (Drake, 1995)

Male patients more likely to be homeless (Westreich *et al.* 1997)

Poorer prognosis (Drake, 1995; Greenfield *et al.*, 1995)

Lack of will to address misuse problem (Dale, 1999)

Management problems

Higher rates of relapse/service use (Drake, 1995)

Non-compliance with treatment (Drake, 1995)

Incarceration/legal problems (Drake, 1995)

Relative isolation

Frequent hospitalization (Drake, 1995; Havassey and Arns, 1998)

Exacerbation/family problems (Bellack and Gearon, 1998)

Housing issues/management problems in residential settings (McKeown and Leibling, 1995)

High level of service use (Drake, 1995)

Higher costs associated with treatment, effects of crime and longer incarceration (Bartels *et al.*, 1995)

Borderline personality disorder (BPD)

People with borderline personality disorder display a pattern of instability of mood, self-image and interpersonal relationships. They exhibit extremes of idealisation and devaluation. Repeated, persistent suicidal threats, gestures and behaviours are common. Impulsive spending, unsafe sex, binge eating or substance misuse can be self-damaging. Clients may experience paranoid ideation and dissociative symptoms. They tend to use substances in chaotic and unpredictable, multiple drug ways. For example, more than one drug can be taken together leading to unpredictable behaviour that is often violent in nature. They often self-medicate with alcohol and other sedative-hypnotic drugs. There can be frequent misuse of benzodiazepines that have been prescribed for anxiety and this often leads to relapse with their primary drugs of choice. Dialectical behaviour therapy has shown some promise in work with people with borderline personality diagnosis (Linehan 1993a,b).

Antisocial personality disorder (APD)

People with antisocial personality disorder usually have a history of chronic antisocial behaviour that begins before age 15 and continues into adulthood. Clients demonstrate a pattern of impulsive, irresponsible, rebellious and reckless behaviour, as indicated by academic failure, poor job performance (if a job is held at all) and illegal activities. There is a diminished capacity for intimacy and clients experience dysphoria. They do not tolerate boredom well and feel victimised. Many people with antisocial personality disorder use substances in a polydrug fashion, involving alcohol, marijuana, heroin, cocaine and methamphetamines. The illegal drug culture corresponds to their view of the world as fast-paced and dramatic and supports their need for a heightened self-image. They may be involved in crime and other sensation-seeking, high-risk behaviours. Individuals with extreme antisocial symptoms tend to favour stimulants such as cocaine and amphetamines. People with less severe antisocial personality tend to use heroin and alcohol to lessen feelings of depression and rage.

Rapists with severe antisocial personality disorder often use alcohol to 'justify' their conquests. Motivation is an important factor in change for any forensic patient and motivational interviewing is used to identify willingness and ability to change in the substance-using mentally ill patient. Finkelhor (1984) gives a model of sex offending and suggests that substances are used to overcome internal inhibitions to offend, so that inclinations to offend are overcome not only by cognitive distortions but also by the use of alcohol or drugs to advance such disinhibition and these are then blamed for the occurrence of the act itself.

Narcissistic personality disorder (NPD)

This involves a recurring cycle of grandiosity, lack of empathy and hypersensitivity to evaluation by others. People with this disorder are often polydrug users with a preference for stimulants. Alcohol has disinhibiting effects on these individuals and may help to diminish symptoms of anxiety and depression. Socially awkward or withdrawn people with narcissistic personality disorder can be heavy marijuana users and some use anabolic steroids to build a sense of physical perfection.

Passive-aggressive personality disorder (PAPD)

Passive-aggressive personality disorder involves a pervasive pattern of negative attitudes and passive resistance to demands for adequate performance in social and occupational situations. Such clients lack adaptive or assertive social skills, especially with regard to authority figures. They generally fail to connect their passive-resistant behaviour with their feelings of resentfulness and hostility toward others. Drug preferences among people with passive-aggressive personality disorder often vary according to gender. Women prefer alcohol and other sedative-hypnotic drugs to sedate negative feelings such as anxiety and depression. Although men may use substances too, they usually choose stimulants to disinhibit aggressive risk-taking behaviours. People with this disorder often complain of somatic problems such as migraine headaches, muscle aches and stomach ulcers. They often seek over-the-counter drugs as well as antidepressant and anti-anxiety medications.

These clinical presentations are often complex and not clear-cut and are only compounded by an unclear service provided in a serial and unintegrated manner. Gournay and Carson (1997), Rasmussen (2000), Dale (2001), and Lowe and Abou-Saleh (2004) have indicated the problems with the provision of serial services to dual diagnosis patients, such as ignorance, bias, lack of cross-trained staff, insufficient resources, overall lack of willingness to take responsibility concerning dual disorder patients, general lack of ownership and professional turf battles. Whether in prison or in hospital services the patient needs to receive integrated services because of the weaknesses and relative failure of consecutive treatment provided in the past by mental health services (Dale, 2001, p. 192). Integrated treatment for clients with dual diagnosis combines services in one unified, comprehensive treatment programme.

Assessment and treatment

Effective treatment has been developed over the last forty years and the principles of such treatment can be seen in Box 13.2.

Box 13.2: Principles of effective treatment.

1. No single treatment is appropriate for all individuals.
2. Treatment needs to be readily available.
3. Effective treatment attends to multiple needs of the individual, not just his or her drug use
4. An individual's treatment and services plan must be assessed continually and modified as necessary to ensure that the plan meets the person's changing needs.
5. Remaining in treatment for an adequate period of time is critical for treatment effectiveness (minimum three months).
6. Counselling (individual or group) and other behavioural therapies are critical components of effective treatment for addiction.
7. Medications are an important element of treatment for many patients, especially when combined with other behavioural therapies.
8. Addicted or drug-abusing individuals with co-existing mental disorders should have both disorders treated in an integrated way.
9. Medical detoxification is only the first stage of addiction treatment and by itself does little to change long-term drug use.
10. Treatment does not need to be voluntary to be effective.
11. Possible drug use during treatment must be monitored continuously.
12. Treatment programmes should provide assessment for human immunodeficiency virus (HIV)/acquired immunodeficiency syndrome (AIDS), hepatitis B and C, tuberculosis and other infectious diseases, and counselling to help patients modify or change behaviours that place themselves or others at risk of infection.
13. Recovery from drug addiction can be a long-term process and frequently requires multiple episodes of treatment.

National Institute on Drug Abuse (1999)

Much of the literature relates to treatment models (Petersen, 2002; West, 1996). However, there is little consensus on which models, if any, provide the way forward in understanding the causes and indications for the treatment of co-morbid problems, particularly co-morbid problems related to personality disorder and forensic patients. McMurran (2002) proposes that two models relate directly to crime:

- The Psycho-Pharmacological Model suggests that the intoxicating effects of illicit substances affect a person's behaviour and so the likelihood for crime is increased. Parker and Auerhahn (1998) provide evidence for a relationship between crack cocaine and violence. There are also fairly clear relationships between personality-disordered special hospital patients with a history of substance misuse who have taken alcohol at the time of the violent index offence as well as substance-related violence and aggression being most likely in those who have a disposition towards aggression (Chermack and Giancola, 1997; Corbett *et al.*, 1998).
- The Economic Necessity Model puts the idea forward that substance misusers need to acquire the means to sustain their habit. Bennett (1998) found that respondents with related drug use and crime had illegal incomes of (on average) £12,000 per annum. This was 2–3 times higher than those where there was no relationship between drug use and crime. Bennett (1998) also found that such crime (burglary, shoplifting and selling drugs) is most closely associated with the use of heroin and crack cocaine.

Assessment and treatment are integrated components of overall care and relate to the index offence that brought the person into the service.

Screening

Screening is the forerunner to assessment and it aims to diagnose that dual disorders exist. Specialist training is required to enable such screening to occur, as particular symptoms, problems and related problems need to be identified. Related problems include such items as severe intellectual/cognitive deficits or severe medical problems including immune system and brain/neurological problems or severe violence and masking of one symptom by another.

Screening is different from assessment, as screening attempts to ask the question 'Is this person ready for treatment?'. Although screening involves taking some assessment information as a baseline on which to ask the question, screening information enables decisions about appropriate placement for care and treatment to be made.

Assessment, on the other hand, enables detailed information about all aspects of the person to be gained to enable direct care and treatment decisions to be made and for care to be given to the person.

Assessment

Assessment is an ongoing process. For example, psycho-active and addictive substances leave residual effects that can mask psychiatric symptoms and withdrawal from substances can make

---

Box 13.3: Assessment areas with some examples of assessment items.

Area	Assessment item examples
Historical	Adjustment; Non-violent offence history; Early maladjustment
Mental health	Active symptoms; Lack of insight; Impulsivity; Personality disorder
Substance misuse	Alcohol/Psycho-active substance history/abuse
Criminal/justice	Index offence; Past history; Breaches of security; Violence
Physical	Infection, e.g. HIV; Physical functioning, Neuro-psychological testing
Psychological	Cognitive state; Behavioural status; Intellectual functioning
Interactions	Psycho-social status and social functioning; Life factors; Never married
Risk	Risk Assessment Instruments e.g. HCR-20; BEST-Index; V-RAG; PCL-R
Recidivism	Failure on prior conditional release; Past history of charges and record
Other clinical	Sexual adjustment/functioning; Response to treatment; Compliance

---

accurate assessment of co-existing problems especially difficult. Examples of assessment are given in Box 13.3.

Assessment for borderline personality disorder/substance misuse dual diagnosis should include such items as:

- Previous treatment, including medication
- Information about sexual abuse
- Dissociative experiences
- Fugue states and psychotic-like thinking
- Suicidal tendencies
- Neurological testing

Assessment for antisocial personality disorder/substance misuse dual diagnosis should include such items as:

- Fire setting, animal abuse or bed wetting as a child
- Thorough sexual history that includes questions about animals or objects
- Information about the client's ability to bond with others
- Questions about possible parasitic relationships
- History of head injuries, fighting and being hit
- Neuropsychological testing

Assessment for narcissistic personality disorder/substance misuse dual diagnosis should include such items as:

- Information about the client's early childhood beliefs with regard to his or her looks, behaviours and thoughts
- A sexual history to identify the ability to be empathic with partners

> ## Box 13.4: Treatment of dual diagnosis.
>
> - Detoxification
> - Prescription
>   - Antagonist
>   - Maintenance
> - Motivational enhancement therapy (MET)
> - Counselling/psychotherapy
> - Cognitive behaviour therapies
> - Family and relationship therapies
> - Therapeutic communities
> - Community reinforcement, care and treatment
>
> Combinations of the above

Assessment for passive-aggressive personality disorder/substance misuse dual diagnosis should include such items as:

- Thorough history/assessment of use/abuse of alcohol and other drugs
- Over-the-counter drugs as well as anti-anxiety and antidepressant medication use
- Assessment of self-care and survival skills and identification of the client's typical passive-aggressive 'manoeuvres or 'scripts' are useful

Treatment

Treatment for all cases of dual diagnosis of personality disorder and substance misuse addresses both the addiction and the personality disorder. Treatment is not as straightforward as Box 13.4 makes it appear. Usually there are treatment challenges involving complex client needs. Dual diagnosis patients almost always require more resources than clients with one diagnosis do (Rasmussen, 2000; p. 333). They tend to exhibit many health and health services problems with higher acute care usage followed by longer and more frequent hospitalisation periods.

Nursing care

Principles and attitudes

There are certain principles involved in nursing the personality-disordered person with an associated substance misuse problem. These are illustrated in Box 13.5. However, these principles are of little use without the right attitudes towards patients with personality disorders and substance

> ## Box 13.5: Forensic nursing principles in dual diagnosis.
>
> - There is a need to engage in a therapeutic nurse-patient relationship with TRUST as the foundation of the relationship and CLARITY in the goal, purpose and direction of the relationship.
> - Appropriate LIMIT SETTING is essential.
> - The person requires assistance with the first phase of the treatment programme: DETOXIFICATION.
> - There is a need to recognise and avoid/deal with POWER STRUGGLES and/or withdrawal.
> - The nurse needs to recognise and obtain help with DISTORTED FORMS OF CARING and to avoid SPLITTING.
> - Develop an appropriate TREATMENT PROGRAMME that includes aspects of both personality disorder and substance misuse treatment/management in an integrated manner.
> - Other health professionals need to be ENGAGED with the treatment programme.
> - MAINTAIN the RELATIONSHIP as it moves fully into the second phase of the treatment programme (remember this is a long-term process).
> - Provide RELATIONSHIP DISENGAGEMENT at the appropriate time.
> - Enable social support mechanisms and other SUPPORT MECHANISMS for both yourself and the patient throughout and after the treatment programme.

misuse problems. As has already been noted, patients with personality disorder suffer because the term is used in a derogatory way and they are seen as incurable. There are similar attitudes towards patients with substance misuse problems, so it is doubly the case that patients with dual diagnosis are seen as being particularly difficult to deal with.

The evidence for the attitudes of forensic nurses towards substance-misusing patients is scant. Foster and Onyeukwu (2003) report that attitudes of forensic nurses are suboptimal (not as good as they should be) on the Substance Abuse Attitude Survey. This accords with similar scores in other groups of mental health and these lower scores have been shown to have an impact on the quality of patient care provided.

Nursing roles, skills and practice

Tennant *et al.* (2000) provide an excellent chapter on working with the personality-disordered offender which provides both an interesting discussion on nursing practice (p. 97) and a sound case study on nursing a personality-disordered sex offender (p. 104).

However, they do not address the issue of a personality-disordered offender with a substance misuse problem. All that they recommend about the nature of the nursing relationship applies equally to those personality-disordered patients with or without a dual diagnosis. Yet there is more than they recommend, because the dual diagnosis patient requires more. For example, where

Tennant *et al.* (2000) discuss the issue of support systems as a part of relationship forming, they recommend the following for staff:

- Clinical supervision
- Professional development
- Peer group
- Formal staff support systems
- Multidisciplinary working
- Informal support systems

What is not discussed is the issue of support systems for the patient, such as enabling access to substance misuse support services or access to groups/buddy systems such as Alcoholics Anonymous or Narcotics Anonymous. This is where the serial service is inadequate for forensic patients and integrated services must be made available where possible.

This also relates to the number and type of skills and roles that the forensic nurse must have in order to adequately intervene with and manage such patients (see Box 13.6). Just as there is a complex clinical picture, so there must be a practitioner with the multiple skills required to deal with it. Box 13.7 shows some of the many and varied types of skills that the forensic nurse requires to be able to use in the care of patients with the multiple and complex presentations that people with personality disorder and substance misuse dual diagnosis present.

There is not the scope within this chapter to detail the specifics of each type of skill. Each of the skills noted in Box 13.7 can be broken down into many component parts. For example, in 'Interpersonal relationship skills', forensic nurses have to set limits with patients who constantly test boundaries and break rules. Schafer (2002) outlines the interventions of limit setting in an expertly written chapter which directly relates to personality disordered patients with substance misuse problems. Included are such items as:

- Unspoken expectations
- Confidentiality
- Power struggles and withdrawal
- Goals/duration/time

Box 13.6: Forensic nursing roles in relation to dual diagnosis.

- Therapeutic use of self
- Practitioner of nursing interventions related to both personality disorder and substance misuse
- Provider of social balance
- Clinical supervisee in clinical supervision/peer supporter and supportee
- Security/risk management agent
- Moral agent
- Spiritual agent
- Educator

> ## Box 13.7: Forensic nursing skills specific to dual diagnosis.
>
> | | | |
> |---|---|---|
> | Interpersonal relationship skills | Observation skills | Counselling skills |
> | Therapeutic use of self | Safety/security/searching skills | Assessment skills |
> | Anger management skills | Psychoeducation skills | Social skills training |
> | Offence-related work skills | Motivational skills | Political skills |
> | Reasoning/rehabilitation skills | Prevention skills | Management skills |
> | Moral reasoning/empathy skills | Therapies and treatment skills | Writing skills |
> | Economic skills | Knowledge/attitudinal skills | Practical skills |
> | Social support skills | Networking skills | Teaching skills |
>
> Other specialist skills such as therapy skills (dialectical behaviour therapy, group therapy, etc)
> and motivational interviewing skills.

- Commitment levels
- Allowing mistakes
- Distorted forms of caring
- Discrepancy
- Understanding significant contextual factors

All of these relate to setting limits and how the nurse can use their own resources within the relationship to the benefit of the patient. Box 13.8 itemises some of the specific forensic nursing interventions related to dual diagnosis.

Clients with dual diagnosis will make excuses, minimise, manipulate, redefine, intellectualise, justify, lie, blame, power play, victim play, ingratiate, somatise, seek drugs in every possible way, self-mutilate and split staff. All of these illegitimate, manipulative, degenerate (Heron, 1986) ways of dealing with staff on the part of the patient should be met with honest, consistent, confronting interventions by the staff. Where necessary, more than one member of staff may be present, but more usually intervention will be either on a one-to-one or a group basis. This tends to be more effective than two or three staff in a room with one patient for confronting interventions.

Education and training

With the evidence that forensic mental health nurses not only do not know enough about dual diagnosis (McKeown and Liebling, 1995) and that their attitudes towards patients with dual diagnosis problems are poorer than is desirable (Foster and Onyeukwu, 2003; Rassool, 1993), education and training are essential. The mental health treatment needs of people with personality disorder and the substance misuse treatment needs of the person both require trained and educated nurses with appropriate attitudes and knowledge.

Box 13.8: Forensic nursing interventions specific to dual diagnosis.

- Individualised assessment of need and care, including specialist psychometric training
- Initial assessment and acute management, especially of withdrawal, including engagement and crisis stabilisation
- Motivational Interviewing
- Comprehensive assessment and long-term management, including individual counselling, group therapy and mutual self-help groups, with a dynamic aftercare plan to prevent relapse and minimise psychiatric crises
- Dialectical behaviour therapy for borderline personality disorder patients
- Special attention to issues such as violence to self or others; post-acute withdrawal; symptom substitution, physical condition and many somatic complaints
- Transference and counter-transference identification and intervention
- Treatment resistance intervention
- Temper control and anger management groups including emotion regulation, distress tolerance and relaxation
- Ability to develop comprehensive treatment plans, including monitoring and recording
- Psychoeducation
- Targeting of criminogenic needs
- Use of active and structured behavioural and social learning techniques (Psychosocial interventions)
- Discharge planning and supervision – care programme approach

Education and training have been shown to positively enable skills, improve attitudes and help to build confidence in working with and the identification of substance misusing individuals (Kennedy and Faugier, 1989; Rassool, 1993).

Conclusion

Despite the high and growing numbers of people with dual diagnosis in forensic services, the problem does not receive the attention or the resources that are urgently required. The powerful point from the literature and from the lack of resources in clinical practice is that integrated treatment and urgent education and training of staff are essential if the patients are to receive the service that they, the staff and the public deserve.

Support mechanisms for staff remain a fundamental part of practice, but staff also require training in developing skills in both substance misuse and personality disorder nursing and intervention. Dale (2000, p. 199) states that:

The extent of the problem is such that it demands integration into pre-registration professional education programmes as well as more focused post-qualifying training .... Staff need to be empowered to tackle often reluctant participants in therapy by having available a range of levers and sanctions to ensure that protection of all concerned, including the individual in need of services, is maximised.

This remains true, and service managers need to continue to work towards integrated services that enable the nursing staff to provide optimal care for dual diagnosis patients.

References

Bartels, S. J., Drake, R. E. and Wallach, M. A. (1995) Long-term course of substance use disorders among patients with severe mental illness. *Psychiatric Services*, **46**(3), 248–251.

Bellack, A. S. and Gearon, J. S. (1998) Substance abuse treatment for people with schizophrenia. *Addictive Behaviours*, **23**, 749–766.

Carey, K. B. (1989) Emerging treatment guidelines for mentally ill chemical abusers. *Hospital and Community Psychiatry*, **40**(4), 341–342, 349.

Champney-Smith, J. (2002) Dual diagnosis. In: Petersen, T. and McBride, A. (eds.) *Working with Substance Misusers: A Guide to Theory and Practice*, Chapter 22, pp. 267–275. Routledge, London.

Chermack, S. T. and Giancola, P. R. (1997) The relation between alcohol and aggression: an integrated biopsychosocial conceptualisation. *Clinical Psychology Review*, **17**, 621–649.

Coid, J., Kahtan, N., Gault, S. and Jarman, B. (1999) Patients with personality disorder admitted to secure forensic psychiatry services. *British Journal of Psychiatry*, **175**, 528–536.

Corbett, M., Duggan, C. and Larkin, E. (1998) Substance misuse and violence: a comparison of special hospital inpatients diagnosed with either schizophrenia or personality disorder. *Criminal Behaviour and Mental Health*, **8**, 311–321.

Dale, C. (1999) Dual diagnosis: the American experience. *Mental Health Practice*, **3**(3), 18–21.

Dale, C. (2001) Dual diagnosis. In: Dale, C., Thompson, T. and Woods, P. (eds.) *Forensic Mental Health: Issues in Practice*, Chapter 18, pp. 189–202. Baillière Tindall, Harcourt Publishers Limited, London.

Dolan, B. and Coid, J. (1993) *Psychopathic and Anti-Social Personality Disorder: Treatment and Research Issues*. Gaskell, London.

Drake R. E. (1995) *Research on Treating Substance Abuse in Persons with Severe Mental Illness*. National Institute of Mental Health, Rockville, MD.

Finkelhor, D. (1984) *Child Sexual Abuse: New Theory and Research*. Free Press, New York.

Havassey, B. E. and Arns, P. G. (1998) Relationship of cocaine and other substance dependence to well-being of high-risk psychiatric patients. *Psychiatric Services*, **49**, 935–940.

Hawkins, J. D., Catalano, R. F. and Miller, J. Y. (1992) Risk and protective factors for alcohol and other drug problems in adolescence and early adulthood: Implications for substance abuse prevention. *Psychological Bulletin*, **112**, 64–105.

Heron, J. (1986) *Six Category Intervention Analysis*. Human Potential Resource Group, Department of Educational Studies, University of Surrey, Guildford, Surrey.

Kennedy, J. and Faugier, J. (1989) *Drug and alcohol dependency nursing*. Heinemann, London.

Linehan, M. M. (1993a) *Cognitive-Behavioural Treatment of Borderline Personality Disorder*. Guilford Press, New York.

Linehan, M. M. (1993b) *Skills Training Manual for Treating Borderline Personality Disorder*. Guilford Press, New York.

Lowe, A. L. and Abou-Saleh, M. T. (2004) The British experience of dual diagnosis in the national health service. *Acta Neuropsychiatrica*, **16**(1), 41–46.

McKeown, M. and Leibling, H. (1995) Staff perception of illicit drug use within a special hospital. *Journal of Psychiatric and Mental Health Nursing*, **2**(6), 343–350.

McMurran, M. (2002) *Expert Paper: Dual Diagnosis of Mental Disorder and Substance Misuse*. NHS National Programme on Forensic Mental Health Research and Development, Liverpool.

National Institute on Drug Abuse (1999) *Principles of Drug Addiciton Treatment: A Research-Based Guide*. NIH Publication No. 99-4180. National Institute on Drug Abuse, Rockville, MD.

Parker, R. and Auerhahn, K. (1998) Alcohol, drugs and violence. *Annual Review of Sociology*, **24**, 291–311.

Petersen, T. (2002) Exploring substance misuse and dependence: explanations, theories and models. In: Petersen, T. and McBride, A. (eds.) *Working with Substance Misusers: A Guide to Theory and Practice*, Chapter 2, p. 23–41. Routledge, London.

Rasmussen, S. (2000) *Addiction Treatment: Theory and Practice*. Sage Publications, Thousand Oaks, California.

Rassool, G. H. (1993) Nursing and substance misuse: responding to the challenge. *Journal of Advanced Nursing*, **18**, 1401–1407.

Rounsaville, B. J., Kranzler, H. R., Ball, S., Tennen, H., Poling, J. and Triffleman, E. (1998) Personality disorders in substance abusers: relation to substance use. *The Journal of Nervous and Mental Diseases*, **186**(2), 87–95.

Schafer, P. (2002) Nursing interventions and future directions with patients who constantly break rules and test boundaries. In: Kettles, A. M., Woods. P. and Collins, M. (eds.) *Therapeutic Interventions for Forensic Mental Health Nurses*, Chapter 4, pp. 36–71. Jessica Kingsley, London.

Tennant, A., Davies, C. and Tennant I. (2000) Working with the personality disordered offender. In: Chaloner, C. and Coffey, M. (eds.) *Forensic Mental Health Nursing: Current Approaches*, Chapter 6, pp. 94–117. Blackwell Science, Oxford.

Verheul, R., van den Brink, W. and Hartgers, C. (1995) Prevalence of personality disorders among alcoholics and drug addicts: an overview. *European Addiction Research*, **1**, 166–177.

Ward, M. and Applin, C. (1998) *The Unlearned Lesson: The Role of Alcohol and Drug Misuse in Inquiries into Homicides by People with Mental Health Problems*. Wynne Howard Books, Ware, Herts.

West, R. (1996) Theories of addiction. *Addiction*, **96**(1), 3–13.

Westereich, L., Guegj, P., Galanter, M. and Baird, D. (1997) Differences between men and women in dual diagnosis treatment. *American Journal of Addiction*, **6**(4), 311–317.

World Health Organization (1992) *The ICD-10 Classification of Mental and Behavioural Disorders: Clinical Descriptions and Diagnostic Guidelines*. World Health Organization, Geneva.

Zimberg, S. (1999) A dual diagnosis typology to improve diagnosis and treatment of dual disorder patients. *Journal of Psychoactive Drugs*, **31**(1), 47–51.

Further reading

Bennett, T. (1998) *Drugs and Crime: The Results of Research on Drug Testing and Interviewing Arrestees*. Home Office, London.

Champney-Smith, J. (2002) Dual diagnosis. In: Petersen, T. and McBride, A. (eds.) *Working with Substance Misusers: A Guide to Theory and Practice*, Chapter 22, pp. 267–275. Routledge, London.

Dale, C. (2001) Dual diagnosis. In: Dale, C., Thompson, T. and Woods, P. (eds.) *Forensic Mental Health: Issues in Practice*, Chapter 18, pp. 189–202. Baillière Tindall, Harcourt Publishers Limited, London.

Foster, J. H. and Onyeukwu, C. (2003) The attitudes of forensic nurses to substance using service users. *Journal of Psychiatric and Mental Health Nursing*, **10**(5), 578–584.

Gournay, K. and Carson, J. (1997) *Stress in Mental Health Professionals and its Implications for Staff Working with Forensic Populations: Review, Critique and Suggestions for Future Research*. Section of Psychiatric Nursing, Institute of Psychiatry, King's College, London.

Greenfield, S. F., Weiss, R. D. and Tohen, M. (1995) Substance abuse and the chronically mentally ill: a description of dual diagnosis treatment services in a psychiatric hospital. *Community Mental Health Journal*, **31**(3), 265–277.

Schafer, P. (2002) Nursing interventions and future directions with patients who constantly break rules and test boundaries. In: Kettles, A. M., Woods. P. and Collins, M. (eds.) *Therapeutic Interventions for Forensic Mental Health Nurses*, Chapter 4, 36–71. Jessica Kingsley, London.

Tennant, A., Davies, C. and Tennant, I. (2000) Working with personality disordered offenders. In: Chaloner, C. and Coffey, M. (eds.) *Forensic Mental Health Nursing: Current Approaches*, Chapter 6, pp. 94–117. Blackwell Science, Oxford.

CHAPTER 14

Nursing interventions in therapeutic communities

Richard Byrt

Introduction

A therapeutic community is an organisation whose total social environment is intended to be therapeutic and of benefit to residents. There are several types of therapeutic community (Kennard, 1998). This section is concerned with the democratic-analytic therapeutic community, which is used in the treatment of individuals with personality disorder (Lees *et al.*, 2004) and has its origins in military hospitals in the Second World War (Harrison, 2000). Box 14.1 lists relevant UK therapeutic communities.

It should be noted that some therapeutic communities avoid terms like 'personality disorder' because of its use by some professionals as a pejorative label (Campling and Birtle, 2001), or its limited utility as a diagnostic category; see Chapter 3 of this text). For example, in certain therapeutic communities, the concept of post-traumatic stress disorder is seen as more useful in understanding and treating individuals' problems (Wright and Woo, 2000).

Features of health service therapeutic communities

In therapeutic communities, all aspects of the social environment are seen as an important part of treatment, including those mentioned in the list below (Bree *et al.*, 2003; Campling and Haigh, 1999; Kelly *et al.*, 2004). In some texts, the social environment is referred to as 'milieu therapy' (Perlin, 2001). Much of the nurse's role is concerned with facilitating a beneficial social environment, including the following:

1. The process of *living together and sharing treatment*, usually in small groups, is seen as important (Campling and Haigh, 1999).

Box 14.1: UK therapeutic communities for individuals with personality disorders.

The Association of Therapeutic Communities lists 30 UK therapeutic communities which admit individuals with personality disorders. These communities include the following. (Unless otherwise referenced, the source is Association of Therapeutic Communities, 2004).

- Therapeutic communities admitting individuals with a wide range of problems. Examples include the therapeutic community at the Royal Cornhill Hospital, Aberdeen, Francis Dixon Lodge, Leicester, and The Cassel Hospital, Richmond.
- Some (non-secure) therapeutic communities provide treatment for individuals, who, in addition to various problems, have histories of offending. This includes the Henderson Hospital, and two recently established therapeutic communities in Birmingham and Crewe, which are based on principles developed at The Henderson (Adie *et al.*, 2002).
- Services admitting individuals who self-harm, including many with a diagnosis of borderline personality disorder. These include the Acorn programme at The Retreat, York (James, 2003), and the crisis and recovery service at Bethlem Royal Hospital. In the latter, 'therapeutic strategies centre on retention of responsibility ... [and] therapeutic risk-taking' (South London and The Maudsley NHS, Trust). This service is described in Cremin *et al.* (1995).
- Therapeutic communities for children and adolescents and their families. These include the Young People's Service, Cambridge, and the Cotswold Community, which is run by National Children's Homes.
- Other voluntary organisation residential projects, including the Arbours Association Crisis Centre in London and Richmond Fellowship houses in Northern Ireland and England.
- Broadmoor Hospital has a high secure modified therapeutic community (Reiss *et al.*, 1996).
- Several prisons have wings run as therapeutic communities, including Grendon (Lees *et al.*, 2004), Gartree, Dovegate, and a therapeutic community for women at HMP Winchester (Rutherford, 2004).

---

2. The *total social environment* of the therapeutic community is also a crucial aspect of treatment. This includes:
   The *relationships* and *communication* between residents and staff.
   The *roles and responsibilities* undertaken by residents.
   All the *activities* shared by residents and staff (Kelly *et al.*, 2004; McCaffrey, 1998).
3. Residents have many opportunities, particularly in psychotherapy and other groups, to '*safely express, and eventually relieve or resolve, painful feelings and problems*' (Byrt, 1999, p. 67), particularly in psychodynamic group psychotherapy (see p. 198).
4. Residents '*learn about themselves and their problems, including relationship difficulties*' (Byrt, 1999, p. 67).
5. There is a '*culture of inquiry. All involved are encouraged to be curious and ask questions*' (Kelly *et al.* 2004, p. 260).

> ## Box 14.2: 'Defining beliefs' of therapeutic communities.
>
> ■ 'Staff are not completely 'well' and residents are not completely 'sick'. There is a basic equality as human beings between staff and residents, who share many of the same psychological processes and experiences.
> ■ 'Whatever the symptoms or behaviour problems, the individual's difficulties are primarily in his or her relationships with other people.
> ■ '*Therapy is essentially a learning process*, both in the sense of learning new skills – how to relate to others or deal more appropriately with distress – and learning to understand oneself and others'.
>
> (Kennard, 2000, p. 1483. Present author's emphasis)

6. Residents also have opportunities to:
   '*take on responsibility and participate in decision making*'
■ '*discover [and] develop aptitudes ... abilities*' (Byrt, 1999, p. 67) *and coping strategies and contribute these to their own and other residents' treatment, and decision making in the therapeutic community* (Kelly *et al.*, 2004).

The 'social climate' of therapeutic communities

Also of importance is the '*social climate*' of therapeutic communities (as measured, for example, on ward atmosphere scales; Timko and Moos, 2004). In therapeutic communities, 'social climate' consists, in part, of the extent that the therapeutic community:

■ Is relaxed
■ Is non-authoritarian

> ## Box 14.3: Ward social environment: a point for consideration.
>
> Think of a mental health service that provides care and treatment for individuals with personality disorders. Consider aspects of the social environment and social climate that are:
>
> ■ (A) Beneficial to these individuals.
> ■ (B) Harmful to them.
> ■ (C) What improvements to patients' social environment would you make if you were the manager of the service?

- Values and enables residents' active participation and their views and ideas (Chiesa *et al.*, 2003).
- Enables residents' safe expression and resolution of difficult feelings.
- Is sensitive to residents' specific needs: e.g. those related to culture and other aspects of diversity.
- Facilitates activities available to residents that are meaningful, fulfilling and contribute to the life of the therapeutic community.
- Avoids dehumanising and unnecessary regimes, routines, rules and restrictions (Kilshaw, 1999).

A resident's treatment in a therapeutic community

The following account, based on the author's experience (Byrt, 1993, 1999) outlines aspects of a resident's treatment in a medium secure therapeutic community. Details have been changed to ensure confidentiality and anonymity.

'Eva' (a pseudonym), a young woman of 20, was a keen gymnast and runner, and a talented artist. She had experienced parental rejection and several changes of children's homes and foster parents, one of whom sexually and physically abused her when she was 12–14 years old. From this time, Eva expressed her considerable distress through cutting herself. She was admitted to a modified therapeutic community in a medium secure unit after setting fire to an empty building.

In her early days in the therapeutic community, Eva understandably found it difficult to trust anyone, often tried to harm herself, and isolated herself from other residents and staff, to whom she was often verbally hostile, and occasionally threatening. Eva's degree of risk to herself and to others was carefully assessed (see Chapter 10). Staff endeavoured to show Eva consistent warmth and concern, and a willingness to listen. Gradually, she became able to trust her Named Nurse and another resident who had similar experiences to Eva. Eva eventually expressed appreciation that people were prepared to listen, and were concerned about her as an individual.

The therapeutic community, unlike some others, combined individual and group work. Initially with her Named Nurse and a psychologist, and later in psychotherapy groups, Eva was able, with the support of other residents and staff, to safely articulate her feelings of hurt, rejection and anger at her abuse and other adverse experiences. Initially this was a painful process, but Eva said that she found it helpful to share how she felt with others, and gradually reported relief from her considerable distress. This was indicated, in part, by a reduced number of nightmares and flashbacks about her abuse, and diminished thoughts of self-harm. Other residents with similar experiences were able to share with Eva how they managed similar problems.

Once she had begun to trust others, Eva was able to use groups to better understand herself and her relationships with residents and staff. This was achieved partly by examining day-to-day events, including a disagreement with another resident (about which television channel to watch), which resulted in Eva making threats. From an examination of this and similar incidents, Eva concluded that she was unable to 'give way' in disagreements because of past experiences where no one had understood or acknowledged her needs. From her positive experiences of others' concern in the therapeutic community, Eva was able to appreciate that some people, at least, would not set out to harm or reject her, and that she did not need to defend herself by being hostile or isolating herself from others.

Gradually, Eva was able to develop her own controls in relation to her thoughts of self-harm and the expression of her anger. She was encouraged to use a diary to monitor her feelings and thoughts. In addition, she recorded the effectiveness of various strategies such as talking about her feelings, finding ways to relax, and expressing and channelling feelings through various activities. These included creative art sessions and use of the Unit's gym and sporting facilities, which also enabled Eva to enjoy herself and develop further skills. Eva reported increases in self-esteem from these activities and from her achievements in contributing positively to the life of the therapeutic community. This included chairing community meetings and contributing to the organisation of ward social events.

Eva was eventually discharged to a hostel run by a voluntary organisation in her home town. Discharge was a gradual process, with Eva spending days in the hostel from the therapeutic community. From the hostel, she was discharged to her own flat, where she was regularly visited by a community mental health nurse. In addition, Eva continued regular counselling with a member of the hostel staff.

The rest of this account is concerned with aspects of the nurse's role in a therapeutic community.

The nurse–resident communication and relationship

A key aspect of nursing interventions in therapeutic communities is communication (Bree *et al.*, 2003; Kelly *et al.*, 2004). This includes the development of an empathetic relationship and a willingness to actively listen to the individual and to develop an understanding of his or her distress. The latter involves an appreciation that some individuals' behaviours and perspectives mirror previous experiences of neglect, abuse and severe trauma (Aiyegbusi, 2004; Wright and Woo, 2000), as was the case with Eva (see Chapter 6 of this text). These experiences may make it difficult for some residents to trust, or to establish therapeutic alliances with staff. Problems in relationships with parents and other significant people may be reflected in relationships with staff. Preparedness to work with the individual, despite such difficulties, appears to be crucial to successful nursing and multi-disciplinary interventions (Bateman and Fonagy, 2004; Campling, 1999).

Some former therapeutic community residents have described the importance to them of consistent, accepting relationships in which staff value them and express interest and concern (Chiesa *et al.*, 2003; Liderth, 2003). The experience of being valued by other residents and staff may constitute a 'corrective emotional experience' (Ratigan and Aveline, 1988), where the individual feels, perhaps for the first time, accepted and viewed positively (as was the case for Eva). This may be a contrast to previous experiences of mental health and other health services. (See Chapter 4 of this text).

Enabling residents to develop their own inner controls

Nurses and other staff are sometimes faced with moral dilemmas concerning the care of individuals with personality disorders. Many of these dilemmas relate to, on the one hand, ensuring the safety of the individual, and sometimes, of others; and on the other hand, enabling the individual's autonomy and freedom. This dilemma can be particularly difficult in therapeutic communities in physically secure health services (Byrt, 1993; Hartman and Smith, 2002) and prisons; and when, sadly, measures to prevent harm to self or others involve a re-enactment of previous trauma (Aiyegbusi, 2004; Norton and Dolan, 1995)

Many individuals with personality disorders have expressed their (often complex) problems through behaviours that result in harm to themselves and/or others (Campling 1999). In some services, this may lead to staff imposing restrictions, such as intensive observation, seclusion or control and restraint, against the individual's will. This is understandable, and at times, apparently unavoidable, as there may be no obvious alternative to prevent serious harm to self or others. However, unfortunately, restrictive measures may be counter-productive, resulting in increases in the individual's sense of disempowerment and despair, and a tendency to engage further in destructive behaviours. The latter may be reinforced because control and restraint and seclusion may (unintentionally) re-enact the individual's childhood or teenage experience of abuse or neglect (Norton and Dolan 1995, Gallop 1999). Because of individuals' past experiences:

> The capacity to contain intense feeling is often limited, and may find expression through anti-social behaviour, which, in turn, elicits an equally negative response from the parent or an alternative authority figure. Sanctions of increasing severity have to be resorted to ... reinforcing in [the individual's] mind the belief that the world is an uncaring place where rules exist only to maintain dominance over the weak ... (Bree, 2003, p. 154)

Therapeutic communities provide an alternative to this situation, as they enable residents to develop their own inner controls. This is partly achieved through the following interventions by nursing and other therapeutic community staff:

■ Facilitating opportunities, particularly in group psychotherapy, for residents to understand the reasons for behaviours that are harmful to themselves or others.
■ With support, enabling residents to practice creative, less harmful ways of expressing distress and other painful feelings. This involves the development of positive coping strategies and skills which residents can apply within the therapeutic community – and, most importantly, in wider society.
■ Whilst there is recognition of staff's specific expertise and skills, there is an emphasis on residents' own aptitudes, both in relation to discovering their creativity and problem solving abilities, and in contributing support and help for other residents (Bree *et al.*, 2003; Byrt, 1999; Kelly *et al.*, 2004).

One study found that, following treatment in a therapeutic community at Grendon Prison, individuals had an 'increased belief in internal locus of control' (Rawlings, 1999, p. 184). ('Internal locus of control' refers to an individual's perception that he or she has some ability to influence events in his or her life; Tones and Green, 2002).

Involving residents in decision making and responsibility

Residents are involved in responsibility and decision making, partly so that they can learn to take responsibility for their lives and for their responses to problems.

> ... As residents, we play a part in setting rules and boundaries. We often test them and sometimes alter them ....

> It is ... about ... taking control over our lives ...

> I have had rules unfairly imposed on me in the past, so I often kicked against rules when I was [a therapeutic community resident]. I wanted to test them, also to see how safe I was within their framework. The rules can be changed, but only after discussion with the whole community ... Some of us kick against boundaries to avoid looking at painful issues. We point this out to each other ... We become able to recognise parts of ourselves by seeing them in other residents ... We identify with each other and feel less alone. Sometimes, I've felt like my own therapist by listening to and watching other residents ...

> I saw people taking control over their lives, giving up their trails of self-destruction, replacing them with healthier ways of coping, finding ways for themselves. I have learned to take control so my impulses don't control me: to direct my feelings outwards, to stop punishing myself (Liderth, 2003, p. 149f).

Although residents are involved in most decision making, all health service and prison therapeutic communities have some basic rules set by staff. These normally include proscription of physical violence, taking of illicit drugs and sexual relationships between residents. The latter can interfere with psychotherapeutic processes. In addition, many therapeutic community residents have histories of sexual abuse and, in some secure therapeutic communities, histories of sexual offending (Cullen, 1997; Ifill, 2002).

Opportunities for residents' decision making and responsibility always occur within the parameters of safety and staff's professional accountability. Staff share decision making in a democratic way, but without abrogating their responsibilities (Byrt, 1999; Kennard, 1998). There is clarity about differences in resident and staff roles. For example, registered nurses have the same professional accountability to ensure resident safety and welfare as in any health service setting. However, there are attempts to avoid unnecessary barriers between staff and patients and between staff of different disciplines, with a 'flattening of the authority pyramid' (Kennard, 1998).

In some therapeutic communities, staff occasionally make unilateral decisions to ensure residents' safety or welfare (Liderth, 2003), and this is likely to occur particularly in secure settings. However, where possible, staff explain the reasons why it was not possible for residents to be involved in a particular decision (Byrt, 1999; Hartman and Smith, 2002). In general:

Each member of the [therapeutic] community has the right to question or express an opinion about any aspect of community life, and, if necessary, vote for things to be done differently. This includes many of the rules (Bree, 2003, p. 154).

According to Liderth (2003), this involvement can result in residents feeling empowered, rather than feeling like victims of arbitrary rules. Bree (2003) outlines how, in one therapeutic community, residents decided to vote for a change on a total ban on social drinking in the evenings and to take responsibility for regulating their own alcohol intake.

Recognising strengths, talents and positive attributes

Rather than being treated as passive 'patients', the strengths, talents and positive attributes of residents are valued and recognised, as are their abilities to contribute to the life of the therapeutic community and to the resolution of not only their own difficulties, but also those of other residents (Kennard, 2000).

Some responsibilities are formal: e.g. chairing community meetings, acting as foreperson of a work group. Residents often have specific responsibilities for cleaning, cooking and other aspects of therapeutic community life, and in some communities are involved in decisions about admission and discharge. In addition, they may contribute particular skills and talents: e.g. in organising social events and other activities, or contributing to a community magazine (Campling and Haigh, 1999; Kennard, 1998).

The nurse's role in periods of crisis: cultures of belonging and safety

Part of the nurse's role is to facilitate this taking on of responsibility, but bearing in mind issues of safety and residents' specific problems and aptitudes. When a therapeutic community has many residents who have made good progress, they may benefit from taking on a wide range of responsibilities in order to practise and develop newly acquired skills and abilities (Kelly *et al.*, 2004). However, early research (Rapoport, 1960) suggests that 'oscillations' occur in therapeutic communities, with alternating periods of relative stability and of crisis. The latter can happen if several newly admitted residents have behaviours that are caused by, and causing, considerable distress. At such times, nurses are more likely to provide greater direction to residents: e.g. to relieve their distress and enable them to express feelings safely (Hartman and Smith, 2002). Specific interventions vary according to residents' needs. Besides regular programmed psychotherapy groups, crisis meetings might be facilitated by nurses to enable residents to express and work through very painful feelings as soon as they occur.

The importance of '*attachment: a culture of belonging*' and '*containment: a culture of safety*' (Haigh, 1999; p. 247f) has been emphasised. This includes the provision of an environment of support, warmth, consistency and safety in relation to residents' overwhelming feelings and their expression (Aiyegbusi, 2004; Bree, 2003; Tolmacz, 2001). Safety issues related to security, whilst clearly inappropriate for many therapeutic communities, need to be considered in prison, secure hospital/unit and psychiatric intensive care unit communities (Byrt, 1993; Hartman and Smith, 2002). In one medium secure unit therapeutic community, staff decided, following a risk assessment, to temporarily lock the kitchen to ensure residents' safety. However, the reasons for this were clearly explained to residents, and attempts to find alternative solutions were discussed with them.

The therapeutic use of activities

Activities shared by residents and staff are an important feature of many therapeutic communities. These may include gardening, cleaning, cooking and engaging in sports, games and creative arts. Nurses' participation in activities with residents has a number of functions. It can promote cohesion, enabling community members to work together effectively. A shared activity may enable the development of therapeutic nurse–resident relationships (Irwin, 1995; McCaffrey, 1998).

Nurses' participation in activities also enables their assessment and understanding of residents' strengths and problems, and provides material that can be considered in psychotherapeutic groups, as described in the section on community meetings (below).

The nurse's role in therapeutic groups

Democratic-analytic therapeutic communities have programmes of structured groups, as follows.

Most therapeutic communities start each weekday with a *community meeting*, where practical issues are discussed and events in the life of the therapeutic community are related to the problems that people face in their lives outside. Anything that happens during shared activities or other aspects of the life of the therapeutic community can be used as 'living–learning situations' (i.e. to enable residents to learn about themselves and the resolution of problems; Jones, 1968; Kennard, 1998). Maxwell Jones, a pioneer of the UK therapeutic community movement, claimed that these organisations were 'microcosms of society', in that the problems that residents encountered in everyday life, before admission, were mirrored in their interactions and ways of resolving problems in the therapeutic community (Hill, 2004; Jones, 1968). A possible problem with Jones's theory is that he may have insufficiently considered the extent that residents' behaviours may be shaped by institutional processes, particularly in therapeutic communities in physically secure health services and prisons (Kilshaw, 1999).

In addition, there are *small psychotherapy groups*. These are often based on psychodynamic principles (Hinshelwood, 1999). Some therapeutic community programmes include psychodynamic groups using one or more arts therapies, e.g. music, drama, writing, painting and other media, to explore individuals' pasts in relation to their present problems, and to enable expression of thoughts and feelings (Liebmann, 1994). There may also be groups using psychodrama, cognitive behavioural therapy, with specific goals (Cullen *et al.*, 1997) and/or creative therapies. The latter use various art forms to enable people to express and enjoy themselves, and 'to find complementary ways of making meaning out of the chaos inside' (Higgins and Newrith, 1999, p. 117). In addition, family therapy is used in some therapeutic communities (Chiesa *et al.*, 2004).

Crisis meetings can be called at any time of the day or night to support residents who are experiencing considerable stress. In the author's experience, crisis meetings can be particularly helpful for individuals with impulsive behaviours or who have urgent needs for relief from very distressing and intense feelings. Crisis meetings can enable residents to safely express these verbally, with opportunities for support from other therapeutic community members (Kelly, 2004). In this way, crisis meetings and other groups can provide substitutes for harming self or others. However, one former resident comments:

> The [therapeutic] community was very intense; you could never get away from it .... An individual or group could call [crisis] meetings any time of day or **night** to express concerns, and everyone was expected to attend (Ifill, 2002, p. 4. Emphasis in the original).

Nurses are involved, with staff of other disciplines, in facilitating psychodynamic and other psychotherapy groups. Some therapeutic community nurses train in psychodynamic psychotherapy. Nursing skills in psychotherapy groups include the following (Bateman and Fonagy, 2004; Campling and Haigh, 1999; Dowson, 1995; Hartman and Smith, 2002):

- Reflective, active listening, including careful attention to residents' non-verbal and verbal communication, c.g. if there is a prolonged silence, nurses and other staff would reflect on its nature and possible causes. If residents appear relaxed, their silence may reflect shared ease at being able to be together without speaking. Anxiety might be indicated by, for example, constant foot-tapping, changes in body posture or other ways that individuals specifically express their anxiety.
- Skills in knowing when to intervene directly, and when to enable residents to contribute thoughts, ideas and views. Direct interventions (e.g. offering support to a newly admitted resident who is very anxious) may be more appropriate at times when residents find it difficult to support each other. Generally, however, it is more important to enable residents to discover their own resources and sources of strength – and to use these to support each other.
- Nurses and other staff need, also, to be aware of group dynamics: the interactions and relationships between different members of the community (Dowson, 1995), e.g. individuals' negative feelings may be directed towards one resident who becomes scapegoated. Two or more residents may reinforce each other's destructive behaviours, with avoidance of efforts to examine and learn from the latter. Staff enable residents to consider these and other group dynamics, and the extent that these may mirror individuals' past relationship difficulties.
- In addition, staff facilitate residents' safe expression of (often complex and very difficult) feelings. Whilst this can be very painful, particularly initially, residents may experience relief and benefit from the support of other community members:

    > [The therapeutic community] gives you the facilities to vent feelings and frustrations ... and know other people are listening. You don't feel the only one with the problem. A problem shared is a problem halved. There are opportunities to talk and share.

... They listen and advise. There are people in the same situation (Anonymous resident, quoted in Byrt, 1996).

Many skills in facilitating groups involve appropriate *timing* of interventions. This relates to staff's appreciation of individuals' readiness to consider particular behaviours or feelings. Most residents, understandably, find group psychotherapy threatening. Many people need time to get used to the experience of being in groups and to openly discussing thoughts and feelings that they find embarrassing or difficult. Part of the role of nurses and other staff is to enable residents to use groups in ways that do not provoke intolerable anxiety (Hartman and Smith, 2002).

Nurses' roles in rehabilitation and in the wider community

One problem with some therapeutic communities, at least in the past, was their provision of a temporary supportive environment which bore little resemblance to individuals' lives in the wider community. This is reflected in the following comment of a therapeutic community resident: 'I know you want us to give our views. But why should I? I don't have any say in my family or the place where I work' (quoted in Byrt and Dooher, 2003, p. 21).

Another problem has been the sudden transition from intensive residential treatment to the wider community, with little support. In response to this problem, some therapeutic communities have developed groups for residents prior to and following discharge (Humphreys and Bree, 2004). In addition, there are a number of community outreach services, such as those developed by the Cassel Hospital. Community nursing interventions provide continued support following discharge from the therapeutic community; and enable individuals to creatively manage the problems and crises they encounter (Chiesa *et al.*, 2004; Pringle and Chiesa, 2001) (see Chapter 9 of this text on community interventions).

Self-awareness, transference and countertransference

Nursing in therapeutic communities requires a high degree of self-awareness and reflection. As a staff member, 'to enter a therapeutic community is to start a journey of learning and personal development' (Overton, 2004, p. 263). It is essential that nurses endeavour to be honest about their feelings about residents. Treatment in therapeutic communities involves intensive exploration and working through intense, and often overwhelming, feelings and experiences. These are often related to very difficult relationships with parents and other significant people. For example, because of their very chaotic early relationships, individuals with borderline personality disorder sometimes have extreme reactions to staff. These may include considerable dislike or idealisation, so that different nurses (or the same nurse at different times) are seen as 'totally bad' or 'totally good' (Bateman and Fonagy, 2004).

In addition, residents may transfer feelings about significant others onto staff. To ensure effective working with these individuals, it is essential that nurses have an understanding of this transference, in relation to residents' adverse experiences of early relationships, and of countertransference (Aiyegbusi, 2004). Many definitions of the latter include two components:

- The influence of the staff member's past relationships and conflicts on her or his communication with, feelings about, and behaviour towards the client (Schafer, 1997).
- The professional's feelings and reactions to the client's transference (i.e. how the client behaves towards the professional, as a result of displacement of feelings originally intended for a parent or other significant person; Bateman and Fonagy, 2004).

Many authorities have stressed that countertransference is a common, 'realistic' response to clients (Bateman and Fonagy, 2004). In order to work therapeutically with residents, nurses need to be aware of the following:

- Their own countertransference and other feelings towards residents: e.g. the development of either negative feelings or of feelings of attraction or strong liking which make it difficult for the nurse to make objective assessments or to work effectively with a particular resident (Overton, 2004).
- Their own needs, and the satisfactions they expect to derive from their work with residents; e.g. a nurse who enjoys residents' dependency on her or him would need to be aware of ways that this could have adverse effects, such as making decisions for residents that they could make themselves (Overton, 2004).
- An understanding that failure to appreciate the presence of countertransference may result in residents' 're-enactment of traumatic experiences' (Aiyegbusi, 2002, p. 147).
- The need to establish and maintain professional boundaries (Nursing and Midwifery Council, 2002). This is particularly important, as some individuals with personality disorder are in particular need of positive and fulfilling relationships that they have never experienced. For this reason, they may seek friendships or close emotional relationships with staff members (Peternelj-Taylor, 2002).

Staff communication, support, clinical supervision and reflection

In order to work effectively and therapeutically with clients, there is a need for the following:

- *Good communication between staff members* to enable understanding of transference and countertransference, and of group and organisational dynamics (i.e. the communication, inter-relationships and roles of community members within psychotherapeutic groups and in the therapeutic community, respectively; Overton, 2004; Rawlinson, 1999).
- Staff communication may be facilitated, in part, through regular *staff support groups*. These provide opportunities for staff to consider their interventions and relationships with patients,

and can increase self-awareness, in relation, for example, to countertransference (Byrt, 1999).

■ *Clinical supervision* may occur individually and/or in a clinical supervision group. The latter may enable staff to share experiences and insights, increase self-awareness, and offer suggestions about effective interventions with particular residents (Bowers, 2002; Schafer, 2002).

■ Also vital are *continuing education* and preparedness to learn from both residents and colleagues, including those in other therapeutic communities (Roberts, 1998). The Association of Therapeutic Communities is a source of information and support. This organisation runs conferences, provides information and publishes a quarterly journal, *Therapeutic Communities*: `http://www.therapeuticcommunities.org/`.

Research on the effectiveness of therapeutic communities

Are therapeutic communities effective? Box 14.4 summarises research findings on various measures of effectiveness.

Closing comments by former residents

I will close with the comments of two former therapeutic community residents:

> Individuals could talk about their problems; but ... this would often mean women talking about their painful and traumatic experiences of abuse, in front of men who had abused women.
>
> ... Not only were you expected to work in a group, you were expected to live in one, too. This had its good aspects, like learning to live in a group, sharing cleaning, cooking, shopping, etc., but on the flip side ... it meant living with people who, at times, you felt damn right uncomfortable about (Ifill, 2002, p. 4).

> There are still times when I want to cut and get drunk, to act out, but I can't. I have tried, but I have changed more deeply than I realise, more than I want. I have to deal with my feelings in new ways. I bear them, live with them and they have not destroyed me – yet (Liderth, 2003, p. 151).

Acknowledgement

My thanks to Michael Coffey for his helpful suggestions and comments, which have been incorporated into this chapter.

Box 14.4: Findings from studies of the effectiveness of therapeutic communities.

A recent meta-analysis of studies, which compared therapeutic community with other treatment methods, concluded that there was evidence of the effectiveness of the former in individuals who complete treatment (Lees *et al.*, 2004). Research findings include the following outcomes from treatment in therapeutic communities (Davies and Campling, 2003; Haigh, 2002; Kennard, 2000; Lees *et al.*, 2004).

1. *High drop out rates* from some therapeutic communities, which means that some residents do not complete their treatment. Therapeutic communities are *not appropriate for all* individuals with personality disorders, particularly people who score highly on Hare's psychopathy checklist (Harris *et al.*, 1994), or who have limited motivation, do not wish to make changes in their lives or find opportunities to explore their problems meaningless or unbearably threatening. Good selection procedures help to identify individuals who are likely to benefit from a therapeutic community (Lees *et al.*, 2004)

2. In many individuals, *reduction in distressing symptoms*, such as anxiety, lack of confidence and low self-esteem, and decreased 'impulsivity and self-damaging behaviour' (Warren *et al.*, 2004, p. 55).

3. *Fewer admissions* to accident and emergency departments, general hospitals and mental health units (Davies and Menzies, 2004).

4. Amongst people treated in NHS non-secure therapeutic communities, *lower recidivism* (repetition of offending) rates (Norton and Warren, 2004).

5. *Mixed results for recidivism* amongst individuals treated in *prison and secure hospitals/units.* Some studies have found increases (Harris *et al.*, 1994) or no change (McMurran *et al.*, 1998; Reiss *et al.*, 1996) in rates of offending. However, at Grendon Prison, reduced recidivism has been found in several studies: e.g. amongst men who stay in a therapeutic community wing for over 18 months (Lees *et al.*, 2004).

6. Several studies of Grendon Prison have reported *reduced aggression* (Rawlings, 1999).

7. *Institutional disturbances* (such as riots) are generally less frequent in prison therapeutic communities, compared with conventional prisons (Rawlings, 1999).

8. Although residential treatment often lasts six months or more, therapeutic communities have been found to be *cost-effective*, because of subsequent reduced use of mental health and general hospital services and, in some studies, reduced recidivism (Davies and Campling, 2003; Davies and Menzies, 2004).

9. Findings suggest that *a briefer period in a therapeutic community, followed by interventions in the wider community is more effective* than a more prolonged stay in a therapeutic community with little or no subsequent nursing interventions and treatment (Bateman and Fonagy, 2004; Chiesa *et al.*, 2004).

10. For individuals with personality disorders, there is evidence that '*specialist facilities* may be a more effective, and ultimately, cost-effective approach' (Chiesa *et al.*, 2004, p. 216).

References

Adie, L., Bracey, A., Prentice, C., Scott, K. and Slade, K. (2002) The first Christmas in a new therapeutic community. *Therapeutic Communities*, **23**(1), 47–60.

Aiyegbusi, A. (2002) Nursing interventions and future directions with women in secure services. In: Kettles, M. A., Woods, P. and Collins, M. (eds.) *Therapeutic Interventions for Forensic Mental Health Nurses*, Chapter 9. Jessica Kingsley, London.

Aiyegbusi, A. (2004) Thinking under fire: the challenge for forensic mental health nurses working with women in secure care. In: Jeffcote, N. and Watson, T. (eds.) *Working Therapeutically with Women in Secure Mental Health Settings*, Chapter 8. Jessica Kingsley, London.

Association of Therapeutic Communities (2004) *Directory of Member Communities and Organisations*. Accessed through: `http://www.therapeuticcommunities.org/diry-need.htm#personality`. Accessed 23 November 2004.

Bateman, A. and Fonagy, P. (2004) *Psychotherapy for Borderline Personality Disorder*. Oxford University Press, Oxford.

Bowers, L. (2002) *Dangerous and Severe Personality Disorder: Response and Role of the Psychiatric Team*, Chapter 1. Routledge, London.

Bree, A. (2003) Untitled section in: Bree, A., Campling, P. and Liderth, S. Empowerment in mental health: the therapeutic community model. In: Dooher, J. and Byrt, R. (eds.) *Empowerment and the Health Service User*, Chapter 10, pp. 151–157. Quay Books, Mark Allen Publishing, Dinton, Salisbury.

Bree, A., Campling, P. and Liderth, S. (2003) Empowerment in mental health: the therapeutic community model. In: Dooher, J. and Byrt, R. (eds.) *Empowerment and the Health Service User*, Chapter 10. Quay Books, Mark Allen Publishing, Dinton, Salisbury.

Byrt, R. (1993) Moral minefield. *Nursing Times*, **89**(8), 63–66.

Byrt, R. (1996) *Freedom in Security: A Therapeutic Community in a Regional Secure Unit*. Unpublished paper.

Byrt, R. (1999) Nursing: the psychosocial environment. In: Campling, P. and Haigh, R. (eds.) *Therapeutic Communities: Past, Present and Future*, Chapter 5. Jessica Kingsley, London.

Byrt, R. and Dooher, J. (2003) 'Service Users' and 'Carers' and their desire for empowerment and participation. In: Dooher, J. and Byrt, R. (eds.) *Empowerment and the Health Service User*, Chapter 1. Quay Books, Mark Allen Publishing, Dinton, Salisbury.

Campling, P. (1999) Chaotic personalities. Maintaining the therapeutic alliance. In: Campling, P. and Haigh, R. (eds.) *Therapeutic Communities: Past, Present and Future*, Chapter 11. Jessica Kingsley, London.

Campling, P. and Birtle, J. (2001) The need for an NHS policy on the role of therapeutic communities in the treatment of 'personality disorder'. *Therapeutic Communities*, **22**(2), 131–142.

Campling, P. and Haigh, R. (eds.) (1999) *Therapeutic Communities: Past, Present and Future*. Jessica Kingsley, London.

Chiesa, M., Fonagy, P. and Holmes, J. (2004) An experimental study of treatment outcome. In: Lees, J., Manning, N., Menzies, D. and Morant, N. (eds.) *A Culture of Enquiry: Research Evidence and the Therapeutic Community*, Chapter 13. Jessica Kingsley, London.

Chiesa, M., Pringle, P. and Drahorad, C. (2003) Users' views of therapeutic community treatment: a satisfaction survey at the Cassel Hospital. *Therapeutic Communities*, **24**(2), 127–141.

Chiesa, M., Wright, M. and Leger, D. (2004) Psychotrophic medication and the therapeutic community: a survey of prescribing practices for severe personality disorder. *Therapeutic Communities*, **25**(2), 131–144.

Cremin, D., Lemmer, B. and Davison, S. (1995) The efficacy of a nursing challenge to patients: testing a new intervention to decrease self-harm behaviour in severe personality disorder. *Journal of Psychiatric and Mental Health Nursing*, **2**, 237–246.

Cullen, E. (1997) Can a prison be a therapeutic community? The Grendon template. In: Cullen, E., Jones, L. and Woodward, R. (eds.) *Therapeutic Communities for Offenders*, Chapter 4. Wiley, Chichester.

Cullen, E., Jones, L. and Woodward, R. (eds.) (1997) *Therapeutic Communities for Offenders*. Wiley, Chichester.

Davies, S. and Campling, P. (2003) Therapeutic community treatment of personality disorder: service use and mortality over 3 years' follow up. *British Journal of Psychiatry*, **182**(Supplement 44), s24–s27.

Davies, S. and Menzies, D. (2004) Economic evaluations in therapeutic community research. In: Lees, J., Manning, N., Menzies, D. and Morant, N. (eds.) *A Culture of Enquiry: Research Evidence and the Therapeutic Community*, Chapter 16. Jessica Kingsley, London.

Dowson, J. H. (1995) Group psychotherapies. In: Dowson, J. H. and Grounds, A. T. (eds.) *Personality Disorders: Recognition and Clinical Management*, Chapter 8. Cambridge University Press, Cambridge.

Gallop, R. (1999) Personality disorder: finding a way. In: Clinton, M. and Nelson, S. (eds.) *Advanced Practice in Mental Health Nursing*, Chapter 9. Blackwell Science, Oxford.

Haigh, R. (1999) The quintessence of a therapeutic environment. In: Campling, P. and Haigh, R. (eds.) *Therapeutic Communities: Past, Present and Future*, Chapter 20. Jessica Kingsley, London.

Haigh, R. (2002) Therapeutic community research: past, present and future. *Psychiatric Bulletin*, **26**(2), 65–68.

Harris, G. T., Rice, M. E. and Cormier, C. A. (1994) Psychopaths: is a therapeutic community therapeutic? *Therapeutic Communities*, **15**(4), 283–299.

Harrison, T. (2000) *Bion, Rickman, Foulkes and the Northfield Experiment*. Jessica Kingsley, London.

Hartman, D. and Smith, L. (2002) Developing community groupwork on a locked psychiatric intensive care unit. *Therapeutic Communities*, **23**(1), 5–16.

Higgins, B. and Newrith, C. (1999) Creativity and play: reflections on a creative therapies group. In: Campling, P. and Haigh, R. (eds.) *Therapeutic Communities: Past, Present and Future*, Chapter 10. Jessica Kingsley, London.

Hill, J. (2004) A living–learning experience. Section in: Kelly, S., Hill, J., Boardman, H. and Overton, I., Therapeutic communities. In: Campling, P., Davies, S. and Farquharson, G. (eds.) *From Toxic Institutions to Therapeutic Environments. Residential Settings in Mental Health Services*, Chapter 25. Gaskell, London.

Hinshelwood, R. D. (1999) Psychoanalytic origins and today's work: the Cassel heritage. In: Campling, P. and Haigh, R. (eds.) *Therapeutic Communities: Past, Present and Future*, Chapter 3. Jessica Kingsley, London.

Humphreys, N. and Bree, A. (2004) Difficulties with attachment and separation: joining and leaving a therapeutic community. In: Campling, P., Davies, S. and Farquharson, G. (2004) *From Toxic Institutions to Therapeutic Environments. Residential Settings in Mental Health Services*, Chapter 6. Gaskell, London.

Ifill, W. (2002) Therapeutic communities. *The Joint Newsletter of the Association of Therapeutic Communities, the Charterhouse Group of Therapeutic Communities, and the Planned Environment Trust*, **6**, 4.

Irwin, F. (1995) The therapeutic ingredients of baking a cake. *Therapeutic Communities*, **16**(4), 263–268.

James, A. (2003) From self harm ... to self-esteem. *Nursing Times*, **99**(33), 36–37.

Jones, M. (1968) *Social Psychiatry in Practice: The Idea of the Therapeutic Community*. Penguin, Harmondsworth.

Kelly, S. (2004) A staff member's journey. In: Kelly, S., Hill, J., Boardman, H. and Overton, I., Therapeutic communities. In: Campling, P., Davies, S. and Farquharson, G. (eds.) *From Toxic Institutions to Therapeutic Environments: Residential Settings in Mental Health Services*, Chapter 25. Gaskell, London.

Kelly, S., Hill, J., Boardman, H. and Overton, I. (2004) Therapeutic communities. In: Campling, P., Davies, S. and Farquharson, G. (eds.) *From Toxic Institutions to Therapeutic Environments: Residential Settings in Mental Health Services*, Chapter 25. Gaskell, London.

Kennard, D. (1998) *An Introduction to Therapeutic Communities*. Jessica Kingsley, London.

Kennard, D. (2000) Therapeutic communities. In: Gelder, M. G., Lopez-Ibor, J. J. and Andreasen, N. (eds.) *New Oxford Textbook of Psychiatry*, Vol. 1, Section 6.3.9. Oxford University Press, Oxford.

Kilshaw, J. (1999) Can medium secure units avoid becoming total institutions? In: Tarbuck, P., Topping-Morris, B. and Burnard, P. (eds.) *Forensic Mental Health Nursing: Strategy and Implementation*, Chapter 11. Whurr, London.

Lees, J., Manning, N. and Rawlings, B. (2004) Therapeutic community research: an overview and meta-analysis. In: Lees, J., Manning, N., Menzies, D. and Morant, N. (eds.) *A Culture of Enquiry: Research Evidence and the Therapeutic Community*, Chapter 2. Jessica Kingsley, London.

Lees, J., Manning, N., Menzies, D. and Morant, N. (eds.) (2004) *A Culture of Enquiry: Research Evidence and the Therapeutic Community*. Jessica Kingsley, London.

Liderth, S. (2003) Untitled section in: Bree, A., Campling, P. and Liderth, S., Empowerment in mental health: the therapeutic community model. In: Dooher, J. and Byrt, R. (eds.) *Empower-*

ment and the Health Service User, Chapter 10, pp. 149–151. Quay Books, Mark Allen Publishing, Dinton, Salisbury.

Liebman, M. (ed.) (1994) *Art Therapy with Offenders*. Jessica Kingsley, London.

McCaffrey, G. (1998) The use of leisure activities in a therapeutic community. *Journal of Psychiatric and Mental Health Nursing*, **5**(1), 53–58.

McMurran, M., Egan, V. and Ahmadi, S. (1998) A retrospective evaluation of a therapeutic community for mentally disordered offenders. *The Journal of Forensic Psychiatry*, **9**, 103–113.

Norton, K. and Dolan, B. (1995) Acting out and the institutional response. *The Journal of Forensic Psychiatry*, **6**, 317–332.

Norton, K. and Warren, F. (2004) Assessing outcome at Henderson Hospital. In: Lees, J., Manning, N., Menzies, D. and Morant, N. (eds.) *A Culture of Enquiry: Research Evidence and the Therapeutic Community*, Chapter 14. Jessica Kingsley, London.

Nursing and Midwifery Council (2002) *Practitioner–Client Relationships and the Prevention of Abuse*. Nursing and Midwifery Council, London.

Overton, I. (2004) A nurse's perspective. In: Kelly, S., Hill, J., Boardman, H. and Overton, I., Therapeutic communities. In: Campling, P., Davies, S. and Farquharson, G. (eds.) *From Toxic Institutions to Therapeutic Environments. Residential Settings in Mental Health Services*, Chapter 25. Gaskell, London.

Perlin, C. K. (2001) Social responses and personality disorders. In: Stuart, G. W. and Laraia, M. T. (eds.) *Principles and Practice of Psychiatric Nursing*, 7th edn, Chapter 23. Mosby, St Louis.

Peternelj-Taylor, C. (2002) Professional boundaries: a matter of therapeutic integrity. *Journal of Psychosocial Nursing and Mental Health Services*, **40**(4), 22–29.

Pringle, P. and Chiesa, M. (2001) From the therapeutic community to the community: developing an outreach psychosocial nursing service for severe personality disorders. *Therapeutic Communities*, **22**(3), 215–232.

Rapoport, R. (1960) *Community as Doctor*. Tavistock, London.

Ratigan, B. and Aveline, M. (1988) Interpersonal group therapy. In: Aveline, M. and Dryden, W. (eds.) *Group Therapy in Britain*, Chapter 3. Open University Press, Milton Keynes.

Rawlings, B. (1999) Therapeutic communities in prisons: a research review. *Therapeutic Communities*, **20**(3), 177–193.

Rawlinson, D. (1999) Group psychoanalytic ideas: extending the group matrix to TCs. In: Campling, P. and Haigh, R. (eds.) *Therapeutic Communities: Past, Present and Future*, Chapter 4. Jessica Kingsley, London.

Reiss, D., Grubin, D. and Meux, C. (1996) Young 'psychopaths' in special hospital: treatment outcome. *British Journal of Psychiatry*, **168**(1), 99–104.

Roberts, J. (1998) Questions of training. In: Kennard, D. (1998) *An Introduction to Therapeutic Communities*, Chapter 12. Jessica Kingsley, London.

Rutherford, H. (2004) Women and offending. In: Jeffcote, N. and Watson, T. (eds.) *Working Therapeutically with Women in Secure Mental Health Settings*, Chapter 3. Jessica Kingsley, London.

Schafer, P. (1997) When a client develops an attraction: successful resolution versus boundary violation. *Journal of Psychiatric and Mental Health Nursing*, **4**, 203–211.

Schafer, P. E. (2002) Nursing interventions and future directions with patients who constantly break rules and test boundaries. In: Kettles, A. M., Woods, P. and Collins, M. (eds.) *Therapeutic Interventions for Forensic Mental Health Nurses*, Chapter 4. Jessica Kingsley, London.

South London and Maudsley NHS Trust (2004) *Clinical Services Directory*. Crisis Recovery Unit [FM1], Bethlem. Accessed through: `http://www.slam.nhs.uk/services/pages/detail.asp?id=432`. Accessed 23 November 2004.

Timko, C. and Moos, R. (2004) Measuring the therapeutic environment. In: Campling, P., Davies, S. and Farquharson, G. (eds.) *From Toxic Institutions to Therapeutic Environments: Residential Settings in Mental Health Services*, Chapter 14. Gaskell, London.

Tolmacz, R. (2001) The secure-base function in a therapeutic community for adolescents. *Therapeutic Communities*, **22**(2), 1.

Tones, K. and Green, J. (2002) The empowerment imperative in health promotion. In: Dooher, J. and Byrt, R. (eds.) *Empowerment and Participation: Power, Influence and Control in Contemporary Health Care*, Chapter 5. Quay Books, Mark Allen Publishing, Dinton, Salisbury.

Warren, F., Evans, C., Dolan, B. and Norton, K. (2004) Impulsivity and self-damaging behaviour in severe personality disorder: the impact of democratic therapeutic community treatment. *Therapeutic Communities*, **25**(1), 55–72.

Wright, D. C. and Woo, W. L. (2000) Treating post-traumatic stress disorder in a therapeutic community: the experience of a Canadian psychiatric hospital. *Therapeutic Communities*, **21**(2), 105–118.

CHAPTER 15

Personality disorder: specialist psychological approaches

Michael Doyle, Anne Aiyegbusi and Paul Burbery

Introduction

Personality disorders are common conditions, although there is considerable variation in severity, and in the degree of distress and dysfunction caused. People with personality disorders are more likely to suffer from drug or alcohol problems and are also more likely to suffer from adverse life events, such as relationship difficulties, housing problems and long-term unemployment (Moran, 2003). The highest prevalence of personality disorders can be found in prison populations where the prevalence of any personality disorder in prisoners can be as high as 78% for remanded males, 64% for sentenced males and 50% for women (Singleton *et al.*, 1998). They are also common in populations of psychiatric patients where they can form the main psychiatric condition or present as co-morbid disorders. The prevalence can be as high as 50% and amongst in-patients with drug, alcohol or eating disorders the prevalence can be as high as 70% (de Girolamo and Dotto, 2000).

Despite the high prevalence of people suffering from personality disorder in mental health services, there is much debate on the issue of treatability (Clift, 1999). Personality disorder is primarily a disorder of interpersonal functioning; its presence is therefore likely to evoke a negative response from carers (Duggan, 2000) and in the public mind there is a strong association between personality disorder and antisocial behaviour where, '... *the use of the concept may appear to be a medical sanctioning of irresponsible conduct*' (Duggan, 2000, p. 155). It has been argued that as a result of the lack of conclusive evidence for effective treatments for people with personality disorder, the likelihood of mental health nurses adopting a therapeutically nihilistic approach is increased (Bowers *et al.*, 2000). This is reinforced by the fact that patients with personality disorder are among the most complex and demanding clients that nurses are likely to encounter.

As the debate about treatability continues to rage extensive literature regarding the treatment of personality disorder has developed. Although the studies are not always of impeccable methodological rigour (McMurran, 2002), there are a number of reviews that suggest that treatment can be effective, but that this may take time (Sanislow and McGlashan, 1998; Target, 1998). In terms of availability of therapies, Byrt *et al.* (2005) noted:

> A few specialist centres provide treatment for individuals with personality disorder diagnoses according to the National Institute for Mental Health in England (2003). These include therapeutic communities in health services (Bree *et al.*, 2003, Campling *et al.*, 2004) and prisons (Davies, 2004; Shine, 2000). In addition, some units offer cognitive behavioural therapy (Rogers and Gournay, 2002; Tennant *et al.*, 2000; Woods, 2001), including dialectical behavioural therapy (Jones, 2002). Rational emotive behaviour therapy has also been used (Sacks, 2004).

Schema therapy has been proposed as an effective treatment that is more appropriate than cognitive behaviour therapy for people with personality disorder (Young, 2003). In addition, a meta-analysis of treatment outcomes with 'Psychopaths' indicates that contrary to popular belief, treatment with this group can be effective, with cognitive-behavioural therapies and psychodynamic approaches showing particular promise (Salekin, 2002).

Although the evidence for effective nursing intervention with this client group is equivocal and far from conclusive (Woods and Richards, 2002), it is important for mental health nurses to be aware of the psychological therapeutic approaches that have shown promise, particularly as the absence of a positive therapeutic approach can lead to the collapse of a rehabilitative ideal with such patients. This can lead to an emphasis upon incapacitation and deterrence that in turn may promote negative and punitive approaches (Palmer, 1992). This chapter will consider three psychological approaches that have shown promise for treating and managing people with personality disorder. These are a psychodynamic approach, cognitive behavioural therapy and schema focused therapy.

Psychodynamic approaches

By operationalising the interpersonal domain, Blackburn (1992, 1998) and Blackburn and Renwick (1996) were able to demonstrate that personality-disordered patients in secure settings present with exceptionally high levels of interpersonal disturbance. This suggests that positive change requires psychological therapy combined with structured, skilfully applied interpersonal interventions in the social environment. Such interpersonal interventions would be required to target the personality-disordered patient's interpersonal disturbance. Nurses, with their professional bases within the social environments of services, would therefore be required to implement a rigorous model of interpersonal change and therefore have a particularly challenging role in the patient's care and treatment. This is especially so because the main therapeutic tool for mental health nurses is the nurse–patient relationship. A psychodynamic nursing approach requires the therapeutic use of self within the context of the nurse–patient relationship to be the main therapeutic tool. The therapeutic use of self would of course be informed and therefore substantially strengthened by a psychodynamic model.

Psychodynamic model and application to nursing practice

As Griffiths and Leach (1998) point out, there has been relatively little attempt in the UK to integrate psychodynamic (or psychoanalytically derived) ideas into mental health nursing practice. This model tends to be well established in the therapeutic communities where specialist treatment for personality-disordered patients is provided. It should probably be borne in mind that the relative absence of a clinical model that enables front line mental health nurses to interact closely with personality-disordered patients has occurred within the context of a mental health system in the UK that has largely excluded personality-disordered people from receiving care and treatment (National Institute for Mental Health in England, 2003). It has been suggested that the absence of a way for mental health professionals to manage the intense emotions provoked by personality-disordered patients who present for care and treatment has contributed to their exclusion from services.

Complex emotions

Hinshelwood (2002, p. 20) gets to the very heart of the matter when he says that: 'The fate of helpers who care for personality disorder is to feel abused by those they aim to help'. For this reason, personality-disordered patients remain disliked by mental heath professionals (Lewis and Appleby, 1988). It is by approaching the task of caring for personality-disordered patients from a relational perspective that it is possible to begin to understand why these people are experienced as difficult to help and emotionally troublesome to professionals attempting to provide care and treatment. A psychodynamic model provides a framework for making sense of the way that personality-disordered patients may make professionals feel uncomfortable in very specific ways. At the core of this model is the conceptualisation of personality disorder as a disturbance that arises as a result of adverse developmental experiences. In the case of what are often referred to as severe personality disorders, these adverse developmental events inevitably arise from such experiences as, loss, toxic separations, deprivation, abuse, abandonment or neglect, typically perpetrated by primary caregivers and others who have been entrusted with their early care and well-being. It is this damaging emotional situation that lends itself to problems with trust and being on the receiving end of care and treatment in later life. For example, the experience of having a fear-inducing primary carer during early development may mean that when in need of care in adult life, the health care professionals who attempt to deliver that care are then experienced as fear-inducing. In psychodynamic terms, the way in which a current carer is unconsciously experienced as if they are a past carer is known as transference. The interaction, should it involve someone with severe personality disorder is unlikely to end there though. Because the traumatic experience with their earliest primary carer has not been processed through thought, it cannot be recognised or communicated verbally. What makes interactions with these patients so emotionally difficult for professionals is the way in which distress is communicated.

The patient is likely to behave in a way that ends up making the professional feel frightened and anxious or angry in a particularly intense and uncomfortable way. In psychodynamic terms this may be referred to as countertransference, or in other words, the way the patient makes the professional carer feel. The patients who are experienced as difficult are those who can only communicate their distress and disturbance through countertransference. Casement (1985) uses the term 'communication by impact' to describe how some patients, who cannot express difficult feelings verbally, do so by making therapists actually experience those difficult to tolerate feelings. The emotional discomfort that professionals are left feeling contributes to their avoidance of these patients. Prolonged, unsupervised contact may result in some professionals becoming drawn into abusive relationships with personality-disordered patients. The result for the patients is that they experience failed care once again.

A destructive cycle

A particular problem that personality-disordered patients present with is the fact that their experiences of failed care have often left them with an unconscious belief that their pain and disturbance cannot be tolerated or contained by anybody. Past experiences have shaped this view, and where there has been a cycle of rejection and mistreatment on the part of caring agencies, including health care services, the patient's belief in their self as a disaster becomes further reinforced. Health care services come to represent, in a concrete way, the care that was denied the patient in early life and thus can also become the focus for anger as well as a stage for re-enacting their early traumatic experience. Davies (1996) describes how forensic professionals can become drawn into these unwritten scripts, acting out roles ascribed by the patient's internal world. Unless professionals know about the patient's early life and what they experienced in terms of negative developmental experiences, they cannot act as free agents or effective clinicians who aim to play a part in discontinuing these destructive cycles. It is therefore important to know what destructive interpersonal cycle requires to be addressed (Davies, 1996; Van Der Kolk, 1996).

Case example

Tyrone is a 25-year-old man who was abandoned when he was ten months old by his mother, who was a single parent. He was found in a shop doorway by a passer-by. His physical state strongly indicated that in his short life he had experienced neglect and deprivation. Tyrone was placed in a Local Authority nursery until he was adopted at the age of two years. Although he experienced good enough care by his adoptive parents, Tyrone was a difficult child who frequently made his adopted family feel he was trying to force them to reject him. Helping him to feel secure was very difficult and he tended to break every rule of the home. Tyrone found it very difficult to manage his relationship with siblings, either ruthlessly competing with them for the parents' attention or disengaging completely in a very passive and disturbing way.

Because of his behaviour in the classroom, Tyrone was excluded from mainstream schooling at the age of eight years. He attended a special school where there was a very high staff to pupil ratio. In this special setting Tyrone was more contained and much better able to concentrate on schoolwork.

When Tyrone reached adolescence his problematic behaviour escalated and came to the attention of police. He regularly stole, and when he developed an addiction to opiates his stealing became prolific in his attempt to fund his addiction. This continued into his early twenties. When burgling a residence, he was interrupted by the arrival home of the single woman who owned the property. For reasons he has never been able to explain, Tyrone was enraged by being disturbed in this way and badly assaulted the victim, both physically and sexually. After a period on remand where his behaviour became out of control, Tyrone was transferred to a secure mental health service. During the assessment process, Tyrone failed to develop a therapeutic relationship with his primary nurse, who he seemed to see only as a vehicle for obtaining prescribed painkiller medication, which he often demanded. He was described as either apathetic or extremely persecutory to professionals and his fellow patients, who he seemed to have extreme difficulty tolerating. Eventually he was transferred back to prison and regarded as untreatable.

Case example discussion

Any mental health treatment agency would need to make sense of the impact that such immense trauma in his early development would have on Tyrone's personality development. Of particular importance would be the early abandonment, rejection, neglect and deprivation at the hands of his mother. After that, a further separation occurred when he was moved from the nursery to his adoptive family. Extraordinarily, given the extent of his early trauma, Tyrone's adoptive family were able to provide an environment that, while struggling to contain him did not reject him outright and did not re-enact the early traumas. This experience, it may be hypothesised, probably enabled Tyrone to progress through childhood and early adolescence without major incident. However, within the family some of his personality difficulties were already evident. His unconscious efforts to bring about rejection and abandonment, for example, could be understood in terms of his trying to take control of an anticipated, unbearable, ending that he felt was inevitable. It would be easier for Tyrone to end a relationship than it would be to tolerate the anxiety of waiting to be rejected. Also, attachment feelings which became intensified by the presence of 'siblings' and the rivalry for parental figures' attention were clearly difficult for him to manage, with Tyrone sometimes becoming apathetic, in keeping with the wounded spirit of an abandoned child in order to manage the agony of competing for his adoptive parents' love, when unconsciously he expects his attempts to be met with rejection. However, at other times he attempted to force himself onto his parents in a way that appeared ruthlessly controlling. The problem of managing situations where he had to compete with 'siblings' was also apparent at school, where Tyrone could not cope in mainstream schooling but was able to manage in a special school with a high staff to pupil ratio.

Hypotheses could (and probably should) be made about the psychodynamics, or unconscious motivations, underlying Tyrone's drug taking and offending behaviour (see Welldon and Van Velsen, 1997). It would be fairly safe to say that he had been robbing others, as he unconsciously felt robbed of his biological mother and the love she was unable to provide. Addiction to drugs could be understood in terms of an attachment to a destructive object, which he in turn was using to self-destruct. This would be in identification with his destructive biological mother, who almost annihilated him psychically (Hinshelwood, 2002). As with many self-destructive behaviours, they often serve multiple functions for the individual. For someone who is extremely anxious and fearful of rejection, an attachment to drugs also provides a way of managing a relationship while avoiding real relationships with human beings. Painkilling medication is sometimes experienced in a concrete way as a method of relieving psychic pain, and in the short term it often does appear to do so.

Tyrone's index offence, it may be hypothesised, was an act of violence driven by rage at his biological mother that for a reason not yet known was triggered in a situation where his quest for care, however perverse, was interrupted by a single woman who was shocked by his unwanted presence.

A psychodynamic nursing assessment of Tyrone's needs prior to admission to the secure service could have provided a proactive mechanism for managing his personality disorder. As it is, the team could be described as blindly acting out the unwritten script of his internal world drama; in other words, when he set up the same relationships as he always had, nothing was in place to discontinue this pattern, with the ultimate conclusion being his rejection and further deprivation (i.e. prison sentence vs. hospital care).

Implementation of a psychodynamic nursing model

After returning to prison, Tyrone received a lengthy prison sentence for his index offence. He was later transferred to a new service designed especially for the needs of men like him, who had been diagnosed as having severe personality disorder but for whom there had previously been little in the way of mental health provision. This service operated a psychodynamic nursing model.

Prior to his arrival on the unit, a pre-admission nursing care plan was put in place in an attempt to be proactive with regard to Tyrone's needs. The primary aim was seen as achieving containment for his fears about being rejected. His anxiety about being dependent on a single carer was identified and a small team of professionals were identified as being responsible for his care. A number of meetings between key workers and Tyrone took place prior to his admission, with the function of assisting the transition. Tyrone was also admitted by a member of his team when he was also informed about the service, the treatment programme and the routine of the ward in an attempt to assuage his anxiety and bewilderment about transferring from one environment to another. Tyrone was also introduced to other patients and informed about how needs were communicated; that is, through the community meeting and in planned one-to-one sessions with nurses and during individual psychotherapy. Again, this structure was in place to provide some containment about being overlooked or in Tyrone's case, neglected by his carers. By getting to know his fellow patients (siblings), he was able to feel less inclined to compete with them in a destructive way.

There were times when Tyrone struggled in the new unit, but his key workers were able to interpret his difficulties in terms of his fears about being rejected. From a nursing perspective, it was possible to make this interpretation by the way Tyrone made the key nursing staff involved in his care feel. By avoiding them and undermining his care plans, Tyrone made them feel incompetent and unwanted. Through supervision it was possible for the nurses to discuss their feelings and understand that they could make sense of these as communications by Tyrone in terms of how he himself was fearful of failing and therefore being rejected.

Summary of psychodynamic nursing approach

A psychodynamic nursing model is of value in the care of people who have personality disorders because it provides a way to manage the intense and usually uncomfortable emotions that these patients stir up in professionals. By using those feelings as a way to understand the patient and inform care plans, it may be possible to overcome the deadlock between service user and professionals that has prevented personality disordered individuals from benefiting from mental health resources in the past.

Cognitive behaviour therapy for personality disorders

Cognitive behaviour therapy (CBT) for personality disorders is a relatively new concept. The traditional cognitive behavioural model developed by Beck *et al.* (1979) emphasises the effect of dysfunctional automatic thoughts, schemas, beliefs and assumptions on dysfunctional behaviour. There are several typical features of CBT in practice. Initially, a thorough assessment is completed that includes consideration of past history, current functioning and contextual factors. Interventions are problem orientated and based on the current 'here and now' time frame. Interventions are based on case formulations (see Figure 15.1) that are developed collaboratively with the patient and, where appropriate, their carers. Focusing on the personal meaning of situations is vital in helping the patient to identify negative thoughts/appraisals about self, the world and the future. How thoughts, feelings and behaviours are linked in maintaining problems is regularly considered. Collaborative hypothesis testing and assignment and completion of between-session exercises are also encouraged. These common stages in applying cognitive behavioural interventions are illustrated in the case example 'David' (see Box 15.1) and the resulting case formulation (see Figure 15.1).

McMurran (2002) reports that cognitive behavioural treatments that purport to treat personality disorders tend to be broad based and address a wide range of interpersonal behaviours, attitudes, cognitions, beliefs and emotional control. In applying the cognitive model to personality disorder, Beck *et al.* (1990) suggested that a simple way to understand personality disorders was to think of them in terms of different interpersonal strategies. When individuals face situations that interfere with the operation of their own particular strategies, the individual can become distressed, depressed or anxious. The strategies become dysfunctional and the diagnosis of personality disorder is appropriate when it causes problems that produce suffering in the patient (e.g. avoidant personality) or difficulties with other people or society (e.g. antisocial personality) (Beck *et al.*, 1990).

Although broad changes in personality may occur as a result of CBT, the primary goal of CBT is not personality restructuring. The goals of CBT for people with personality disorder are usually developed collaboratively between the therapist and the patient. These typically involve aiming to alleviate the patient's distress by applying 'eclectic' interventions that deal with behaviours, attitudes, cognitions, beliefs and emotional control. Due to the often complex nature of the problems experienced by people with personality disorder, attempts have been made to modify the

Box 15.1: Case example 'David'.

David is a 24-year-old man admitted to a Regional Psychiatric Secure Unit from prison whilst serving a two-year sentence for sexually assaulting an adult woman. He has a history of similar offences and a history of brief admissions to local psychiatric units following episodes of self-harm.

David's early years were traumatic; he frequently witnessed his father and stepfather physically assaulting his mother. Both his father and stepfather were violent towards him. His mother was an alcoholic and not affectionate. From an early age David was often left alone at home or in the care of a maternal aunt who was five years older than him. He was teased and bullied by his aunt, and from the age of 11 to 13 his aunt and a boyfriend sexually abused him.

At school he was shy and withdrawn. Often the victim of bullying, he would frequently truant and he left school at 16 with no qualifications. When he was 17 his mother and stepfather forced him out of the family home following a violent altercation. Shortly after this incident he committed his first indecent assault, which was quickly followed by his first psychiatric admission. He has had a number of unskilled jobs, but these have always been short-lived due to the high levels of anxiety he experiences in social situations.

Whilst serving his most recent sentence David made a number of attempts to harm himself. These resulted in a referral to a Forensic Psychiatrist who recommended he be transferred to his local Regional Secure Unit.

Following his admission, David presented as very withdrawn and isolated. He frequently rebuffed attempts by staff and his peers to get to know him, on occasions becoming aggressive and threatening if he felt the interaction was too intrusive. He would spend long periods of time on his own in his bedroom or the smoke room and would refuse to become involved in any ward-based activities such as community meetings or one-to-one sessions with his Primary Nurse. He would frequently challenge ward policies, for example by smoking in non-designated areas or refusing to get out of bed to engage in a therapeutic activity.

David completed Young's Schema Questionnaire and was assessed as having a 'mistrust/abuse' schema. Patients with this schema have the belief that, given the opportunity, other people will use the patient for their own selfish ends. For example, they will humiliate, abuse, cheat, manipulate or lie to the patient. They also believe that this harm is intentionally inflicted rather than neglectful. This schema is most likely to occur when an individual has been repeatedly subjected to abuse or intentional harm during childhood.

traditional CBT approach applied to Axis 1 and emotional disorders (Freeman and Jackson, 1998; Pretzer and Beck, 1996) to avoid problems frequently encountered when treating people with personality disorders, including treatment resistance and attrition. Some special considerations for working with people with personality disorder are summarised in Box 15.2.

Although there is a wealth of empirical evidence for the efficacy of CBT for emotional disorders such as depression and anxiety (Beck, 1993; Blackburn and Davidson, 1995; Dobson, 1989) the evidence for treating personality disorder is limited. Nevertheless cognitive behavioural approaches have shown promise in treating people with antisocial and borderline personality dis-

Figure 15.1: Cognitive behavioural case formulation 'David'.

Early experiences
Witnessing violence towards mother
Left alone for long periods of time
Teased and bullied at school
Bullied and sexually abused by aunt and her boyfriend

↓

Formation of unconditional schematic (core) beliefs
People cannot be trusted; they will reject me or try to hurt me
No one likes me

↓

Formation of conditional schematic beliefs
I must not get close to people; they will only hurt me
If I trust people they will take advantage of me
I am not worthy of being liked, I deserve to be hurt and abused

↓

Critical incident
↓
(Assumptions activated)

↓

Negative automatic thoughts
Don't trust the staff: they don't really care and they will only let you down
I am worthless and deserve to be punished
I deserve to be hurt and abused

AFFECT
Sad, guilty, shame, hostile, angry

PHYSIOLOGY
Tense, tremor, butterflies in stomach

BEHAVIOUR
Isolates self, solitary activities, harms self, ignoring others, confrontational interactions with staff and peers

COGNITIVE PROCESSES
Ruminating on past experiences, poor concentration

Summary of formulation
By isolating himself and rebuffing others attempts to engage, often in an aggressive manner, David is not allowing himself the opportunity to test out his belief that others cannot be trusted. How David compensates for and maintains his schemas influences his interactions with others. These difficult interactions merely reinforce his beliefs that others cannot be trusted, that he is not worthy of being liked and that he deserves to be abused.

Recommendation for nursing management
Nursing interventions should be aimed at disconfirming David's schemas. Staff need to understand that his social withdrawal and anti-authoritarian attitude are driven by his beliefs about himself. Reassurance should be given that he will not be abused or rejected and that staff are here to protect him.

Box 15.2: Special considerations when using cognitive behaviour therapy with people with personality disorder.

1. Increased activity of therapist in sessions focusing more attention on engagement and development of therapeutic relationship
2. Be prepared for long-term therapeutic engagement with client
3. Place emphasis and spend extra time on developing shared case conceptualisation
4. Collaboratively develop clearly defined, shared goals with emphasis on self-management
5. Introduce efficacy-enhancing and anxiety-reducing interventions early to enhance confidence
6. Attempt to link early maladaptive schemas with 'here and now' thoughts, feelings and behaviour
7. Focus on modifying core underlying beliefs and early maladaptive schema
8. Maintain stable framework and structure of treatment
9. Constant awareness of potential boundary violations paying careful attention to transference and counter-transference
10. Be aware of environmental and pharmacological influences on behaviour
11. Ongoing assessment of risk to self and others
12. Anticipate problems with compliance and prepare constructive response

---

order (Davidson and Tyrer, 1996), psychopathy (Salekin, 2002; Hughes *et al.*, 1997) prisoners (Reiss *et al.*, 1996) and people detained in a specialist personality disorder unit (McMurran *et al.*, 1999; Warren *et al.*, 2003). A derivative of traditional CBT is *Dialectic Behaviour Therapy* developed by Marsha Linehan. This has been found to effective in treating parasuicidal behaviour, anger and social adjustment in females with borderline personality disorder (Linehan, 1993) and in females with co-morbid borderline personality disorder and substance abuse (Linehan *et al.*, 1999). Furthermore, cognitive-behavioural approaches have generally been found to be more effective than any other psychotherapeutic interventions in treating people with personality disorder (McMurran, 2002; Salekin, 2002) and formulation-based cognitive behavioural interventions are seen by many as the psychological treatment of choice when working with violent and forensic populations (McGuire, 1995; Novaco, 1997; Thomson, 2000; Wong and Gordon, 2000). In summary the research to date suggests that CBT can have a positive impact on the problems resulting from personality disorder. Although we do not yet have sufficient empirical data, evidence to date suggests that CBT is likely to be superior to other forms of psychotherapy.

The application of CBT for personality disorders focuses more on altering underlying belief structures rather than a reduction in symptoms. Application of cognitive-behavioural principles to nursing practice and collaborative care plans, must therefore concentrate on a patient's underlying belief structures as well as attempting to manage the symptoms displayed by the individual. This should assist the nurse in gaining a more comprehensive understanding of the origin, development and maintenance of the person's behaviour and symptoms, which in turn should result in more client-centred, effective nursing interventions. This approach should foster improved communication between staff and ensure that nurses are less likely to focus solely on patients' behaviour.

Despite the promise of CBT for people with personality disorder, Young (2003) argues that short-term cognitive therapy is unlikely to be successful for patients with personality disorders because for cognitive therapy to have any chance of success the patient must have seven basic characteristics that are often lacking in patients with personality disorders. These include lacking ability or willingness to access feelings, thoughts and images, having little motivation to complete homework assignments and to learn self-control strategies, and problems engaging in a collaborative relationship with the therapist within a few sessions.

Three main characteristics of personality disorders – rigidity, avoidance and long-term interpersonal difficulties – lead to considerable difficulty in applying CBT because these characteristics are not compatible with the features of CBT described above. For example, for short-term cognitive therapy to succeed patients have to have relatively easy access to their thoughts and feelings. However, in many personality disorders thoughts and feelings are often avoided because of the pain they cause to the patient.

Young (2003) proposes that for cognitive therapy for personality disorders to have a chance of success the cognitive therapist needs to primarily focus on the deepest level of cognition, the *Early Maladaptive Schema*. If the therapist were to primarily focus on automatic thoughts, cognitive distortions and underlying assumptions as is the case with short-term cognitive therapy they would not be able to overcome the rigidity, avoidance and interpersonal difficulties that have developed as a result of a person's maladaptive schemas.

Schema-focused therapy

Patients with personality disorders will have maladaptive schemas that underlie their patterns of dysfunctional behaviour (Scott *et al.*, 1993). Segal (1988, p. 150) defined schema as:

> Organised elements of past reactions and experiences that form a relatively cohesive and persistent body of knowledge capable of guiding subsequent perception and appraisal.

These schemas are typically entrenched underlying beliefs that bias interpretations of events in a consistent manner, and in some conditions may appear delusional in intensity. For example, people with psychopathic traits or antisocial personality disorder may hold key beliefs such as 'I have to look out for myself' and 'people will get me if I don't get them first'. The person with paranoid personality disorder may believe 'I cannot trust other people' and 'I have to be on guard at all times'. The importance of these beliefs is that they are the primary focus of treatment in cognitive therapy of personality disorders (Beck *et al.*, 1990; Young, 2003). A person views the world through their schemas, as they are important feelings and beliefs that the person holds about themselves and the environment and they are accepted without question. Therefore schemas operate as relationship templates: they allow a person to make sense of themselves within relationships and also influence the predictions a person makes about how they will be treated in future relationships (Murphy and McVey, 2001).

As a result of maladaptive schemas, the strategies that people with personality disorder use to interact with the world, develop relationships or deal with interpersonal problems are often ineffective (Scott *et al.*, 1993). The differing behavioural pathologies of the various personality disorders are linked to specific clusters of characteristic schemas (Beck *et al.*, 1990). For example a person with a dependent personality might assume that '*I cannot live alone*' or '*if he (she) leaves me I'll die*'. Whereas a person with a schizoid personality might believe '*I will always be alone*' or '*keep away from others*' (Scott *et al.*, 1993, p. 371). Some schemas common in people with personality disorder are illustrated in the case of 'David' (see Figure 15.1).

During childhood, schemas can be very adaptive (Murphy and McVey, 2001) and people are very often reluctant to abandon their schemas. In later life, schemas can become dysfunctional. A child abandoned by her father who she felt very close to may develop a schema that predicts that '*men who show me affection will abandon me*'. This could become generalised to all men and would prevent her from engaging in genuinely warm and loving relationships. Therefore, schema can be maladaptive when they are applied to all interactions with people beyond the family (or original providers of care) because they cause people to predict that many different people will all treat us in an identical fashion (Murphy and McVey, 2001).

Thus far, Young (2003) has identified 18 common schema patterns that cluster into five broad domains. Each of the five domains represents an important component of a child's core needs. Schemas interfere with the child's attempts to get the core needs met within each domain. The five domains are: (1) disconnection and rejection; (2) impaired autonomy and performance; (3) impaired limits; (4) other directedness; (5) over-vigilance and inhibition.

Young (2003) hypothesises that there are three processes that perpetuate the presence of maladaptive schema: schema maintenance, avoidance and compensation. Avoidance is the strategy that individuals use to prevent the activation of particular schemas, as the triggering of maladaptive schemas will usually result in high levels of affect, such as fear, anxiety, intense anger, sadness or guilt. An example of this could be a girl who has been sexually abused by her father might avoid entering into adult sexual relationships with men (Murphy and McVey, 2001). Schema maintenance refers to the process by which early maladaptive schemas are reinforced. Strategies used include cognitive distortions or self-defeating behaviour; individuals reinforce their schemas because the early maladaptive schemas form the cornerstone of their self-concepts. For example the sexually abused child may repeatedly place herself in situations of sexual vulnerability, such as prostituting herself or engaging in relationships with sexually dominant or sadistic males. Compensatory strategies refer to the behaviour that an individual adopts that, for all intents and purposes may appear to contradict the schema, but it is adopted out of a need to overcompensate. For example, some people who have experienced significant emotional deprivation as children behave in a narcissistic manner as adults. The sexually abused child who manages her schema in a compensatory manner may engage in sexual relationships where she is the dominant sexual partner or even a sexual abuser (Murphy and McVey, 2001).

Schema compensation and avoidance are used by an individual to try to resist a recreation of their childhood experiences; however, all three processes mentioned above actually perpetuate the schema; compensatory and avoidant strategies prevent the individual from having new experiences that may enable them to broaden their repertoire of expectations of interpersonal relationships (Murphy and McVey, 2001, p. 10). It is often the case that these strategies elicit the type of response from others that is exactly the type of experience that the strategy is designed to avoid.

Treatment phases and strategies in schema-focused therapy

There are two phases to schema-focused therapy (SFT). The first phase consists of assessment and conceptualisation, while the second phase focuses on schema change (Young, 2003). The aim is to weaken the early maladaptive schemas as much as possible and then strengthen the individual's healthy side (Bricker and Young, 1993).

Young (2003) identifies four major treatment strategies: cognitive, behavioural, interpersonal and behavioural. Cognitive strategies include reviewing the evidence that supports the schemas, critically examining the supportive evidence, reviewing evidence that contradicts the schema, illustrating to the patient how he or she discounts contradictory evidence, the development of flashcards that contradict the schema and challenging the schema whenever it is activated inside or outside therapy. Experiential techniques include creating imagery dialogues with the patient's parents and emotional catharsis. Interpersonal techniques include the use of the interpersonal relationship itself, to provide a therapeutic relationship that counteracts early maladaptive schemas and group therapy exercises. The aim of behavioural techniques is to change schema-driven behaviours; this involves pushing the patient to change long-term behaviour patterns that have reinforced the schemas for most of the patient's life (Young, 2003).

Young (2003) identifies a number of differences between schema-focused therapy and short-term cognitive therapy. These include less use of guided discovery and more confrontation. There is more use of the therapeutic relationship as a vehicle for change. The therapy is lengthier, as there is more resistance to change and the level of affect is much higher during schema-focused therapy sessions. The therapist is more concerned with identifying and overcoming cognitive, affective and behavioural avoidance and much more time is spent exploring the childhood origins of schemas and experiential techniques surrounding these early experiences.

Schema-focused therapy retains many of the important elements that differentiate Beck's approach from more traditional client-centred or psychoanalytic therapies. These include the higher levels of therapist activity, much more systematic change techniques and a strong emphasis on self-help homework assignments. The therapeutic relationship is collaborative rather than neutral and the schema-focused approach is much more rapid and direct than conventional psychotherapy. Finally, the therapist uses an empirical approach, as the analysis of evidence is a crucial aspect of schema change.

Applying a schema-focused approach to nursing practice

Moran and Mason (1996) suggest that to be able to effectively nurse patients with personality disorders the nursing staff need to be less reliant on the medical model as a guide for their interventions and that they should incorporate a psychological understanding into their care and treatment. Murphy and McVey (2001) identified five core areas of difficulty that posed particular challenges to the nursing staff. Firstly, nursing training inadequately prepares nurses for this work. Secondly, personality-disordered patients are more demanding and less reinforcing than mentally ill patients. Thirdly, the role of providing nursing care to personality-disordered patients is high in conflict. Fourthly, the role of providing nursing care to this group of patients is traumatising and finally those nursing a person with personality disorder require specific skills and qualities.

Murphy and McVey (2001) describe a training project aimed at overcoming these core areas of difficulty for nurses in an inpatient setting. The case example 'David' in Figure 15.1 illustrates the key stages of schema-focused interventions leading to recommendations for nursing management. Following schema-focused training and supervision the nursing team gained a common language that allowed them to have a shared understanding of each patient. The involvement in the development of such a cognitive milieu would offer the nurses the opportunity for the development and application of their own therapeutic skills (Bowler *et al.*, 1993). The patients reported that they felt more strongly validated by the nursing staff and both staff and patients felt that they had a common language with which to communicate with each other and that a shared understanding of the patients' difficulties had been established. The involvement of the nursing staff in this way has allowed this particular ward to develop from what Wright *et al.* (1993) describe an 'add-on' model of cognitive milieu (where the ward has its own milieu and cognitive therapy is provided as a supplement) into a much more comprehensive model.

Chapter summary

Despite the high prevalence of people suffering from personality disorder in mental health services, there is much debate on the issue of treatability. Although the evidence for effective treatment of personality disorders remains at best inconclusive, it is important for mental health nurses to be aware of the psychological therapeutic approaches that have shown promise in order to avoid therapeutic nihilism. Three contrasting psychological approaches have been briefly described above. All have shown a certain promise in treating people with personality disorder, but as yet the evidence base is limited. Whereas a psychodynamic nursing model may provide an effective way to manage the intense and uncomfortable emotions that these patients stir up in professionals, cognitive-behavioural approaches appear to have the strongest empirical evidence base. Despite this, extensive modifications to the traditional CBT approach have been made and are currently under development in an attempt to understand the role of underlying schemas in influencing the problems and needs of people with personality disorder. In light of recent government initiatives, it is likely that research currently under way will finally begin to unravel the complexities of the disorders of personality and offer new directions in psychological treatment. In the meantime mental health nurses who are expected to care for and treat this client group need to keep up-to-date on the developments in positive psychological approaches to management and treatment.

References

American Psychiatric Association (1994) *Diagnostic and Statistical Manual of Mental Disorders*, 4th edn (DSM-IV). American Psychiatric Association, Washington.

Beck, A. T., Rush, J., Shaw, B. and Emery, G. (1979) *Cognitive Therapy of Depression*. Guilford Press, New York.

Beck, A. T. (1993) Cognitive therapy: past, present and future. *Journal of Consulting and Clinical Psychology*, **61**(2), 194–197.

Beck, A. T., Rush, J., Shaw, B. and Emery, G. (1979) *Cognitive Therapy Of Depression*. Guilford Press, New York.

Beck, A. T., Freeman, A. and Associates. (1990) *Cognitive Therapy of Personality Disorders*. Guilford Press, New York.

Blackburn, I. M. and Davidson, K. (1995)*Cognitive Therapy for Depression & Anxiety*. Blackwell Science, London.

Blackburn, R. (1992) Criminal behaviour, personality disorder and mental illness: the origins of confusion. *Criminal Behaviour and Mental Health*, **2**, 66–67.

Blackburn, R. (1998) Criminality and the interpersonal circle in mentally disordered offenders. *Criminal Justice and Behaviour*, **25**(2), 155–176.

Blackburn, R. and Renwick, S. J. (1996) Rating scale for measuring the interpersonal circle in forensic psychiatric patients. *Psychological Assessment*, **8**(1), 76–84.

Bowers, L., McFarlane, L., Kiyimba, F., Clark, N. and Alexander, J. (2000) *Factors Underlying and Maintaining Nurses' Attitudes to Patients with Severe Personality Disorder*. Final report to the National Forensic Mental Health R&D, City University, London.

Bowler, R. A., Moonis, L. J. and Thase, M. E. (1993) The role of the nurse in the cognitive milieu. In: Wright, J. H., Thase, M. E., Beck, A. T. and Ludgate, J. W. (eds.) *Cognitive Therapy for Inpatients*, pp. 247–272) Guilford Press, New York.

Bree, A., Campling, P. and Liderth, S. (2003) Empowerment in mental health: the therapeutic community model. In: Dooher, J. and Byrt, R. (eds.) *Empowerment and the Health Service User*. Quay Books, Mark Allen Publishing, Dinton, Salisbury.

Bricker, D. and Young, J. E. (1993) *A Client's Guide to Schema Focused Therapy*. Cognitive Therapy Centre, New York.

Byrt, R., Wray, C. and 'Tom' (2005) Towards hope and inclusion: nursing interventions in a medium secure service for men with 'personality disorders'. *Mental Health Practice*, **8**(8), 38–43.

Campling, P., Davies, S. and Farquharson, G. (eds.) (2004) *From Toxic Institutions to Therapeutic Environments: Residential Settings in Mental Health Services*. Gaskell, London.

Casement, P. (1985) *On Learning from the Patient*. Brunner-Routledge, East Sussex.

Clift, I. (1999) Personality disorder: time for a new approach? *Mental Health Practice*, **2**(10), 35–38.

Davidson, K. M. and Tyrer, P. (1996) Cognitive therapy for antisocial and borderline personality disorders: single case study series. *British Journal of Clinical Psychology*, **35**, 413–429.

Davies, R. (1996) The interdisciplinary network and the internal world of the offender. In: Cordess, C. and Cox, M. (eds.) *Forensic Psychotherapy: Crime, Psychodynamics and the Offender Patient*, Chapter 9, Part 2, Mainly practice, pp. 133–144. Jessica Kingsley, London.

Davies, S. (2004) Secure psychiatric services. In: Campling, P., Davies, S. and Farquharson, G. (eds.) *From Toxic Institutions to Therapeutic Environments: Residential Settings in Mental Health Services*, Chapter 12, pp. 233–243. Gaskell, London.

de Girolamo, G. and Dotto, P. (2000) Epidemiology in personality disorders. In: Gelder, M. G., Lopez-Ibor, J. J. and Andreasan, N. C. (eds.) *New Oxford Textbook of Psychiatry*, Vol 1, pp. 959–964. Oxford University Press, New York.

Dobson, K. S. (1989) A meta-analysis of the effectiveness of cognitive therapy for depression. *Journal of Consulting and Clinical Psychology*, **57**, 414–419.

Dolan, B. and Coid, J. (1993) *Psychopathic and Antisocial Personality Disorders: Treatment and Research Issues*. Gaskell, London.

Duggan, C. (2000) Personality disorder – what role for the mental health services? In: Gregoire, A. (ed.) *Adult Severe Mental Illness*. GMM, London.

Freeman, A. and Jackson, J. T. (1998) Cognitive behavioural treatment of personality disorders. In Tarrier, N., Wells, A. and Haddock, G. (eds.) *Treating Complex Cases: The CBT Approach*, pp. 319–339. Wiley, London.

Griffiths, P. and Leach, G. (1998) Psychosocial nursing: a model learnt from experience. In: Barnes, E., Griffiths, P., Ord, J. and Wells, D. (eds.) *Face-To-Face with Distress: The Professional Use of Self in Psychosocial Care*, Chapter 1, pp. 5–41. Butterworth-Heinemann, Oxford.

Hinshelwood, R. D. (2002) Abusive help – helping abuse: the psychodynamic impact of severe personality disorder on caring institutions. *Criminal Behaviour and Mental Health*, **12**, S20–S30.

Hughes, G., Hogue, T., Hollin, C. and Champion, H. (1997) First-stage evaluation of a treatment programme for personality disordered offenders. *Journal of Forensic Psychiatry*, **8**, 515–527.

Jones, A. (2002) DBT and treating personality disorder. *Mental Health Nursing*, **22**(2), 6–9.

Lewis, G. and Appleby, L. (1988) Personality disorder: the patients psychiatrists dislike. *British Journal of Psychiatry*, **153**, 44–49.

Lindsay, M. (1983) A critical review of the validity of the therapeutic community. *Nursing Times*, **78**, 105–108.

Linehan, M. M. (1993) *Cognitive Behavioural Treatment of Borderline Personality disorder*. Guilford Press, New York.

Linehan, M. M., Schmidt, H., Dimef, L. A., Craft, J. C., Kanter, J. and Comtois, K. A. (1999) Dialectal behaviour therapy for patients with borderline personality disorder and drug-dependence. *American Journal on Addictions*, **8**, 279–292

McGuire, J. (ed.) (1995) *What Works: Reducing Reoffending: Guidelines from Research and Practice*. Wiley, Chichester.

McMurran, M. (2002) *Expert Paper: Personality Disorders*. NHS National Programme on Forensic Mental Health Research and Development, Liverpool.

McMurran, M., Egan, V., Richardson, C. and Ahmadi, S. (1999) Social problem solving in mentally disordered offenders. *Criminal Behaviour and Mental Health*, **9**, 315–322.

Moran, P. (2003) *The Epidemiology of Personality Disorders*. http://www.doh.gov.uk/mental-health/moran.pdf.

Moran, T. and Mason, T. (1996) Revisiting the nursing management of the psychopath. *Journal of Psychiatric and Mental Health Nursing*, **3**, 189–194.

Murphy, N. and McVey, D. (2001) Nursing in-patients with personality disorder: a schema focused approach. *British Journal of Forensic Practice*, **3**(4), 8–15.

National Institute for Mental Health in England (2003) *Personality Disorder: No Longer a Diagnosis of Exclusion. Policy Implementation Guidelines for the Development of Services for People with Personality Disorder.* Department of Health, London.

Novaco, R. (1997) Remediating anger and aggression with violent offenders. *Legal and Criminological Psychology*, **2**, 77–88.

Palmer, T. (1992) *The Re-Emergence of Correctional Intervention.* Newbury Park, London.

Pretzer, J. L. and Beck, A. T. (1996) A cognitive theory of personality disorders. In: Clarkin, J. F. and Lenzenweger, M. F. (eds.) *Major Theories of Personality Disorder*, pp. 36–105. Guilford Press, New York.

Reiss, D., Grubin, D. and Meux, C. (1996) Young 'psychopaths' in special hospital: treatment and outcome. *British Journal of Psychiatry*, **168**, 98–104.

Rogers, P. and Gournay, K. (2002) Nurse therapy in forensic mental health. In: Kettles, A. M., Woods, P. and Collins, M. (eds.) *Therapeutic Interventions for Mental Health Nurses*, pp. 151–164. Jessica Kingsley, London.

Sacks, S. B. (2004) Rational emotive behaviour therapy: disrupting irrational philosophies. *Journal of Psychosocial Nursing and Mental Health Services*, **42**(5), 22–31.

Salekin, R. T. (2002) Psychopathy and therapeutic pessimism: clinical lore or clinical reality? *Clinical Psychology Review*, **22**, 79–112.

Sanislow, C. A. and McGlashan, T. H. (1998) Treatment outcome in personality disorders. *Canadian Journal of Psychiatry*, **43**, 237–250.

Scott, J., Byers, S. and Turlington, D. (1993) The chronic patient. In: Wright, J. H., Thase, M. E., Beck, A. T. and Ludgate, J. W. (eds.) *Cognitive Therapy with Inpatients.* Guilford Press, New York.

Segal, Z. (1988) Appraisal of the self-schema: construct in cognitive models of depression. *Psychological Bulletin*, **103**, 147–162.

Shine, J. (ed.) (2000) *A Compilation of Grendon Research.* HMP Grendon, Aylesbury.

Singleton, N., Meltzer, H., Gatward, R., Coid, J. and Deasy, D. (1998) *Psychiatric Morbidity Amongst Prisoners.* Office of National Statistics, London.

Target, M. (1998) Outcome research on the psychosocial treatment of personality disorders. *Bulletin of the Menninger Clinic*, **62**, 215–230.

Tennant, A., Davies, C. and Tennant, I. (2000) Working with the personality disordered offender. In: Chaloner, C. and Coffey, M. (eds.) *Forensic Mental Health Nursing: Current Approaches*, pp. 94–117. Blackwell Science, Oxford.

Thomson, L. D. (2000) Management of schizophrenia in conditions of high security. *Advances in Psychiatric Treatment*, **6**, 252–260.

Van Der Kolk, B. A. (1996) The complexity of adaptation to trauma: self regulation, stimulus discrimination, and characterological development. In: Van Der Kolk, B. A., McFarlane, A. C. and Weisaeth, L. (eds.) *Traumatic Stress: The Effects of Overwhelming Experience on Mind, Body and Society*, Chapter 9, pp. 182–213. Guilford Press, New York.

Warren, F., McGauley, G., Norton, K., Dolan, B., Preedy-Fayers, K., Pickering, A. and Geddes, J. (2003) *Review of Treatments for Severe Personality Disorder.* Home Office, London.

Welldon, E. V. and Van Velsen, C. (1997) *A Practical Guide To Forensic Psychotherapy*. Jessica Kingsley, London.

Wong, S. and Gordon, A. (2000) *Violence Reduction Programme: Phases of Treatment and Content Overview*. Regional Psychiatric Centre, Saskatoon, Saskatchewan, Canada.

Woods, P. (2001) Personality disorders. In: Dale, C., Thompson, T. and Woods, P. (eds.) *Forensic Mental Health: Issues in Practice*, pp. 169–178. Baillière Tindall/Royal College of Nursing, Edinburgh.

Woods, P. and Richards, D. (2002) *The Effectiveness of Nursing Interventions with Personality Disorders: A Systematic Review of the Literature*. University of Manchester, School of Nursing, Manchester.

Wright, J. H., Thase, M. E., Beck, A. T. and Ludgate, J. W. (1993) The cognitive milieu: structure and process. In: Wright, J. H., Thase, M. E., Beck, A. T. and Ludgate, J. W. (eds.) *Cognitive Therapy with Inpatients*, pp. 61–90. Guilford Press, New York.

Young, J. E. (2003) *Cognitive Therapy for Personality Disorders: A Schema-Focused Approach*. Professional Resources Press, Sarasota, Fl.

CHAPTER 16

Conclusions: themes, action and research for the future

Alyson McGregor Kettles, Phil Woods and Richard Byrt

Introduction

In this text, we have offered up-to-date and, where possible, research-based accounts of how forensic and mental health nurses can care for people with a personality disorder. We hope within this short chapter to highlight some of the main themes which have emerged. Some key areas of care have been presented and discussed. We have tried to ensure that some of the contributions that forensic and mental health nurses make to the professional care, intervention and treatment of this group of patients have been addressed. Such insights can only provide a basis on which ideas, thinking and future research can be developed around the ways that nurses' roles and interventions can enable the best possible care to be given to the person with a personality disorder.

It is heartening that attention is at last beginning to be paid to this major problem. However, the paucity of evidence for the nursing care of this group of patients and nursing interventions for them has been corroborated throughout the book, and this lack of evidence, in turn, supports the results of the systematic literature review by Woods and Richards (2003). Commonly, staff consider that patients have been receiving treatment by the 'back door', so treatments have been applied under the guise of another mental health problem, such as schizophrenia, substance misuse or depression. This has resulted in the lack of knowledge about specific treatments and interventions suitable for this group of people with this personality disorder as their primary problem.

There is a continuing tendency to apply generic mental health concepts directly to the care of a person with personality disorder in forensic and other mental health environments. This is deleterious to the individual with a personality disorder, as their primary problem is ignored, or treated as unimportant or as a secondary issue with secondary interventions. At worst, the person is not admitted for care when this is needed.

Emerging themes

To us, eleven key themes appear to emerge from this text and these may indeed not come as any real surprise to practitioners. Despite forensic and mental health nurses' move towards professional recognition, nurses have not made much in the way of determined efforts to generate new care pathways for people with personality disorder in their care up until now, although this is beginning to change. Also, despite building an encouraging evidence base for care of individuals with histories of offending associated with mental illness, little specific nursing intervention attention has been paid to the care of the person with a personality disorder who is an offender (Woods and Richards, 2003).

Theme 1: The nurse–patient relationship

There is no doubt that the nurse–patient relationship is the primary vehicle for enabling nursing care for clients and patients with personality disorder. Aiyegbusi (Chapter 6), Collins, Davies and Ashwell (Chapter 11), Kettles and Woodally (Chapter 12) and Byrt (Chapter 14), amongst other authors in this book, all show that forensic and mental health nursing is fundamentally a relational endeavour. As Aiyegbusi states 'the effective treatment of personality disorder requires an interpersonal process ... underpinned by a robust clinical framework and delivered through the effective relational skills of practitioners' (p. 85). This relationship must remain fundamental to the care of this client group. Also of importance, as indicated by several contributors to this book, is a willingness, on the part of the nurse, to endeavour to appreciate the perspectives and (often very painful) experiences of individuals with personality disorder. The engendering of hope, and nursing interventions based on sensitivity to the person's spiritual, cultural, psychosexual, gender and other diversity needs are also crucial aspects of care (see Chapters 5 and 8).

Theme 2: Attitudes

Attitudes are an important feature of any care given. Whilst some staff have very positive attitudes towards individuals with personality disorder, there are many who do not. Many chapters in this text have highlighted this and suggested that a move towards positive changes, both from an individual and an educational shift, needs to be a focus for future care. For example, what has traditionally been termed 'attention-seeking' behaviour needs to be reframed as 'attachment seeking'. Moreover, attention should be, and already is, focusing on the attitudes of policy makers, healthcare managers, educators, and the public. Many of the chapter authors within this text have referred to the attitudes of the staff caring for people with personality disorders and the sense of a 'lack of real care' that pervades the NHS for people with these diagnoses. No matter that personality disorder has not, historically, been recognised as a *dis-ease* in the way that schizophrenia or leukaemia have been; it is still a disorder that affects the person and sometimes, other people in an adverse way. This, alone, requires help and care from empathic and sympathetic staff, no matter whether the presentation is of a primary or a secondary nature.

Theme 3: Stigma

Closely linked to the theme of attitude is the stigmatisation that individuals with personality disorder often find, frequently in terms of 'attention seeking' or 'being aggressive'. Many of the authors who have contributed to this text have acknowledged both this stigmatisation and the difficulties of working with people with a personality disorder. However, nurses are generally well versed at dealing with problems of working with ill people in any environment. Therefore, working with people with personality disorder in conditions of security should be no exception. Several authors (e.g. in Chapters 3, 4, 6, 14 and 15) discuss the particular problems facing people with personality disorders. The diversity issues discussed in Chapters 5 and 8 of this text also apply to this group and they should not be stigmatised in the ways that they have been in the past.

Theme 4: Risk assessment and risk management

Chapters 10 and 11 of this text indicate that risk assessment and risk management are the essential basis for all nursing intervention. Without measures to ensure the safety of the individual and others, other interventions may be ineffective, as Mick Collins, Steffan Davies and Chris Ashwell indicate in their chapter. These authors refer to Collins' and Davies' (2001) Security Needs Assessment Profile, and the need to ensure that aspects of security meet individuals' assessed needs, rather than 'blanket' protocols for security being imposed.

Theme 5: Nursing policy for people with personality disorders

What has emerged is that there is a need for special nursing policy and research with respect to individuals with personality disorder, along with multi-professional care packages and working. There has been some attention paid to people with personality disorders by the NHS National Programme on Forensic Mental Health Research and Development, but this has not been a nursing approach. An expert paper on personality disorders (McMurran, 2002) was written from a psychological point of view. However, given the state of evidence as presented in this text, it is a matter of urgency that nursing people with personality disorders should be given a priority in both policy and research.

Theme 6: A political role for nurses

Central government policy related to individuals with personality disorder often appears to be influenced, to a large extent, by political factors and media and public pressures (see Chapter 3), which can impinge on both the care of individuals with personality disorders and the role of forensic and other mental health nurses (Byrt, 2001). It can be argued that nurses can (and, we would argue, should) have a political role (Byrt, 2000), e.g. through professional associations, trade unions and organisations such as the National Forensic Nurses' Research and Development Group, the Forensic Psychiatric Nurses Association and the Forensic Nurse Consultant Group. Influencing central government policy can be in collaboration with service users, carers and other professionals, as currently occurs in the Mental Health Alliance's efforts to influence new mental health legislation in England and Wales (Mental Health Alliance, 2005).

The nurse's political role particularly applies to proposed or implemented policies and legislation which both fail to contribute to public safety and adversely affect the care or rights of individuals with personality disorders; or result in their receiving services in levels of security greater than is warranted by their assessed levels of risk. Examples of related policy include the 'dangerous and severe personality disorder' (DSPD) services (see Chapter 3), and the increase in levels of security in high-security hospitals, following the Government's implementation of recommendations following the Tilt Report (Department of Health, 2000). Soon after the implementation of the Tilt Report recommendations, the Mental Health Act Commission reported serious and deleterious consequences to patients, related, in part, to the effects of increased security, with consequences for nurses' work with patients (Brindley, 2001).

Theme 7: Attention to education for nurses

Education for nurses is urgently required at both pre- and post-registration levels. Watson and Kettles, in Chapter 7, clearly identify that there is inadequate preparation of nurses. Both educationalists and service managers need to be aware of the 'emotional impact' (see Chapter 6) on nurses caring for individuals with personality disorders, and this needs to be considered in the provision of support, clinical supervision and education and training. As many authors in this book have commented, education needs to be particularly related to issues of safety: and to nurses' attitudes, self-awareness and ethical awareness. In particular, nurses require support, clinical supervision and education which enable them to understand, without rejection, the reasons for individuals' reactions and behaviours; and to find creative ways of coping with the difficult feelings these may arouse (Aiyegbusi, 2002; Bowers, 2002).

Theme 8: Public education and prevention

There is also inadequate public education, with personality disorder remaining invisible despite high-profile anti-stigma campaigns (Crisp *et al.*, 2004). Two mental health nursing roles that could be developed include public education about individuals with personality disorder; and preventative work with children and young people at identified risk of developing personality disorder (Farrington, 2003; Moran and Hagell, 2001).

Care of people with personality disorder has some similarities with other treatment programmes, but we do not know what differences are required because the care applied to this group becomes integrated into mainstream mental health. For example, cognitive behavioural therapies can be applied to a person with a personality disorder. However, it is not clear whether there are any specific differences in the way that these therapies should be applied for the person with an obsessive-compulsive disorder compared with the person with personality disorder. Given the differences in the nature of the disorders, it seems reasonable to assume that there may be application differences. The same can be said for nursing interventions. In Chapters 9–15 these specific issues have been addressed and applied to the care and treatment of the person with a personality disorder.

Theme 9: Integrated health and social care

Another theme to emerge from the text is that of the need for integrated care. Fundamentally, people with personality disorder need to have not only their mental health addressed but assistance with all other areas of their functioning. These areas cannot be dissociated and split up into neat compartments. For this reason, working with other professionals and good multidisciplinary and multi-agency communication are essential if care for people with personality disorder is to have any chance of working at all. Other authors (Chapters 9, 13, 14 and 15) also draw attention to the need for integrated and joined up care services.

Theme 10: Developing the evidence and intervention base in forensic and mental health nursing for people with personality disorders

Ways forward are beginning to be identified. Empirical science has begun to show that there is neuroscientific evidence (Eisenberger *et al.*, 2003) at the heart of this particularly human problem. This small but growing amount of evidence will develop into a body of knowledge that enables nurses to care for patients in a much more appropriate way and to develop the skills and interventions necessary to implement that care. However, nurses have to play an active part in that development process. Some creativity is going to be needed, as well as sound, rigorous, meticulous quantitative research work for treatment and intervention methodology and sound transferable qualitative research work for the relational components of care.

The respective Mental Health Acts in Scotland, England and Wales and Northern Ireland will help with pushing the agenda forward, by at last including personality disorder within the same boundaries as other mental health problems.

Services are developing at all levels of security, and the complexity of such development has been shown and discussed in Chapter 11. However, what we have not addressed in detail is the issue of dangerous and severe personality disorder (DSPD) (Feeney, 2003). Currently services are being developed within prison and high-security environments and we can only await the evaluation of these. However, as any person cared for within the DSPD units will have a clinical diagnosis, as described in Chapter 2, any and all of the discussion in the book relates to them.

Theme 11: A framework for care

Currently, there is no single framework to 'pin' service development or integrated care on. Any framework could be well informed by issues considered in this text. Such a framework would

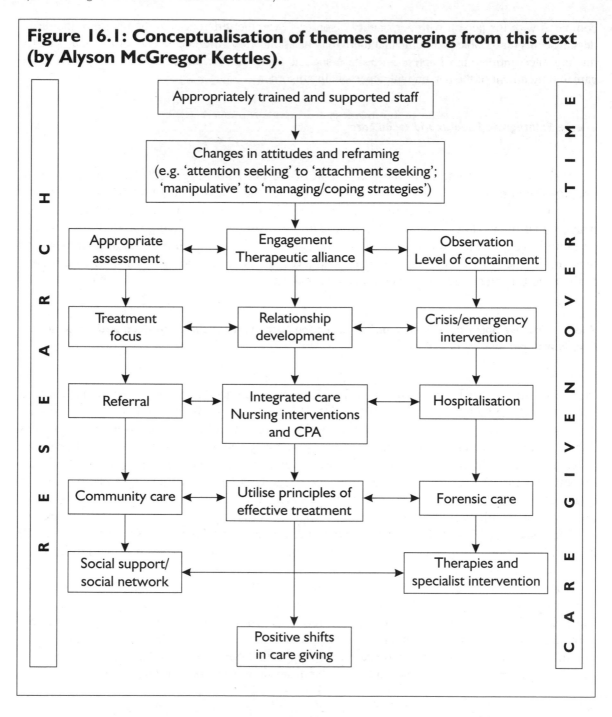

Figure 16.1: Conceptualisation of themes emerging from this text (by Alyson McGregor Kettles).

need to begin with appropriately trained and supported staff with positive attitudes, including the reframing of attitudes of staff in general, to enable the therapeutic process to begin. Some hospitalisation may be required for short periods of time or the longer term involvement in therapeutic communities and community care, with therapies and specialist interventions. Research is required at all points of the process and throughout the process. We have conceptually mapped out such a framework informed from issues emerging from this text. Whilst we are careful not to offer this as a model of care or a definitive framework, we do offer it as a way of developing thinking that will hopefully assist practitioners in developing their own models of care (see Figure 16.1). This tentative framework incorporates what is currently known and what can be done in the future to provide for a greater integration of care. An example is where care is already given over time but the focus on periods of hospitalisation needs to change so that patients are not excluded, admitted for secondary issues or for longer terms than they require, given what is known about observation and engagement with the person with a personality disorder.

Conclusion

We hope that the outcome of this text will be the following:

- That what is known about care can be appropriately used in practice to the benefit of people in any level of security with a diagnosis of personality disorder.
- That this text helps in the education of nurses towards working with people with personality disorder and so care can move forward.
- That the literature presented here helps to inform the way forward and to contribute to the development of appropriate policy, services and interventions.

We hope that you have enjoyed reading this book as much as we have enjoyed writing and editing parts of it. We will close with this quotation from Carl Rogers (1978):

The individual has within himself/herself vast resources for self-understanding, for altering his/her self-concept ... attitudes, and ... self-directed behaviour ... These resources can be tapped if only a definable climate of facilitative psychological attitudes can be provided (Rogers, 1978, p. 7, quoting Rogers, 1974, p. 116).

References

Aiyegbusi, A. (2002) Nursing interventions and future directions with women in secure services. In: Kettles, A. M., Woods, P. and Collins, M. (eds.) *Therapeutic Interventions for Forensic Mental Health Nurses*, Chapter 9. Jessica Kingsley, London.

Bowers, L. (2002) *Dangerous and Severe Personality Disorder: Response and Role of the Psychiatric Team*. Routledge, London.

Brindley, D. (2001) Watchdog hits at special hospitals' tighter security. *The Guardian*, 4 December. Accessed through: http://www.guardian.co.uk/. Accessed 28 April 2005.

Byrt, R. (2000) Dangerous proposals? A response to 'Managing dangerous people with severe personality disorder. *Mental Health Practice*, **3**(10), 12–17.

Byrt, R. (2001) Power, influence and control in practice development. In: Clark, A., Dooher, J. and Fowler, J. (eds.) *The Handbook of Practice Development*, Chapter 10. Quay Books, Mark Allen Publishing, Dinton, Salisbury.

Crisp, A., Cowan, L. and Hart, D. (2004) The college's anti-stigma campaign, 1998–2003: a shortened version of the concluding report. *Psychiatric Bulletin*, **28**, 133–136.

Department of Health (2000) *Report of the Review of Security at the High Security Hospitals*. Department of Health, London.

Eisenberger, N. I., Lieberman, M. D. and Williams, K. D. (2003) Does rejection hurt? An FMRI study of social exclusion. *Science*, **302**(5643), 290–292.

Farrington, D. P. (2003) Advancing knowledge about the early prevention of adult antisocial behavior. In: Farrington, D. P. and Coid, J. W. (eds.) *Early Prevention of Adult Antisocial Behavior*, Chapter 1. Cambridge University Press, Cambridge.

Feeney, A. (2003) DSPD. *Advances in Psychiatric Treatment*, **9**, 349–359.

McMurran, M. (2002) *Expert Paper: Personality Disorders*. NHS National Programme on Forensic Mental Health Research and Development, Liverpool.

Mental Health Alliance (2005) Website: `http://www.mentalhealthalliance.org.uk/`. Accessed 28 April 2005.

Moran, P. and Hagell, A. (2001) *Intervening to Prevent Antisocial Personality Disorder: A Scoping Review (Home Office Research Study 225)*. Home Office Research and Statistics Directorate, London.

Rogers, C. (1978) *Carl Rogers on Personal Power: Inner Strength and Its Revolutionary Impact*. Constable, London.

Woods, P. and Richards, D. (2003) Effectiveness of nursing interventions in people with personality disorders. *Journal of Advanced Nursing*, **44**(2), 154–172.

Index